Big-time Shakespeare

Shakespeare has made the big time in the idiomatic sense of cultural success and widespread notoriety. Other literary figures may achieve canonical status within the academic community based on claims for artistic distinction, but Shakespeare is unusual in that he has also achieved contemporary celebrity. His aptitude for controversy constantly keeps his name in the public eye.

Bristol discusses the supply side of cultural production and argues that Shakespeare retains his authority, at least in part, because suppliers of cultural goods have been skillful at generating a social desire for products that bear his trade mark and in creating merchandise to satisfy that desire. *Big-time Shakespeare* suggests that his plays represent the pathos of our civilization with extraordinary force and clarity. His characters remain interesting because we recognize what they are going through. Shakespeare's contradictory understanding of the social and cultural past is also examined through readings of *The Winter's Tale*, *Othello*, and *Hamlet*.

Bristol attempts to bridge the gap between conservative demands for unreflective affirmation of the ideals and achievements of Western civilization and the equally unhelpful oppositional programs of compulsive resistance and critique.

Michael D. Bristol is Professor of English at McGill University.

Big-time Shakespeare

Michael D. Bristol

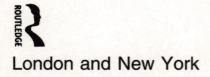

London and New York

First published 1996
by Routledge
11 New Fetter Lane, London EC4P 4EE

Simultaneously published in the USA and Canada
by Routledge
29 West 35th Street, New York, NY 10001

© 1996 Michael D. Bristol
Michael D. Bristol asserts his moral right to be acknowledged as
author of this work

Typeset in Baskerville by BC Typesetting, Bristol

Printed and bound in Great Britain by
Clays Ltd, St Ives plc

British Library Cataloguing in Publication Data
A catalogue record for this book is available from the British Library

Library of Congress Cataloging in Publication Data
Bristol, Michael D.
    Big-time Shakespeare / Michael D. Bristol.
        p. cm.
    Includes bibliographical references and index.
        1. Shakespeare, William, 1564–1616—Criticism and interpretation.
    2. Shakespeare, William, 1564–1616—Stage history.   3. Canon
    (Literature)   4. Theater—History.
    PR2976.B658   1996   95-48493
    822.3'3–dc20

ISBN 0-415-06016-8 (hbk)
ISBN 0-415-06017-6 (pbk)

Contents

To the memory of my parents

Gertrude Shapiro Bristol 1912–1971
Edward Bristol   1912–1978

Preface

Are the Beatles timeless? Or is it all just hype? This is the question for Radio Noon, broadcast on CBC on Monday, 20 November 1995, just after the release of *The Beatles Anthology* on compact disk. The discussion is lively. For some callers the new album is an embarrassment. The Beatles are innocuous, passé, the expression of an outdated sensibility. For others, however, the Beatles represent a more durable value, something that goes beyond the ephemeral fashion of a particular generation. Despite obvious differences in taste, all the callers understand that they must address a larger problem of value. But the callers also understand that the determination of value will necessarily be distorted by corporate promotion of *The Beatles Anthology*, by the 'hype' that stands in opposition to any claim of durable and authentic worth.

The most interesting caller is a 12-year-old girl, who affirms that the Beatles are her favorite group. At first, she admits, she was encouraged to listen to the Beatles by her parents. In time, however, this passive and derivative habit gave way to a deeper, more personal appreciation of this music that she was able to share with friends of her own age. For this young caller, the act of recognizing and taking possession of the Beatles represented both an enhancement of her self-concept and an expansion of her social horizons. This personal value is precisely what appears to go beyond mere fashion, publicity and commercial interest. At the same time, discovering the value of the Beatles for herself entails a complex and even paradoxical redefinition of her relationship with her parents. Sharing the Beatles with friends of her own age depends crucially on feeling empowered to exclude parents from playing a role in the determination of cultural values. But in the very act of such an exclusion, the Beatles are identified as a point of reference across generational lines.

In July 1992 I was invited to appear as a guest on a radio program in Melbourne, Australia to discuss the work I had done in *Shakespeare's America/America's Shakespeare*. After summarizing some of my arguments about the ideological recruitment of Shakespeare in North America, I was asked to respond to listeners on an open line. Many of the callers were troubled by the very notion of putting the value of Shakespeare in question and refused to countenance the suggestion that they were deluded in their appreciation of his plays. The most complex and in some ways the most angry response came from a man who began by identifying himself as 'working class'. This caller had no trouble understanding how Shakespeare might have been used to shore up the position of a dominant class. But he took no comfort in the idea of an exposé of the ideological appropriation of Shakespeare by and for privileged white males. For this caller, the problem of appropriation was just not that interesting. The real issue for him was that his lack of education deprived him of full access to what he recognized as a genuine good. Like the 12-year-old girl who discovered the Beatles on her own, this self-educated student of Shakespeare was firmly convinced as to the reliability of his judgement. For me to have suggested that his appreciation of Shakespeare was simply false consciousness, or that he might be happier enjoying a football match with his mates, would have been a manifest and inexcusable insult.

The everyday practical criticism of Shakespeare and of the Beatles I've just described suggests what's at stake for me in this project. Although vernacular critics frankly acknowledge that buying and selling play an enormously powerful role in our civilization, they nevertheless express a deeply felt belief in values above and beyond those of the market. The present work is also concerned with this problem of value, and specifically with how the value of Shakespeare's works has been sustained and transmitted over time. A basic assumption here is that Shakespeare, like the Beatles, is ambiguously positioned with respect to cultural goods and services that circulate in the commercial marketplace. There can be no doubt that Shakespeare is one of the great show business success stories. *Big-time Shakespeare*, as the title suggests, is concerned with the commercial initiatives that account for the remarkably durable and endlessly renewable fortune of Shakespeare's works. Whether the Beatles – or Elvis – can support this kind of sustained money-taking opportunity over a period of several centuries simply cannot be known or reliably predicted. But even the Beatles may represent a value beyond ephemeral distraction and vitiated commodity exchange. And notwithstanding hype, aggressive commercial promotion, and even the relentless encouragement of parents, successive generations have discovered genuine value in Shakespeare for themselves.

The difficulty of articulating Shakespeare's value begins with the complex semantics and patterns of usage associated with his name. Shakespeare is a term with extraordinary currency in a wide range of discursive practices as a complex symbol of cultural value. It is widely used in vernacular idiom and throughout the genres of popular culture from advertising to situation comedies where it refers equivocally to a particular man, an author, a body of works, a system of cultural institutions, and, by extension, a set of attitudes and dispositions. It defines taste communities and cultural positioning. But Shakespeare is not just a token of cultural worth and significance. The term has multiple and ambiguous valences, especially in its vernacular usage, where it may also signify privilege, exclusion, and cultural pretension.

Oddly, one area where Shakespeare's name is conspicuous by its absence is in promotional material for filmed versions of his plays. Reviews, advertising, and even the film credits themselves speak of Zeffirelli's *Hamlet* and Kenneth Branagh's *Henry V*. Film trailers and television commercials inform viewers that Castle Rock Entertainment will present *Othello*. But of course the force of these commercial messages is in the way they prompt viewers to supply the omission by invoking the name of Shakespeare for themselves. The box-office success of these films depends crucially on the mobility of cultural consumers and this is what accounts for producers' reticence about overt reference to Shakespeare's name. By avoiding explicit utterance of Shakespeare's name, film producers successfully evade the admonitory accent of parental encouragement. Mel Gibson, Kenneth Branagh, and Laurence Fishburne are effective surrogates for Shakespeare for the purposes of commercial hype. The implied promise here is that Gibson, Branagh, and Fishburne will provide a comfortable and convenient way to access larger pay-offs in the enjoyment of Shakespeare's works.

The mobility of Shakespeare's works in the commercial market for cultural goods and services is the initial focus of *Big-time Shakespeare*. In the opening chapters of this book I intend to focus on suppliers of cultural goods, beginning with the early modern period. The argument here is that Shakespeare's currency depends on the initiatives of entrepreneurs in both book publishing and show business. The circulation of various cultural products between these competing industries is a necessary condition for sustaining a high level of public interest in Shakespeare's works. Shakespeare is important because publishers and impresarios see to it that Shakespeare is prominently and conspicuously positioned in the cultural market. Indeed, it ought to be self-evident that without widely available and inexpensive editions of his works, the *longue durée* of Shakespeare as a value within our public culture is simply inconceivable. Commercial profit rather than a wish to guarantee the durable public value of Shakespeare is the motive that best accounts for the diverse enterprises of book publishers, theater managers, film-makers and television producers.

The supply side of culture has evolved as a series of initiatives taken in response to technical as well as financial innovation in the way cultural goods and services are distributed. But, as the Preface to *The First Folio* already implies, there has never been a consensus about what kind of product or service really is Shakespeare. Beginning with the period in which they were actually composed, the material reproduction of Shakespeare's works has been accomplished within the opposing jurisdictions of print culture and of show business. Chronic tension between a more exclusive culture of the book and a more popular culture of performance has contributed to the propagation of Shakespeare's authority by making his work available in new market sectors. Shakespeare is a term that refers to the large and still expanding aggregate of cultural products and services, almost like a trademark or corporate brand name.

The remarkable social mobility of Shakespeare's work over time is not well described in terms of local and ephemeral ideological recruitment. Ideological appropriation is simply too iterative and too mechanical a model to make a very good story. I'm not convinced that radical ideological reduction provides an adequate answer to the question of Shakespeare's long-term authority. Narrow accounts of the local utilities of Shakespeare's works not only forbid attribution of transcendent value; they go much further in effacing the effective social significance of this material over time. In my view, Shakespeare's authority is not simply the accumulated dead weight of a series of fragmentary appropriations designed to further the ideological interests of dominant groups. In one sense this claims too much in the way of intellectual or political commitment for the supply side of culture. The actual suppliers of cultural goods bearing the Shakespeare trademark are as likely as not quite indifferent to the ideological payloads carried by their products. And there is no reason to think that Shakespeare's works are always successful in achieving disciplinary effects, even when media of transmission have been organized to accomplish the purpose of social regulation. Even when it can be shown, moreover, that the design and distribution of cultural products is intended to privilege feelings and beliefs favored by a particular social class, it is by no means certain that such beliefs and feelings will actually favor the interests of that social class. Men and women who enjoy the advantages of a privileged social position may prefer to adopt certain beliefs because that is how they want to interpret their world. This kind of wishful thinking, typical of ideology, is likely to be both untrue and ineffectual in the long run.

Technical innovation, along with the appeal of cross-over markets, tends to out-pace and eventually overrun cumbersome ideological agendas in the production of cultural goods like the works of Shakespeare. Although competition between show business and the printed book has remained in a state of relative equilibrium for a considerable period of time, in the long run I think it is indisputable that show business has become the dominant public form. The disburdening appeal of the technology of spectacle – theatre, cinema, video – is finally much greater than the more difficult form of the printed book. This is now apparent in the way so many of our best students find that the task of reading Shakespeare is more trouble than its worth, and who may not even see much point in reading it at all. But Shakespeare has adapted very well to new media such as film and television. And in an odd way the striking adaptability of Shakespeare within the market for cultural goods and services tends to confirm the vernacular intuition that his works have some real social worth and importance above and beyond their contingent market value.

Although I favor the most candid acknowledgement of the profit motive governing the reproduction of Shakespeare, this does not persuade me that his works are only alienating products of a commercial trade in leisure activity. The most opportunistic market initiatives may express, though in a dim and often grossly distorted way, the conviction that Shakespeare's works have had extraordinary saliency for the successor cultures of early modern England.

The brisk circulation of Shakespeare's works in the cultural market may in fact hint at a more durable basis for the value and authority of these artifacts. Professional critics, theatrical producers and cultural consumers have sustained their belief in the possibility of such a durable value at least since the time of Dryden and Davenant. The sheer tenacity of such convictions suggests, to me at least, that no one should presume that belief in Shakespeare's authority is either self-deluded or self-serving. There is really no question that this material has had an effective and socially consequential life in the *longue durée* of Western civilization. The difficulty is in knowing how best to articulate the cultural authority sedimented in Shakespeare's works. Can such artifacts actually widen and enhance democratic participation in our public culture, or do they just reinforce acrimonious social divisions?

In the second half of *Big-time Shakespeare* I intend to reopen the possibility that Shakespeare is the common possession of Western modernity and a definitive expression of its experience. Such a claim, which in the not very distant past would have seemed altogether self-evident, is likely to strike many contemporary readers as controversial and even inflammatory. The argument I hope to advance is not, however, that Shakespeare is a hypostatized body of reliable social wisdom and moral certainty or that his works ought to have the function of secular scripture. Shakespeare is a common possession, though not unambiguously a common good. In my view, Shakespeare's authority is linked to the capacity of his works to represent the complexity of social time and value in the successor cultures of early modern England. One of the crucial features common to these successor cultures is the way individuals and institutions must constantly adapt to the exigencies of a market economy. Our extended historical dialogue with Shakespeare's works has been one of the important ways to articulate values more durable than those which circulate in current markets.

Contemporary debate over Shakespeare's cultural authority has now reached an impasse in the 'Bardbiz' debate, a major battleground in the deplorable public spectacle known as the culture wars. The culture wars are an example of adversarial debate characteristic of a society where the exigencies of commodity exchange tend to dissolve every more durable form of social authority. The authority of Shakespeare will continue to have a substantive value only as long as it remains possible to sustain belief in communal solidarity with the past. The possibility of such solidarity would, however, depend on a full and candid assessment of all the cultural endowments held by the successor cultures. Dogmatic celebration of the achievements of the past would be as unhelpful as the compulsive rebelliousness often proposed as an alternative.

Shakespeare's works are some of the most complex artifacts we possess in common. But these commonly held bequests do not contribute equally to the happiness and prosperity of every beneficiary within the successor cultures. Consider, for example, a Jewish reader who engages with *The Merchant of Venice* in a social setting where 'Shylock' is common street language for a loan shark. For such a reader, critical appreciation of this text is likely to be complex and painful. But it can also be valuable as a way to grasp the way chronic anti-Semitism endures among the discourses and institutions of Western modernity. The point, however, is that these are discourses and institutions in which we must find ways to live together. *Big-time Shakespeare* is an aggregate of commodities fashioned to offer distraction from the continuing pathos of Western modernity. *Big-time Shakespeare* is also the common endowment of Western modernity, quite distinct from the market circulation of cultural goods and services. The problem of social continuity and sustained cultural authority depends on the effort to engage both of these contradictory intuitions with equal honesty. This is, I take it, the crucial insight expressed in the vernacular criticism with which I began. *Big-time Shakespeare* is a preliminary effort to give formal articulation to that insight.

Montréal, 25 January 1996

Acknowledgements

This project began to take shape with my reading of Mikhail Bakhtin's brief remarks on Shakespeare in his 'Response to a Question from the *Novy Mir* Editorial Staff'. I'm grateful to James Nielson for providing me with his own original translations of the discussion of *bolshoe vremja* as well as for his insights in putting the idea of Big Time into the context of Bakhtin's extraordinary career. Many people have sent me newspaper clippings and other Shakespeareana from contemporary popular culture. I owe specific debts to Howard Ziff for Ziff's Law, to Peter Ohlin for Red Buttons, to Susan Baker for Joseph Sobran, to Susan Fox for Tony Horwitz, to Caroline Thomas for George Neavoll, and to Universal Press Syndicate for *Calvin and Hobbes*. Jordan Raphael led me to Morpheus, King of Dreams, and Lord Morpheus showed me how to bring this project to an end. And since this book is about long-term authority, this is probably as good a time as any to thank teachers and mentors, especially Harry Berger Jr, Harold Bloom, D. W. Robertson, Thomas P. Roche, and Irving Zeitlin for helping me to discover my vocation, such as it is. I'm extremely grateful both for their timely attention and their equally timely inattention.

Parts of the argument here have been road-tested at meetings of The Association of Canadian University and College Teachers of English, The Modern Language Association, The Mid-West Modern Language Association, and The Shakespeare Association of America. I also wish to thank my hosts at The Hudson Strode Seminar at the University of Alabama, Melbourne University, Dalhousie University, The New York Shakespeare Society, The Ogden Glass Distinguished Speakers Series at Bishops University, and Muhlenberg College for their generosity and encouragement with various parts of the project. An earlier version of Chapter 6 has been published in *Shakespeare Quarterly*, 41, Summer 1991, pp. 145–168. Earlier versions of Chapter 7 have appeared in *Renaissance Drama*, N.S. XXI, 1991, pp. 3–21 and in *True Rites and Maimed Rites*, Linda Woodbridge and Edward Berry (eds), Urbana: University of Illinois Press, 1992. Part of Chapter 8 is included in *Shakespeare's Books: Contemporary Cultural Politics and the Persistence of Empire*, Marion Campbell and Philip Mead (eds), Melbourne: Melbourne University Literary and Cultural Studies, Volume I, 1993.

My work on *Big-time Shakespeare* has been funded by generous grants from the Social Sciences and Humanities Research Council of Canada and from the Québec Fonds pour la Formation de Chercheurs et l'Aide à la Recherche. Thanks to these agencies I have had the unusual opportunity to work with exceptionally resourceful assistants. I'm extremely grateful to Susan Johnston, Marcus Librizzi, Marcel DeCoste, Jessica Sights, and Michael Morgan Holmes for their enthusiasm and intelligence, not to mention enough research material to fuel several careers. McGill University has very generously supported my research by providing me with sabbatic leave. In 1992–1993, I had the rare good fortune to receive a Folger Library Long-Term Fellowship funded by the National Endowment for the Humanities and I thank Werner Gundesheimer for making this possible. I had expected to complete this project during my tenure there, but the more I talked to people at tea, the more complicated and difficult the issues became. So thanks a lot, everyone! I want to express particular appreciation to Betsy Walsh and the staff of the Folger Reading Room for their alacrity in responding to my requests. Fellow fellows Lee Bliss, Tom Cartelli, and Joe Levine contributed much more than they know by listening and by patiently explaining their own projects. I'm also grateful to Folgerians Leeds Barroll, Barbara Mowat, Lena Orlin, Georgianna Ziegler, Michael Neill, Peter Blayney, Bruce Smith, and Gail Paster for the gossip, the political shmoozing, and in general for the extraordinary dialogue at all those noisy lunches at various Capitol Hill watering holes. James Shapiro, Paisley Livingston, and someone who wishes to remain anonymous read the completed manuscript. Their suggestions were extremely helpful in the fine-tuning of various arguments. Talia Rodgers has been saintly in her patience as I wrestled with my demons. And thanks and thanks again to everyone who has debated these issues with me, whether they wanted to or not: to Doris Bristol, Jean Howard,

Part I
The supply side of culture

Chapter 1

Introduction

> I am thy father's spirit,
> Doomed for a certain term to walk the night. . . .
>
> (*Hamlet*: 1.5.10)

> The good time is the small time, the big time is the hard time.
>
> (Red Buttons, 1956)

Shakespeare has made the big time. No less than the Beatles or Liberace, Elvis Presley or Mick Jagger, Shakespeare is big-time in the idiomatic sense of cultural success, high visibility, and notoriety. Other literary figures may achieve canonical status within the academic community based on claims to artistic distinction, but Shakespeare is unusual in that he has also achieved contemporary celebrity. Such an achievement entails an aptitude for controversy that keeps Shakespeare's name above a certain threshold of public attention. Notwithstanding a long history of challenges to his cultural authority, Shakespeare has been a celebrity for just about as long as the social state of being a celebrity has existed. Other stars of the culture industry – David Garrick, let's say, or, to choose a more properly literary example, Lord Byron – have had nothing like Shakespeare's durability. Such extraordinary cultural stamina will be the primary focus of this book.

When he was still alive, Shakespeare was not much of a public figure. He seems to have avoided publicity, and as far as anyone knows, preferred a relatively modest and retiring existence. On the other hand, the evidence of the *Sonnets* suggests that Shakespeare had hoped for and expected considerable public renown for his poetry, though there is a perhaps naïve insistence here on the genuine worthiness of his performance as the main reason for his fame. In Sonnet 65 Shakespeare writes of the 'miracle' of 'black ink' as the solution to the problem of 'sad mortality' and suggests that his 'powerful rhyme' can outlive 'marble and the gilded monuments of Princes'. As a private aspiration, fame is simply a wish to be remembered after one is dead. But in the traditional understanding of fame it clearly matters exactly what one hopes to be famous for. Fame, in the sense intended in Shakespeare's sonnets, is the consequence of virtuous acts and exemplary achievements. From the perspective of the community, the moral dignity achieved by famous people through their famous deeds enhances the cohesion of society over time.

Shakespeare's own desire for fame has been gradually transmuted into something radically different in the form of contemporary celebrity. Unlike fame, celebrity is a form of social being that does not rest on any particular claim for distinction. Indeed, it is quite possible to achieve celebrity without excelling at any particular craft. The class of celebrities can include not only show business performers and creative artists, but also politicians, sports figures and journalists, certain popular religious leaders, as well as mobsters and serial killers. Public visibility, regardless of how it has been achieved, is the only necessary requirement for claiming the status of celebrity. A celebrity is simply 'a person who is known for his well-knownness' (Boorstin 1962: 57). The achievement of celebrity status is perhaps more complex than Boorstin's picture of mass deception and mass credulity seems to imply (Gamson 1994). Nevertheless, celebrity requires neither extraordinary competence nor exceptional virtue. It demands only energetic self-assertion and adroit public relations directed towards a public socialized to the habits of mass consumption.

THE BIG TIME AND THE SMALL TIME

Shakespeare's name, together with his image, has extraordinary currency in contemporary culture at a time when the practice of reading and careful study of his works appears to be in decline. In the nineteenth century Shakespeare societies were organized in communities all over the English-speaking world for the purpose of reading and discussion of the plays. To judge by their newsletters and other ephemera, these reading clubs seem quaint and even eccentric by contemporary standards. They were often more preoccupied with the social etiquette of club meetings or with the menus planned for club dinners than with serious critical scrutiny of the plays. Nevertheless, the Shakespeare clubs were important in providing a public forum where citizens could practice the art of critical deliberation using Shakespeare to moot a range of social or political topics. The use of Shakespeare for enhancing socialization in these contexts is linked primarily to the idea of his fame, since it is motivated by respect for his virtues. Shakespeare's celebrity, on the other hand, is primarily the result of his circulation as a mass-cultural icon (Charnes 1993: 155).

Although he is probably not as bankable as, say, Clint Eastwood, there is nevertheless a considerable market for a range of cultural goods that carry the Shakespeare trademark. Film versions of the plays such as Kenneth Branagh's *Henry V* and *Much Ado About Nothing* or Zeffirelli's *Hamlet* and his earlier *Romeo and Juliet* have shown that Shakespeare can be profitable in the context of commercial film production. Even more remarkable perhaps is the success of such *avant-gardiste* productions as William Reilly's *Men of Respect*, Peter Greenaway's *Prospero's Books*, and Gus Van Sant's *My Own Private Idaho*, all of which rely on their audience's prior knowledge of a Shakespeare text. In general the overall level of economic activity in publishing, movies, video production, and commercial theater that exploits the general public's knowledge of Shakespeare remains very high. In this sense to speak of Shakespeare's currency is an apt usage, since his image actually appears on VISA cards issued by certain banks in the UK, and a scene from *Romeo and Juliet* is depicted on the back of £20 notes.

In an age where everyone can expect to be famous for at least fifteen minutes in the sense of sheer visibility and vulgar recognition, neither publicity nor sheer dollar volume nor any combination of these two factors provides a complete account of large-scale cultural success and recognition. There is a temporal dimension to this success as well. Contemporary celebrity is ephemeral; nothing seems more dated or more lame than the popular music enjoyed by one's parents. The typical career of a media star is likely to be characterized by extraordinary peaks of notoriety and public attention, followed in many instances by complete oblivion. One of the rather more difficult tasks I have had to face in composing this chapter has been to think of examples of celebrities whose currency will not already have depreciated by the time the book is actually published.

Celebrities come and go, but only a few achieve promotion to the big time. The experience of such big-time status, moreover, is complex and evokes deeply ambivalent attitudes. In the course of a long career as a comedian in vaudeville, television, and film, Red Buttons experienced many ups and downs. In 1956, when his career was on the skids, he summarized his experience in a vaguely poetic aphorism: 'the good time is the small time, the big time is the hard time'. For those who aspire to it, the big time is distant, alien, and cold. The regime of the big time diminishes and forbids small-time felicity. The seductive glamor of celebrity status is offset by exorbitant costs in personal sacrifice, self-discipline, compromise, and aggression. In the end celebrity status may prove extremely evanescent and transitory, offering no immunity against 'sad mortality'.

Despite the risks and the rigorous exactions, however, it's clear that small-time satisfactions offer no serious challenge to the rewards of the big time. Red Buttons' season of big-time celebrity, such as it was, could not have been accomplished without a willingness to sacrifice enjoyment of the small time. Shakespeare's own apparent preference for the small time did not, however, prevent his eventual succession to the big time. Paradoxically, there is an important sense in which big-time Shakespeare is a collectively produced phenomenon generated out of the innumerable small-time accomplishments of actors and directors, advertising copy-writers, public relations specialists, as well as scholars, editors, and educators. In another sense, however, big-time Shakespeare is a scandal and a reproach to these efforts, an index of the transience and marginality of small-time incapacity to serve the hard time of serious cultural ambition and achievement.

Celebrity demands hard time. Its value to individual aspirants may be quite high, though there is no doubt that it is also very costly. But what about the value of big-time celebrity for the community at large and for the vast majority of people who have no serious big-time aspirations? Since it is not based on any pattern of exemplary conduct, big-time celebrity has no binding force for a community over time. The more homely and familiar world of the small time, for example, an extended family, or a religious congregation, or even a professional organization of like-minded people with a common history, provides for satisfaction of basic needs such as material comfort, emotional reassurance, and a sense of moral as well as social orientation. Big-time achievements are in many ways inimical to the needs of ordinary people and the values of everyday life.

The idea that big-time achievements are in some important ways irrelevant and even antagonistic to the concerns of everyday life is given powerful articulation in the ruminations on Shakespeare of Mr Ramsay, in Virginia Woolf's *To the Lighthouse*.

> he slipped, seeing all this, smoothly into speculation suggested by an article in *The Times* about the number of Americans who visit Shakespeare's house every year. If Shakespeare had never existed, he asked, would the world have differed much from what it is to-day? Does the progress of civilization depend upon great men? Is the lot of the average human being better now than in the time of the Pharaohs? Is the lot of the average human being, however, he asked himself, the criterion by which we judge the measure of civilization? Possibly not. Possibly the greatest good requires the existence of a slave class. The liftman in the Tube is an eternal necessity. The thought was distasteful to him. He tossed his head. To avoid it, he would find some way of snubbing the predominance of the arts. He would argue that the world exists for the average human being; that the arts are merely a decoration imposed on the top of human life; they do not express it. Nor is Shakespeare necessary to it.
>
> (Woolf 1932: 70–71)

It is not clear whether Mr Ramsay actually believes his own conclusions, since his desire 'to disparage Shakespeare' seems motivated largely by the tiresome demands of preparing for a guest lecture. Whatever readers may make of this character in the context of Woolf's novel, however, he does raise a troubling question, viz. Is Shakespeare really important in the *longue durée* of culture, and if so why?

By asking whether 'civilization' would be any different if Shakespeare had never existed, Mr Ramsay assigns a radical privilege to the claims of ordinary life and to all those ordinary people whose exclusive daily concern is with repetitive labor and the struggle for subsistence. What Mr Ramsay challenges here is the kind of lofty universalist claim, often unexamined, that Shakespeare in some way expressively defines social being within 'civilization'. Mr Ramsay's intuitions here suggest a further shift in the comparative valence assigned to the categories of big time and small time. He certainly acknowledges that Shakespeare is one of the historically great figures of his culture, but he does not interpret this status as in any way fundamental to the values of civilization.

Mr Ramsay proposes instead a strong claim for the moral dignity of ordinary life, against which the claims of art can be dismissed as merely arrogant and frivolous. This powerful affirmation of ordinary life as the sovereign ethical purpose of civilization goes beyond transvaluation of the idea of the big time. The very definition of what is genuinely enduring is tied, not to the grandiose ambitions of big-time celebrity, but rather to the anonymity of the small time. The arts are merely a superficial diversion when considered in light of the more solid permanence of things and places – 'familiar lanes and commons'.

The conventional value assigned to Shakespeare is connected with the belief that his works are in some way essential to the 'progress of civilization'. Appreciation and understanding of Shakespeare would then somehow be constitutive of membership in civilized society. Mr Ramsay's thought is that any such belief in the achievements of 'great men' simply reflects the interests of an elite class. Shakespeare's importance is illusory; people can get along perfectly well without him. But Virginia Woolf does not present Mr Ramsay's affirmation of ordinary life without considerable irony.

> Not knowing precisely why it was that he wanted to disparage Shakespeare and come to the rescue of the man who stands eternally in the door of the lift, he picked a leaf sharply from the hedge. All this would have to be dished up for the young men at Cardiff next month, he thought.
>
> (Woolf 1932: 71)

Mr Ramsay's defense of ordinary life against the claims of art and high culture is destined for an audience of university students, many of whom doubtless aspire to wealth and distinction. But these 'young men' are at Cardiff, not Oxford or Cambridge, and his lecture will be 'dished up' as intellectual leftovers to the sons of shopkeepers and tradesmen. His challenge to the importance of 'great men' is complicated by an obscure resentment of this audience and by his irritation with his own contradictory institutional situation. The planned lecture will attest to the moral centrality of ordinary life. But at the same time the act of 'dishing up' such a lecture to the young men at Cardiff simply instantiates the social relations of privilege, exclusion, and complacency it is intended to challenge.

In *A Room of One's Own*, Virginia Woolf presents a very different account of Shakespeare's authority and its relation to everyday life. Her discussion suggests that literary creativity is sustained in and through broad social participation, that it is an effect of communal life. Shakespeare's works are built up from comprehensive borrowing of preceding literary works and from an unselfconscious absorption of the speech types of the common people.

> For masterpieces are not single and solitary births; they are the outcome of many years of thinking in common, of thinking by the body of the people, so that the experience of the mass is behind the single voice. Without . . . forerunners, Jane Austen and the Brontës and George Eliot could no more have written than Shakespeare could have written without Marlowe, or Marlowe without Chaucer, or Chaucer without those forgotten poets who paved the ways and tamed the natural savagery of the tongue.
>
> (Woolf 1929: 98)

Woolf's immediate concern is with the revolutionary and epochal emergence of the institution of women writing, an event she thinks of 'greater importance than the Crusades or the Wars of the Roses' (p. 97). Such an emergence takes place through the initiative of an exceptional singular agent, but the pre-condition of such originality is the existence of a shared expressive life among the socially excluded and unvoiced.

The most powerful figure for the silenced and subordinated community in *A Room of One's Own* is Woolf's description of Judith, Shakespeare's 'wonderfully gifted sister' (p. 70ff.). As Woolf has no doubt correctly insisted, a woman with a Shakespearean capacity of expressivity and a determination to use that capacity publicly would almost certainly have been denounced and punished as a witch or demon. Judith Shakespeare is a casualty of the patriarchal order and its violent policing of language. William Shakespeare himself is not, however, indicted for the generic persecution of Judith or for any of his anonymous sisters. Furthermore, the voice of the doomed sister can in fact be heard resonating through the work of the brother. Shakespeare is, for Woolf, a maternal figure, a fecund and nurturing precursor for her own alter ego, Anon (Schwartz 1991: 722).

Woolf's account of Shakespeare as 'mother and muse' to the long-silenced expressive potentiality of women writing suggests a second, contrasting meaning that the term 'big-time Shakespeare' has for this project. On one level I certainly intend to stress the sheer vulgar celebrity Shakespeare has enjoyed for a period of several hundred years. But the expression 'big time' is also an idiomatic translation of Mikhail Bakhtin's phrase *bolshoe vremja*, which is usually given the more formal academic rendering in English of 'great time' or even 'macrotemporality' (Morson and Emerson 1990: 287–288). The translation of *bolshoe vremja* as 'big time' evokes a show business idiom of long runs and return engagements that usefully suggests Shakespeare's success in the entertainment industry. Bakhtin's intention with this phrase, however, is more closely equivalent to the classical proverb *ars longa, vita brevis* than it is to contemporary notions of show business celebrity.

The notion of 'great time' is obviously related to the concept of *longue durée* as this has been developed by historians of the *Annales* movement, and indeed Bakhtin read and admired the early *Annales* historians, particularly Marc Bloch (Holquist 1986: xxi). But where Bloch and the other *Annales* historians were primarily concerned with the historical record of material culture left by anonymous peasants and artisans, Bakhtin focuses on the more dynamic and eventful long-term existence of individual artistic works:

> It seems paradoxical that . . . great works continue to live in the distant future. In the process of their posthumous life they are enriched with new meanings, new significance: it is as though these works outgrow what they were in the epoch of their creation.
>
> (Bakhtin 1986: 4)

This view of the durable permanence and the gradual 'coming-into-being' of the work of art is summed up in one of Bakhtin's proverb-like formulations – 'nothing is absolutely dead: every meaning will have its homecoming festival' (p. 170). This aphorism seems to offer the possibility of an eventual reconciliation of big time with small time in a sense not suggested by the observations of Red Buttons or Mr Ramsay. The pastoral and domestic resonances suggested by McGee's translation of Bakhtin's *prazdnik vozrozhdeniya* suggest that there is something to come home to, some feeling of solidarity or sense of community that links the present with the past. In the original Russian the idea has a more specifically religious connotation. A more literal translation would be 'festival of rebirth'. James Nielson interprets Bakhtin's phrase as the equivalent of Easter and suggests 'every meaning will celebrate its day of resurrection' as a translation that more exactly captures the spirit of Bakhtin's idea in this fragmentary passage, probably the last thing he wrote before his death in 1975.

Bakhtin's idea of 'great time' focuses on the extended life of the community as encompassing and also as linking together the much briefer tenure of individual lives. This is a view of social time primarily in terms of its intersubjective and ethical aspects, in which people are related not only through spoken dialogue, but also through reciprocal economic obligations, and even physical intimacy. Bakhtin arrived at his notions of the big time late in his career as an extension of his central theme of dialogue. The dialogic context has neither linguistic boundaries nor temporal limitations. Even the 'alien word' of historically distant contexts remains capable of revealing new meanings to dialogue partners who could never have been envisioned at the moment of the utterance. Shakespeare, in this view, has become both an enduring institution *and* a source of cultural authority not by virtue of cheap and meretricious celebrity but because the works produced are already richly dialogized and thus answerable to unforeseen social and cultural circumstances.

Shakespeare's works are not closed discursive formations, nor are they limited to expressing the concerns and interests of a narrowly circumscribed historical period. They have potential for generating new meanings in successive epochs. Bakhtin argues that there is something paradoxical in the way certain works exist in epochs far removed from the time of their composition. In effect, the works outgrow the meanings and purposes for which they may have been intended and acquire new significance during an extended afterlife.

We may say that neither Shakespeare himself nor his contemporaries knew the 'great Shakespeare' that we know today. . . . The treasures of meaning invested by Shakespeare in his works arose and accumulated over centuries and even millennia – they were lurking within language, and not just literary language, but also in those strata of the popular language, which prior to Shakespeare, had not penetrated into literature. . . . Shakespeare, like every artist, constructed his works not out of dead elements,

>not out of bricks, but out of forms already heavy with meanings,
>filled with them.
>
>(Bakhtin 1986: 4)

Shakespeare was a writer who was vitally in touch with the richest possible sources from a wide range of past cultural formations. His works constitute a vast archive or library of 'lost voices' that retain their potential to be heard with new force and intonation in the perspective of the big time.

It's possible that Bakhtin was led to the notion that lost meanings may enjoy a 'homecoming festival' in consequence of his own return from political exile. For Bakhtin the great works of literary culture provide a rich resource that allows us to connect with other human beings, even in situations of isolation and extreme deprivation. Such works enable much wider social participation in great time:

>The mutual understanding of centuries and millennia, of peoples,
>nations, and cultures, provides a complex unity of all humanity,
>all human cultures (a complex unity of human culture), and a
>complex unity of human literature. All this is revealed only on
>the level of great time.
>
>(Bakhtin 1986: 167)

For Bakhtin, the great works of world literature provide the basis for this sort of ecumenical vision on a grand scale. It's important to distinguish here between abstract notions of universality and Bakhtin's intuitions about a complex unity of human culture. Universality in both its anthropological and axiological usages has been subjected to a withering critique, although this criticism does not always do full justice to the complexity of the idea. The 'complex unity of human culture' to which Bakhtin refers in these cryptic notes is neither abstract nor totalizing. Human cultures and indeed individual human voices are characterized not by a shared essence or common underlying structure but rather by otherness and outsideness.

The existence of others is the basic condition for a dialogue by means of which a differentiated unity of human culture is revealed over time. What Bakhtin envisions here is more than a dogmatic affirmation of transgression and otherness. The uncritical celebration of a mere plurality of contending voices simply leads to a disorienting moral relativism. Bakhtin's notion of dialogue here is as opposed to relativism as it is to the authoritative monologue. The contingent and concrete particularity of everyday practical morality is grasped in dialogue. Such dialogue would have no conceivable purpose, however, in a world of pure difference and radically unstable identities.

Shakespeare's plays, along with other great works of art, enter into great time in the sense that these works have a long and significant cultural afterlife. It would be a crude and disingenuous oversimplification of Bakhtin's notion however, to equate this idea of a vital afterlife with vague romantic idealizations of Shakespeare's 'immortality'. Nor is it anything like the oddly farcical 'haunting' described so vividly by Marjorie Garber in *Shakespeare's Ghost Writers* (Garber 1987: 88–90). The afterlife of the great work of art is the work of living social agents whose interpretations accomplish the re-accentuation of the author's utterance. Interpretation is thus a form of inquiry that reveals a 'new intonation' that would not have been intelligible to the original public of the author.

The entry of the art work into 'great time' corresponds to its 'answerability' to the needs of successor societies to articulate standards of practical morality (Bakhtin 1990; Clark and Holquist 1984: 63–94). This is true of all literary objects, but it is most vividly manifested in the theatrical performance of dramatic works. Every staging of a Shakespeare play results from a dialogue between the historical moment of its creation and the contemporaneity of the *mise-en-scène*. At the same time, the thought of the author and of his community continues to resonate even in the most self-consciously modernizing interpretation. The interpreted work thus takes on a 'double intention' as it participates in dialogue about focal concerns and practical morality (Morson and Emerson 1990: 65ff.).

In its contemporary form the requirement that art must serve the needs of practical morality has often been expressed as a demand for commitment on the part of the author. The notion of commitment, however, is primarily a form of authoritative monologue which would in the end exclude genuine moral inquiry. Furthermore, as Emmanuel Levinas has argued, the creation of an art work may not in itself be a morally good action. The socialization, indeed the humanization of the art work is the task of interpretation and criticism:

> Art then is not committed by virtue of being art. But for this
> reason art is not the supreme value of civilization, and it is not
> forbidden to conceive a stage in which it will be reduced to a

source of pleasure . . . all this is true for art separated from the criticism that integrates the inhuman work of the artist into the human world. Criticism already detaches it from its irresponsibility by envisaging its technique.

(Levinas 1987: 12–13)

Levinas apparently wants to reinstate the romantic doctrine of artistic autonomy here, but without the romantic idealization of that autonomy. Works of art have a mode of existence that exceeds their marginal social utility. Interpretation is required to socialize the art work, which otherwise remains 'inhuman' and 'irresponsible'. Criticism reconciles what is otherwise alien to an everyday world of ordinary people.

In suggesting that 'art is not the supreme value of civilization', Levinas acknowledges the claims of ordinary life. On this view art, even big-time art, may be seen as merely an optional extra. Levinas identifies criticism as the means for socialization of the art work. Mr Ramsay, on the other hand, almost seems to suggest sheer ignorance as a solution to the problem of the great work of art, which is in any case outside the regime of ordinary life and unnecessary for its purposes.

Despite his own situation of isolation and extreme persecution, Bakhtin remained committed to the idea that literary works have a significant temporal dimension, a vital afterlife in cultural dialogue that leads to mutual understanding across generational and cultural boundaries. Great time, with its potential for ecumenical recognition of all the diverse forms of human experience, is distinct from history, or at least from the interpretation of history so vividly described by Walter Benjamin as a whirlwind of catastrophes interrupted only by the vindictive and gloomy triumphal processions of winners over losers (Benjamin 1969: 256). Bakhtin's ideas about the inexhaustible potential of great literary works and their co-ordination in a complex unity of human cultures is likely to strike many contemporary readers as nothing more than wishful thinking, especially in light of ever increasing racial, religious, and ethnic violence in many different parts of the world. Red Buttons' wry intuitions about the alienating and competitive nature of the big time may well on the whole seem more plausible.

Bakhtin's intuitions recall those of such earlier observers as Ralph Waldo Emerson and Virginia Woolf, who also believed that Shakespeare's works transcended the local and contingent circumstances of their original creation. With all due caution, therefore, I propose in this project to reopen the question of 'the great work of art' as it is defined by Bakhtin in his notion of the work's entry into 'great time'. In pursuing this question I do not intend simply the mechanical application of ready-made ideas derived from Bakhtin's theoretical writings. However, the ideas of dialogue and of great time do constitute a normative horizon for much of my discussion, especially in the final chapters of the book, where I hope to show in more detail how the latent semantic potentiality of *The Winter's Tale*, *Othello*, and *Hamlet* become manifest.

Despite the relatively stable value or hierarchical position of Shakespeare within different milieux over time, there has been no stable or durable consensus as to the reasons that best account for his long-term cultural success. The already vast and increasingly diverse body of interpretation of these works also suggests that the long-term value of these texts is not well explained in relation to any well-defined ensemble of determinate meanings. The question raised by this observation is how the value of Shakespeare is sustained and transmitted over time against a background of rapidly shifting cultural frameworks. Furthermore, it is no longer possible to investigate the *longue durée* of great works such as *Hamlet* or *The Winter's Tale* without acknowledging the complex political ramifications of Shakespeare's authority within an increasingly diverse and conflicted contemporary culture. Unfortunately, discussion of this problem has deteriorated over the past few years into an increasingly belligerent and unproductive polemic.

ADVERSARIAL DEBATE AND THE DOCTRINE OF FRAGMENTARY APPROPRIATION

Shakespeare's authority has become a topic of bitter controversy, not only among academics but also within a wider community represented by journalists, and other opinion leaders. Debate over Shakespeare forms part of an even larger argument over such issues as canon, curriculum, and the role of classical literary works in sustaining the identity of Western civilization. The emotional fervor of this controversy can be seen in the 'Bardbiz affair' that raged in *the London Review of Books* for more than a year between February 1990 and September 1991. 'Few things unhinge the British as much as doublet and hose.' So begins Terence Hawkes' essay reviewing a number of recent books on Shakespeare, including my own

Shakespeare's America/America's Shakespeare (1990). The essay is, among other things, a lively exposé of the 'Bardbiz', drawing attention to the commercialism of a number of cherished institutions in England.

Within a month the first attack appeared, in the form of a letter by James Woods denouncing Hawkes for treating specific Shakespearean works as 'an ideological sponge'. Alan Sinfield immediately launched a counter-attack, condemning Woods for a 'panic reassertion of . . . Shakespeare'. What ensued quickly came to resemble a pie-throwing contest from a silent comedy, except for the sour ill-humor of the combatants. The quarrel eventually faded from the *London Review of Books*, but it continues to echo through cyberspace, where the 'flaming' of opponents has developed into a minor art-form. In light of the crude and radically polarized state of our wider public discourse, this is perhaps not altogether surprising. What is particularly troubling about these more specifically intellectual controversies is that the parties do not appear to have any interest in reaching an understanding. There is a tacit agreement that both sides are engaged in a winner-take-all power struggle. Unhappily, escalation of the conflict has led the various parties to adopt mutually incompatible theoretical positions.

On one side of this debate are cultural critics who view Shakespeare's work as a numinous source of binding cultural authority, of whom the most notorious, and it must be said the most successful in attracting wide public attention have been Alan Bloom and William Bennett. Works like Helen Gardner's *In Defence of the Imagination*, Richard Levin's *New Readings vs. Old Plays*, Brian Vickers' *Appropriating Shakespeare: Contemporary Critical Quarrels*, and Graham Bradshaw's *Misrepresentations: Shakespeare and the Materialists* represent more reasoned and academically responsible versions of this viewpoint. Their opponents in the debate are led by a group of British academics who rally together around the doctrines of cultural materialism. Terence Hawkes' *That Shakespeherian Rag*, and *Meaning by Shakespeare*, Graham Holderness' *The Shakespeare Myth*, and Alan Sinfield's *Faultlines* are among the more important articulations of this position. Their research focuses on the institutional provenance of Shakespeare and the ideological interests that motivate interpretation of his works.

Helen Gardner explains Shakespeare's durable value according to a belief that his works are an abundant source of reliable intuitions about the most durable aspects of 'human nature'. Shakespeare's crucial role in the education of the young derives from the ability of his works to transcend parochial interests:

> the dissemination of knowledge and understanding of the past through its literature is a prime source of society's sense of its own identity and cohesion, something very precious without which it can become a mere ant-heap or beehive devoted to the increase of the Gross National Product.
>
> (Gardner 1982: 45)

There is undeniable cogency in Gardner's implied claim that a society must be something more than a market apparatus. Since the publication of *In Defence of the Imagination* in 1982, however, the ideology of market economics has been promoted increasingly aggressively. Fredric Jameson has argued that the identification of the free market with human nature is 'the most crucial terrain of ideological struggle in our time' (1991: 263–264). Jameson interprets this struggle in terms of the accelerating disintegration of social life and the rapidly diminishing sense that the polity should even attempt to control its own destiny. Gardner's diagnosis of this problem as early as 1982 was in some ways prophetic. Her idea that the teaching of literature might help to resist such a tendency, however, is perhaps more wishful thinking than anything else (Elster 1982: 123–149).

Conservative culture critics like Helen Gardner believe that the capacity of literature to foster harmonious social relations is immanent in the literary artifacts themselves. For Gardner, the values and insights of literary texts are fully actualized at the moment of their creation. The task of reading is simply to recognize and to acquiesce in the author's intentions:

> we are conscious as we read a book or a poem that we are reading the expression of an individual mind and sensibility, and that this is conveyed to us by an individual manner of expression that, like a voice, belongs to one person.
>
> (Gardner 1982: 6)

Literary works, in this view, can offer emancipatory as well as reconciliatory benefits, but only on the condition that reading is oriented by a commitment to 'the plain sense' of the text. Here the locution 'plain sense' conveys the idea that meanings are simple and also obvious. Interpretations that miss the plain sense are prompted by perverse resistance to what is salutary in the literary object.

Shakespeare should not be contaminated with the voices of more nearly contemporary authorities, for example, Freud, or Marx. Such interpretive promiscuity privileges the moment of the text's reception and thus reverses both the ethical and ontological priority of the author's originating word.

Reading that sets out to interpret Shakespeare's works in active dialogue with contemporaneity is condemned by Gardner as a surrender to the 'confinement to present circumstances'. Such reading would 'deny the possibility of any communication of mind with mind by the medium of the written word' (p. 7). This affirmation of an encounter between two minds seems to imply a notion of dialogue. However, the model of communication adopted here does not envision anything like a fully interactive dialogue between literary works and readers in historically distant contexts.

Gardner is right to stress the author's intention in her account of the historically extended social life of literary artifacts. A literary object is the deliberate and purposeful work of a human agent. However, it is one thing to argue that a literary work has been created on purpose with a particular set of initial goals, and quite another matter to maintain that the author's intention remains fully transparent and effective over time once it has been activated in a text. Furthermore, the idea that a text can have social effects all by itself is based on a faulty ontology of literary artifacts. Literary objects have no power to bring about social effects without intervention by knowledgeable agents who engage with those objects (Livingston 1991: 63ff.). Gardner's model insists on a strong picture of the author's role in a historically extended cultural dialogue, but it fails to give an even minimally adequate account of the contribution to that dialogue of the recipients and beneficiaries of literary works.

The larger aim of *In Defence of the Imagination* is to express militant opposition to what are described as the vitiated and ideologically distorted practices of contemporary reading. This opposition takes the form of a violent attack on the new theoretical movements that began to emerge in the 1970s and became professionally dominant in the 1980s. At one point Gardner characterizes herself as a kind of academic Rip Van Winkle returning to the field of literary criticism after a long slumber and finding it virtually unrecognizable.

It is these new, theoretically dense and unfamiliar discourses that prompt Gardner to undertake a defense of the imagination. Following the maxim that the best defense is a good offense,

Gardner moves to an aggressive attack mode, condemning adherents to the new doctrines as 'enemies of humanity' (Kermode 1982: 87–102). Gardner's treatment of the new theories she encounters is neither competent nor particularly engaging. She complains bitterly about the 'strange and new vocabularies' used in contemporary interpretations, though without making much effort to understand the purpose behind the novel terminology. Her harshest objections, however, are reserved for the openly political character of recent critical movements.

Of course, many recent interpretations make no secret of their contingent political aims. However, Bakhtin specifically rejects the view that the reception of literary works in historically distant contexts should be condemned as ideological distortion. Meanings that could not have been fully grasped by the author are latent in great works of literature; they appear in successor cultures as acts of genuine discovery. Gardner would, of course, deny that literary works should be answerable to historically contingent interests. Interpretation should be concerned only with accurate re-articulation of an author's plain meaning. However, her account underestimates both the rich semantic potential of Shakespeare's texts and the complexity of active hermeneutic reflection on which the extended life of those texts depends (Morson and Emerson 1990: 284–290). Furthermore, the suggestion that interpretation can simply be a matter of reading for 'the plain sense' is not only theoretically inadequate; it is also politically disingenuous.

There have been many more recent articulations of the positions taken in *In Defence of the Imagination*. Brian Vickers engages with contemporary theory in much fuller detail than Gardner, though his general aims are very similar (Vickers 1993; see also Bevington 1994). Graham Bradshaw's work is a more specific rejoinder to British cultural materialists (Sinfield 1994: 4–5). Both of these writers develop their argument by means of much more detailed reading of Shakespeare's actual works than Gardner provides. In the United States Richard Levin has been indefatigable in challenging the work of feminists as well as cultural materialists. Nevertheless, Helen Gardner's close ties to an earlier generation of literary critics that includes F. R. Leavis and T. S. Eliot make her an apt representative for a set of doctrines that has been vigorously attacked by Jonathan Dollimore (1984) as the heresy of 'essentialist humanism'. His argument unfolds in the context of an innovative analysis of Jacobean tragedy as a form of radical social critique.

Dollimore maintains that the great tragic drama of the Jacobean period is created in opposition to a prevailing ideology of Christian humanism. The various plays, on this account, work to reveal the historically contingent human practices that are concealed and at the same time justified by the ideological fiction of a natural, providentially ordained hierarchy. Dollimore's strongest criticism is, however, reserved for a secular transformation of Christian humanism that only emerges after the Enlightenment. Essentialist humanism, on this account, is the doctrine of a universal essence of 'Man' fully expressed in each and every individual (Dollimore 1984: 250). This belief is variously said to be misguided, dishonest, and mostly just plain wrong, though Dollimore does not really take account of any arguments that might plausibly be used to defend such a view. The humanist view is wrong because it 'mystifies suffering and invests man with a quasi-transcendent identity' (p. 190). A more correct view, according to Dollimore, would be one that privileges historical difference, change and struggle.

Dollimore's critique of humanism is confined to its 'essentialist manifestations'. In a tantalizing footnote he explains that he is not concerned with the validity of 'other forms of humanism' and alludes to 'humanistic trends in the Renaissance' that encouraged political critique, resistance, and social change (pp. 283–284). Dollimore, writing in the tradition of Antonio Gramsci, Louis Althusser, and Raymond Williams, sees the overriding purpose of cultural inquiry as the overcoming of domination. In a crucial passage he demonstrates that the beliefs expressed by Hume and by Kant in an unchanging human essence and in an abstract human individuality are directly connected to their self-assured racism (p. 256). Successful resistance to the justification of institutionalized domination then calls for an intellectual orientation based on 'certain objectives: not essence but potential, not the human condition but cultural difference, not destiny but collectively identified goals' (p. 271).

In this, the final sentence of *Radical Tragedy*, Dollimore enunciates the broad agenda of what might be called a radical humanism. The emphasis on potential, cultural difference, and collective goals seems in a way to echo Bakhtin's intuitions about the 'complex unity of human cultures'. Unfortunately, the implementation of this agenda by oppositional critics has focused almost exclusively on cultural difference and struggle, with almost no attention given to ideas of 'potential' or 'collectively identified goals'.

However salient the critique of essentialist humanism may have been in the context of Dollimore's *Radical Tragedy*, in its derivative usages the expression has now become little more than a dismissive epithet. None of the critics he confronts use the term in their own self-understanding. The label of essentialist humanism is simply the interpellation of a diverse group of traditionally oriented critics by their opponents. There may be any number of family resemblances among the various critics who have been so interpellated, but it's not really clear that critics with a traditional orientation to the exegesis of literary works have been committed either to an idealist picture of meaning or to a politics of surveillance and domination. Nor is it apparent in exactly what precise philosophical sense any of this earlier work ought to be described as essentialist. The massive rejection of a wide-range traditional scholarship as the uniform expression of a misguided 'essentialist humanism' has often focused on the most vitiated and self-serving expressions of the humanist faith. This rather selective strategy misrepresents a set of insights with some genuine value for understanding Shakespeare's long-term cultural importance.

Some of the more recent examples of criticism defending the humanist tradition have been ignorant and mean-spirited, not to mention racist, and sexist, and this has made the broader attack on essentialist humanism seem more plausible and compelling. I nevertheless believe that even in the most egregious instances of conservative culture criticism certain important issues are raised. The basic intuitions of conservative culture criticism are that culture persists over time, that societies promote a sense of belonging through the practices of cultural memory, and that there are overarching values that usefully transcend the parochialism of identity politics. Related to this is the idea that we have some sort of obligation to the past, usually expressed through such notions as legacy, patrimony, or heritage. In this view the role of teachers in the humanities is to foster a sense of obligation in their students through the study of valued literary works. I'm not convinced that conservative culture critics are always sincere in their profession of such beliefs. However, the beliefs themselves merit serious attention, not least by oppositional critics committed to the progressive social agenda set forth by Jonathan Dollimore.

Oppositional criticism has attempted to dislodge the 'essentialist' view of Shakespeare's authority by arguing that it is based on a disingenuous metaphysic of textual value. Dollimore's *Radical Tragedy*

(1984) supplied the initial terms for the counter-attack against traditional criticism. This was followed by three influential collections of essays, *Political Shakespeare* (1985), edited by Dollimore and Alan Sinfield, and *Alternative Shakespeares* (1985), edited by John Drakakis, and *The Shakespeare Myth* (1988), edited by Graham Holderness. All these interventions shift attention away from analysis of text-immanent properties to study of literature as a set of institutions. One of the most original, and certainly the wittiest discussion of Shakespeare as a cultural institution has been in the recent work of Terence Hawkes.

That Shakespeherian Rag was a path-breaking study which set out to expose the hidden political agenda in some of the most venerated works of Shakespeare scholarship. Hawkes analyzes the various ideological preoccupations that motivate the work of A. C. Bradley, Sir Walter Raleigh, and John Dover Wilson. The discussion of Dover Wilson's recruitment of Shakespeare as an ally in the struggle against bolshevism and labor unrest has been an important model for a great many similar investigations. In some ways, however, the title essay, which focuses on T. S. Eliot's curious relationship with Shakespeare, is the most interesting section of Hawkes' work. Bradley, Dover Wilson, and Raleigh are responsible for creating an overly solemn, joyless, and stuffy picture of Shakespeare as the central icon of British national culture. For Hawkes it is T. S. Eliot, with his lifelong interest in vocalization and his sensitivity to 'that Shakespeherian rag', who recognizes the jazz – or jouisance – in Shakespeare's writing.

That a political and religious conservative like T. S. Eliot should be assigned the role of playful and transgressive outsider already tells us a great deal about Hawkes' view of the politics of literary culture in contemporary England. But Eliot is important for Hawkes' argument as the representative of an alternative intonational dispensation for the reception of Shakespeare based on the spontaneous and improvisatory polyphony of jazz. Eliot's appreciation for the sound of Shakespeare's language is contrasted with Bradley's preoccupations with language as the unvoiced 'expression' of the 'author's mind'. This appreciation for the physicality of language is no doubt enhanced by Eliot's 'American accent' and his sensitivity to a wide range of speech types: 'Being an American helped him to recognize something that Bradley, being English, missed: the sound of the human voice and the demand for dialogue, for joining in the chorus, that it embodies' (Hawkes 1986: 90). It is perhaps a little odd to think of Eliot as a proto-Bakhtinian critic of Shakespeare, but Hawkes does try to show that Eliot's poetry, if not his criticism, is committed to a polyphonic view of language. Jazz Shakespeare then is proposed as a replacement for an essentially moribund classical Shakespeare.

T. S. Eliot's irreverent handling of Shakespeare suggests a way to return his works to the participatory interaction and playful dialogue of popular culture. Hawkes sees jazz as a model for the production of aesthetic experience as a form of improvisation.

> The essence of that native American musical tradition . . . blues and jazz, lies . . . in its reaching out to and invasion of its listener's being below the conscious levels of thought and feeling, in the identification with the performance that it demands from an audience, and in the identity it insists on between performance and performer: a performance in which 'interpolations' in and on to the original 'text' . . . literally constitute the music and make the player, music, and audience simultaneously part of the same momentary whole.
>
> (Hawkes 1986: 88)

Jazz is derivative creativity, a synthesis of lawful or pre-ordained structure with spontaneous expressive individuality. This is an extremely interesting metaphor to describe the interactive reception of a work by Shakespeare, especially in the way it assigns an equal privilege to the most ephemeral aspects of the moment of a work's reception and to the presumably more durable features that constitute the work's identity. In proposing jazz as his preferred model for interpretation, Hawkes appears to endorse a fully interactive theory for explaining Shakespeare's cultural authority. However, Hawkes' commitment to the idea that Shakespeare's works participate in a temporally extended dialogue is in fact as one-sided as Gardner's.

For Hawkes, a Shakespeare work has no specific identity or being in itself. Works of literature exist only as loose aggregates of contingent local appropriations. This view is hinted at in *That Shakespeherian Rag*; it is prosecuted much more forcefully, however, in the 1992 volume, *Meaning by Shakespeare*.

> Traditionally, critics, producers, actors and audiences of Shakespeare have assumed . . . that the 'meaning' of a play is bequeathed to it *ab initio* and lies – artfully concealed perhaps – within its text. Each account, or production of the play, then

offers to discover and lay hold of this meaning, hoisting it triumphantly, like buried treasure, into view. . . . However, these essays rest on a different, almost opposite principle. . . . Suppose we have no access to any 'essential' meaning nestling within Shakespeare's texts and awaiting our discovery (any more, let it be said, than Shakespeare did). Then what can their purpose be? If they do not transmit the meaning intended and embodied within them by their author, what on earth do Shakespeare's plays do? How do they work? And what are they *for*?

The answers proposed here suggest that, for us, the plays have the same function as, and work like, the words of which they are made. We *use* them to generate meaning. In the twentieth century, Shakespeare's plays have become one of the central agencies through which our culture performs this operation. That is what they do, that is how they work, and that is what they are for. Shakespeare doesn't mean: *we* mean *by* Shakespeare.

(Hawkes 1992: 3)

This, it seems to me, moves destructively away from the very promising idea of interpretive dialogue suggested by jazz Shakespeare in its unequivocal assertion of the work's semantic emptiness ('Shakespeare doesn't mean'). On Hawkes' account, literary artifacts endure precisely because of this emptiness. Shakespeare's works (and presumably the works of all other valued authors) possess no real value or determinate meaning in themselves, though they do possess instrumental utility.

By focusing exclusively on the socially pragmatic uses of Shakespeare's works, Hawkes' analysis seeks to replace a dogmatic essentialism with an equally dogmatic, self-defeating functionalism. The category of the semantically determinate work is eliminated in favor of an account of the aggregate of its social functions as a text. This is clearly the obverse of an essentialist picture of the numinous work whose metaphysical reality is radically disengaged from its social existence. Hawkes' inarticulate functionalism is, however, neither more cogent nor more helpful than the so-called essentialism it sets out to replace. Literary works certainly have a variety of social and psychological functions over the duration of their existence, and they have frequently been recruited in the service of ideological interests. However, many of the specific uses of a work within successor cultures are unanticipated and unintended consequences of the work's semantic potentiality. To maintain that such unforeseen consequences could have any significant bearing on the formal and semantic configuration of a work is to mystify the actual creation of literary artifacts by introducing a confused and occulted teleology. Indeed, any theory that attempted to account for a work's particular shape based only on its social afterlife would lack even a minimal descriptive and explanatory competence.

Jon Elster has pointed out that functional explanation has cogency only when applied to a recurrent pattern of actions and events.

> Functional explanation is applicable when a pattern of behavior maintains itself through the consequences it generates; more specifically, through consequences that benefit some group, which may or may not be the same as the group of people displaying the behavior.
>
> (1986: 32)

The central claim of the contemporary oppositional critique is that the use of Shakespeare has been of enduring benefit to a particular group. Recent research emphasizing the social provenance of Shakespeare's works has been concerned with demonstrating how he has been enlisted by a social and economic regime to serve the interests of a white, Christian, middle-class, predominantly male and heterosexual mainstream. For these critics, Shakespeare's cultural authority cannot be explained on the basis of any immanent properties of his work. That authority must be understood as the artifact of various institutional practices. The study of these institutional practices has been prompted by a commitment to exposing the function of Shakespeare in furthering class or gender domination and social discipline. This is clearly a project of an adversary culture within the academy. The success of this research agenda has made it increasingly difficult to defend the older, apparently naïve view of Shakespeare's authority as flowing naturally from intrinsic properties of the works.

It is now clear, I believe, that manifold institutional practices, supported by massive investment in concrete institutional infrastructure, have jointly contributed to the cultural position of Shakespeare and have shaped the reception of his works. Clearly a literary artifact cannot be grasped in isolation from its complex social history. In *Shakespeare's America/America's Shakespeare* (Bristol 1990) I have sketched the difference between the Shakespeare of England and the Shakespeare of the United States. Important research is also being done on the role of Shakespeare in the national culture of Canada, Australia, Germany, and India. However, overly restrictive attention to the local utilities served by particular works does not provide an adequate account of that work's larger social history. The danger inherent in particularistic research of this kind is that it may promote an unnecessarily fragmented picture of Shakespeare as a random aggregate of local practices and partisan ideological appropriations.

A model of cultural authority based exclusively on fragmentary appropriations and local historical struggle tends to obscure larger social continuities. It also tends to overlook the specific properties of literary artifacts. As Elster has shown, the cogency of any functional analysis depends on establishing the existence of feedback mechanisms in order to account for the functional persistence of various practices. In other words, there must be some kind of causal link between a given pattern of activity and the historically downstream behavior that reflects or reproduces it. In the case of a literary work this causal connection is easy to demonstrate, since such an artifact is itself an example of a feedback mechanism. Shakespeare's works do not consist of empty signifiers freely available for opportunistic appropriation. They are already 'thick with interpretations', exactly as Bakhtin suggests. The ideological uses of this material are not well described as unilateral appropriations; these 'uses' are more correctly viewed as the discovery of latent semantic potentiality. Some of the most persuasive scholarship produced by oppositional critics has shown how the ideological effects of plays like *King Lear* or *The Tempest* are prompted by the narrative and linguistic shapes of the works in question.

The central arguments of Hawkes' *Meaning by Shakespeare* depend very heavily on the insights of deconstruction, with its central principle of the semantic dispersal of texts into a generalized textuality or *écriture*. The realization that texts lend themselves to a variety of sometimes incompatible interpretations was, of course, obvious to readers in antiquity long before anyone had ever heard of literary deconstruction. In many social and interpretive contexts, however, this insight simply does not seem all that compelling. St Augustine pointed out the arbitrariness and instability of the verbal sign, but only to warn about the dangers of wilful and wayward interpretation. Similarly, as a written text the Koran is no less an unstable construction of semiotic difference than the works of Shakespeare, yet for astute Muslims such an observation completely misses the real significance of a unique historical event of divine revelation. In the Islamic community there could be no practical reason to contemplate the free play of signification; the purpose of reading is to understand and to obey the will of Allah more fully. In such a context the insights of deconstruction are likely to be seen not so much as heretical as simply frivolous.

Shakespeare's plays certainly display considerable semantic ambiguity, and this is no doubt a property they share with every other textual artifact. However, instead of uncritically celebrating the indeterminacy of texts as if this in itself were a truly liberating discovery, it may be more productive to reflect on the kind of society in which just this peculiar property of verbal artifacts seems the salient and important feature to notice about them. The possibility of multiple textual meaning only takes on importance in societies where institutional monopolies of interpretation give way to the practice of open discussion typical of the liberal and democratic public sphere. Deconstruction argues for an even more radical dissolution of the signifier into an anonymous and unstable textuality. The notion that signification is perpetually mobile, changing, and incommensurable actually describes the increasingly absolute sovereignty of the free market in contemporary society, where the fading away of reliable meaning in discursive practices such as advertising has become a familiar feature of everyday life.

Hawkes is certainly right to argue that the interpretation of a literary work is never a simple matter of passive submission to an author's intention. The activity of interpretation is always socially interested. However, it does not follow from these insights that literary works are themselves vacuous. To suggest that a verbal artifact as complex as for example, *Hamlet*, contributes nothing of its own to the practices of exegesis, interpretation, and stage performance is to trivialize those very practices. 'Even bricks', says Bakhtin, 'have a definite spatial form, and consequently, in the hands of a builder, they express something' (1986: 4).

The Bardbiz debate has unfolded as an increasingly scandalous altercation over the proper allocation and administration of Shakespeare's cultural authority. The strife, however, is really much less about the Bard than it appears to be, and more about the biz. Gardner clearly sees the encroachment of the market as a threat, but fails to realize how Shakespeare is already fundamentally implicated in commercial relations. Hawkes' doctrine of semantic indeterminacy, on the other hand, is a misrecognition of the socially disorienting effects of market economics. The partial and distorted awareness of the economic aspects of cultural experience suggests a provisional approach to big-time Shakespeare as the product of what I will call the supply side of culture.

My preliminary hypothesis is that once a certain threshold of public familiarity has been achieved, the long-term success of a line of cultural products can become self-financing. New cultural products succeed by tapping a pool of demand that has already been created by previous patterns of consumption. The role of the supply side is now evident in the simultaneous appearance of new editions of Shakespeare's works from several major publishers, and the consequent redeployment of the scholarly labor force. These new editions have relatively little philological significance. They do reflect the contemporary spirit of economic deregulation, however, and the potential payoffs for the winners in the marketing competition may be considerable. The discussion of the supply side hypothesis will focus on cultural markets and on the commercial value of Shakespeare's plays to the producers of cultural goods and services. Shakespeare retains his authority, at least in part, because suppliers of cultural goods have been skillful at generating a social desire for products that bear his trademark and in creating merchandise to satisfy that desire.

My initial 'text' for this discussion of the supply side of culture will be the familiar story of the early modern theaters and the way they interact with an emerging print culture. The early modern theaters as well as the printers and booksellers competed in a lively market for cultural goods and services. My central argument here will be that Shakespeare's plays were composed within the context of an early and prototypical culture industry. I then consider the parallel development in the eighteenth century of publishing and entertainment as businesses within the larger framework of the public sphere. The focus here will be on some of the primary institution builders, including William Davenant, David Garrick, and Edmond Malone. Particular attention is given to the initiatives of the publishing house of Jacob Tonson and his heirs in generating a market for printed editions of Shakespeare's works. The final chapter of Part I examines the way cultural capital has been transformed into capital pure and simple within the contemporary cultural market. I will look at a few salient examples of the commercial production of Shakespeare's works in the contemporary cultural market. This will be followed by a discussion of the journalistic promotion of Shakespeare's celebrity. I conclude my discussion of the supply side hypothesis in Part I with a more broadly theoretical examination of contemporary mass culture. This preliminary hypothesis helps to clarify the semantics of Shakespeare's name in our culture, but it does not try to account for any specific properties of Shakespeare's works. In Part II of this book, therefore, I adopt a substantially modified perspective that will provide a more complex account of big-time Shakespeare.

Chapter 2

The bias of the world

Since Kings break faith upon commodities, Gain be my Lord, for I will worship thee.

(King John: 2.1.573)

It is a matter of increasing controversy and scandal whether or not the works of Shakespeare are foundational works of Western civilization. There is, however, considerably less uncertainty that they are founding documents in the history of modern show business. By the time Shakespeare began his professional career in London there was already a very lively market for a diverse range of cultural products and services. This market offered an array of alternatives to the participatory and collective forms of traditional culture to a new constituency of consumers. The appearance of anonymous customers for these products marks off a specialized sense of culture as a sphere of activity separate from the social and religious imperatives of the traditional community. Shakespeare's works enter this market by way of two different and in some sense fundamentally opposed forms of production: theatrical performances and printed books.

In this chapter I intend to analyze the complex relationship between these emerging media without assigning a privilege either to a theatrical or to a bookish Shakespeare. Instead of taking sides on this troublesome question, I will suggest that competition between these institutional regimes is a necessary part of any explanation of Shakespeare's durable importance. The aim here will be to explore the early institutional formation of Shakespeare's cultural authority and to suggest a pattern of long-term continuity in that institutional formation. I will look first at theater and then at printing in early modern England as both cultural and economic practices. In order to articulate the question of authority more precisely, I will then turn to the vexed and increasingly confused question of Shakespeare as an author, a question I hope to reformulate in terms of the broader issue of Shakespeare's vocation.

NO BUSINESS LIKE SHOW BUSINESS

The earliest permanently housed commercial theaters were established in London while Shakespeare was still a boy in Stratford. Considerable symbolic importance has been assigned to the simultaneous construction of no fewer than three new playhouses in 1576, but, as William Ingram's research makes clear, the events of that year were possible only on the basis of complex antecedent developments (Ingram 1992: 119–150). There are at least three distinct stages in the formation of this early modern entertainment industry. The first stage corresponds to the emergence of a number of more or less permanent repertory companies that provided a decent livelihood for their members by performing in rented spaces. The moderate success of these repertory companies evidently suggested the idea of capital investment in permanent infrastructure for a nascent entertainment business. In this crucial second stage, purpose-built playhouses were constructed to be leased on various terms to established companies. To proceed with such capital ventures, investors would have to be convinced that there is already a viable market for dramatic performances. The third stage in the development of this prototypical show-business would be what economists call vertical integration as the members of the repertory companies themselves invested in theater buildings and eventually even formed partnerships with booksellers for the distribution and sale of printed editions of selected plays.

Given the combination of surveillance by state power, hostility from the civic authorities in London, and religious anti-theatricalism, it has seemed to some observers that the early playhouse projects must have been fundamentally subversive of social order and stability. The early theaters have been analyzed by Louis Montrose and Steven Mullaney in terms of their marginality relative to a dominant ceremonial culture of the crown and the city companies (Montrose 1980; Mullaney 1986; Tennenhouse 1986). Mullaney interprets this marginality as a paradoxical manifestation of power.

> Some of the . . . most equivocal acts of cultural definition and per-
> formance were reserved for the margins of early modern society:
> for that culturally, socially, and politically ambiguous domain
> outside the city walls, where the powers of city, state, and church
> were most resolutely plural and most equivocally defined.
>
> (Mullaney 1986: 24)

Mullaney approaches the history of the early modern theater with
the skills of a sensitive ethnographer in order to foreground and
de-familiarize the distinctive features of the Elizabethan city as a
historically distant and in many ways exotic cultural formation.
My own orientation, by contrast, aims at a re-familiarization with
a view towards highlighting institutional and cultural continuities.

Mullaney's research is an important contribution to an ongoing
debate over the political impact of early modern theaters and their
possible role in fostering social change. The vigorous opposition to
the novel institution of the commercial theaters voiced by various
religious and civic authorities has suggested to some that the
activities of the repertory companies must have been effective in
expressing opposition to important segments of the dominant
culture. Other critics have argued that even the most extreme forms
of theatrical license should be seen as part of a larger dialectic of
surveillance and social discipline (Greenblatt 1988: 110–116).
Jean Howard has recently tried to adjudicate this issue by analyzing
various dramatic works performed in the theaters as the articulation
of diverse ideological interests (1994: 1–22). However, even the
most detailed investigation of the contradictory pattern of ideological interests in which theater is implicated is unlikely to settle
the issue. Part of the problem with the debate may be that it depends
too heavily on the evidence of a vividly polemical anti-theatrical
literature. The rhetorical intensity of this literature, together with
its graphic depictions of moral and social degeneracy may in fact
give us a very distorted and exaggerated picture of the actual effects
of early modern theaters on the general population.

The debate over theatrical subversion and its containment has
been inconclusive partly because it depends on conceptions of power
and ideology that seriously underestimate the exigencies of a market
economy. Recent studies by Jean Christophe Agnew, Richard
Halperin, and Douglas Bruster have stressed the more narrowly
economic dimensions of theater practice in relation to the cultural
marketplace (Agnew 1986; Bruster 1992; Halperin 1991). These

studies have unfortunately focused too heavily on unnecessarily abstract notions such as 'the placeless market' or 'primitive accumulation', with the aim of interpreting the overall cultural significance of the early theaters. Viewed in retrospect, the early playhouse may well have had some function in the expression of such vague notions as class struggle, marginality, socio-sexual anxiety, or the appearance of new forms of social discipline. However, the early history of theater as a business suggests that there were more immediate practical issues at stake both for the proprietors of the new playhouses and for the sharers in the newly formed joint-stock companies.

Without wishing to deny the importance either of anti-theatrical polemics or of the critical scholarship it has inspired, I nevertheless want to suggest that in many ways the urban environment of London in the late sixteenth and early seventeenth century provided highly advantageous circumstances for the formation of an early entertainment industry. The sharers in the new joint-stock companies had good reason to believe in the likelihood of their own success. It is difficult to reconstruct from the very scanty evidence that has survived exactly what might have prompted such early entrepreneurs as James Burbage or John Brayne to invest in the construction of a building for the risky and possibly illicit purpose of staging plays. It seems highly probable, however, that their desire for a lucrative return on their investments was at least as important as any artistic aspirations they may have had or any political agenda they may have intended to pursue.

The evolution of a trade in cultural goods, which includes a specific demand for performance services, was not an abrupt emergence. The rather far-fetched scheme of earning a steady livelihood by charging admission to dramatic performances only makes sense within a well-developed money economy. Speculators in early modern show business had to hope that their potential customers would understand exactly what they proposed to offer. Even more basic than any specific 'purpose of playing' in this context was the elementary notion of purchasing a commodity.

> The city of London standeth chiefly upon the traffic and intercourse of merchants and the use of buying and selling of their sundry commodities.
>
> (*A breefe discourse* 1584: 21)

The circulation of cultural commodities by ballad-mongers and itinerant players was already a well-established practice in the towns and rural fairs all over England (Würzbach 1990). The more diversified forms of production and distribution typical of a rudimentary culture industry developed within the highly favorable economic environment of London.

One way to grasp the intensely commercial character of the early modern theaters is to consider how the specialized *métier* of the professional players differs from the social role of performers in traditional community-based pageantry. Robert Laneham, in a letter composed in 1575, describes a special performance for the Queen's visit 'by certain good hearted men of Coventry' of the traditional Hock Tuesday play. The featured role of Gawain in this unusual revival was performed by 'captain Cox . . . by profession a Mason' (Ingram 1982: 273). According to Laneham, Cox was a man of multiple attainments. He was a master story-teller, whose repertoire included a vast range of folk material along with such items as 'Gargantua' and 'Elynor Rumming'. And he was also widely read in moral and natural philosophy, 'to guess by the omberty of his books (p. 274)'. Cox was also prominent in the local militia, where his judgement was taken as the best in the parish; he was regularly chosen to serve as an officer over his social superiors.

It's clear from Laneham's account that Cox was deeply committed to the traditions of his community. The Hock Tuesday play had served to represent and celebrate historical narratives with considerable local importance in Coventry. The Queen's visit in 1575 provided the occasion for a revival of this custom which, like other forms of popular theatricality, had been actively discouraged by increasingly severe preachers. 'Playing' in this context is a particularly vivid and engaging form of social participation, a 'pastime' used for purposes of conviviality and the expression of shared social meaning. It has only marginal economic significance. Cox and the other 'good-hearted Coventry men' accepted a generous gratuity from the Queen for their performance, but the Hock Tuesday play was not performed as a commercial venture.

The suppression of popular theatricality by Church authorities may actually have provided a commercial advantage for the professional companies by helping to open up a market niche for their services. Players like Tarlton, Burbage, Alleyne, and Kemp offered a more specialized version of the skills possessed by Captain Cox. As professionals in the entertainment field, however, they are not deeply embedded in the manifold activities of everyday community life. Their performances are convened not in accordance with a traditional festive calendar but by a regularly publicized commercial schedule. Attendance at theatrical performances in the public theaters might be, among other things, an occasion for conviviality, but there is now a marked social distance separating the performers from the spectators. This social distance is a crucial factor in the emergence of the novel institution of the star performer.

The most prominent players in the early modern entertainment business are not only purveyors of cultural products, they are themselves extremely valuable commercial properties. The new theaters are simply a specialized market environment for these living commodities, and plays are often composed as vehicles for certain performers. A star of the magnitude of Will Kemp was able to capitalize on the simple fact of being Will Kemp (Wiles 1987: 24–43). Kemp is an exemplary case of show business celebrity. He was widely known not only in England, but throughout Western Europe. The autobiographical *Nine Daies Wonder* suggests that Kemp was popular not only for particular skills but also for his personality, much in the way of modern celebrities. Despite his success, however, the big time was hard time for Kemp as he evidently died penniless (Wiles 1987: 41). The commercial entertainment industry he helped found, however, continued to thrive in London and elsewhere.

Several factors account for the hospitality of London to an emerging trade in cultural commodities and specifically for dramatic entertainments performed by full-time professional actors. London's hospitality to 'the use of buying and selling of . . . sundry commodities' has already been noted. But London also had a distinctive political culture in which the strategic pursuit of economic advantage was well understood and carefully protected (Hexter 1980: 17). In many ways the civic institutions of London at this time also anticipate some of the typical features of the liberal political institutions that would emerge more fully during the eighteenth century.

the manner of their government, whereat strangers do no lesse envy than admire seeing so populous a city, containing by true estimation more then 500 thousands of all sorts of inhabitants managed not by cruel viceroys, as is Naples or Milan . . . but by a man of trade or a mere merchant.

(*A breefe discourse* 1584: 15)

The virtual sovereignty of men of trade leads to a situation where economic self-determination is strongly defended, mainly through litigation and precedent, but also through statutory law. There is a strong consensus that people have the right to enjoy the benefits of property accumulated through their own labor. Brayne, Burbage, and the other early theatrical speculators were all themselves men of trade. Whatever theoretical objections might be raised to the idea of 'harlotry players', the right of tradesmen to dispose of their own capital assets would nevertheless be widely recognized.

Despite the open hostility of the city authorities, the early theatrical speculators could count on a potentially large clientele already familiar with complex cultural negotiations in their everyday life. Individual cultural consumers might conceivably find particular plays distasteful on ideological grounds, but the larger principles of theatrical representation would pose no immediate challenge to their sense of social order. The citizens, apprentices, and foreign visitors in London during the early modern period were, of course, familiar with a public culture of spectacle and pageantry within a variety of social contexts. Dramatic performances were important in the social life of guilds, in universities, in aristocratic households and in the popular festive traditions of small communities (Billington 1991; Bristol 1986; Laroque 1991). These performances were intended as significant expressions of community solidarity and of the values of corporate life, and participation in this form of spectacle provided for a greatly enhanced experience of conviviality. The larger processions staged by the Crown, the Lord Mayor, and the great livery companies, on the other hand, were more frankly expressions of power and authority. What was novel and perhaps disruptive about the commercial theaters could not have been the simple fact of theatrical performance in itself. What the theaters were able to accomplish was the transformation of otherwise familiar performance practices into cultural merchandise. To grasp the implications of this development it is important to examine more closely the notion of commodity.

A commodity is an article of commerce exchanged with a view to purely economic advantage among people who remain strangers to each other. Anthropologists frequently distinguish between commodity exchange and gift exchange in terms of their bearing on the ethical relations between the participating agents. In sixteenth-century usage, however, commodity has additional, related advantages of both expediency and convenience. Albert Borgmann, in his study *Technology and the Character of Contemporary Life* (1984), has adopted these earlier meanings as part of an ambitious critique of technology. I will discuss this critique at greater length in Chapter 4. What's important to note about Borgmann's analysis here, however, is the distinctive appeal of a commodity as a means for securing a desired utility without the complications of reciprocal obligation and social engagement that prevail in a gift economy. Dramatic performance in the early modern commercial playhouse offers the commodities of spectacle, narrative, and conviviality without the long-term social commitment that would be required to obtain these goods in a traditional social setting.

Theatres like the Globe or the Curtain are paradigmatic examples of commodity exchange as this has come to operate in the sphere of cultural goods and services. The public who paid for admission to these performances were able to enjoy cultural goods at their pleasure as self-reliant consumers, without the time-consuming burden of direct participation. Dramatic presentation in the commercial playhouses is no longer tied to the traditional schedules of the liturgical calendar, nor is it dependent upon the ceremonial life of guilds or the patronage of great households. Although the major repertory companies retained important links with powerful aristocratic benefactors, commodity really is the bias of the show-business world in the sense that theatrical incomes are independent of the social status of its paying customers.

The playhouses make performance available, through direct purchase, to a new social constituency of cultural consumers. Affiliation with a corporate body gives way to disposable income as the basic qualification for participation in a cultural event. This confers at least a temporary social equality on all consumers of the same product. The socially undifferentiated consumer of cultural services is the most important invention of the early modern theater. The perceived danger of this social undifferentiation is prominent in many anti-theatrical pamphlets. Fears connected with theatrical representation are linked to larger anxieties about independent sources of secular authority. Certainly with the acceleration of trade in cultural goods and services, authority becomes discretionary – a matter of money rather than of close embedding in a traditional community with its patterns of solidarity, deference, and personal obligation.

The denunciations of the anti-theatrical pamphleteers have been diagnosed as a set of basically irrational anxieties about the nature of theatricality itself. However, as Mette Hjort has shown in her analysis of William Prynne's *Histrio-Mastix*, there is a certain cogency in the anti-theatrical literature (Hjort 1993: 187–195). What Prynne saw in the exchange of cultural commodities was the substitution of strategic economic calculation for the Christian virtues of gravity, modesty, and sobriety (pp. 190–195). Prynne's crucial insight is that the mutual enfranchisement of the commercial theaters and their clientele would have far-reaching implications for the moral authority of many traditional social institutions. His concern is perhaps best understood by considering the corporate and legal status of the repertory companies.

Although it was an adjunct to the corporate life of guilds, theatrical performance was not a free-standing traditional craft practice in its own right. The itinerant players of late medieval and early modern England never received a royal charter as a guild, even though acting is similar in many respects to skilled craft labor. Craft guilds are typically conservative social organizations with firmly established traditional privileges tied to a permanent location. Authority within the guilds is reserved for the master craftsmen who regulate production and set standards of quality. However, once the period of servitude as an apprentice has been completed, membership in a guild or livery company was a franchise to practice a craft under the general supervision of the corporation and to enjoy the status of citizen or freeman. The early travelling players led a life in many ways similar to that of the journeymen in the established crafts, but they were journeymen who could never look forward to the privileges and social status of settled masters in a trade. As players they did not enjoy any formal charter to practice their art, and in this sense they were not really very different from ordinary vagabonds.

Even well-established groups of players were excluded from the system of entrenched livery companies in London. Individual players were citizens, but only by virtue of their affiliation with other established trades. The collective security that comes with recognition as a legitimate profession was only available to theatrical companies as a gift of the Crown. Without a royal charter, companies of players could sustain themselves only through adroit social and economic improvisation. In order to distinguish themselves from the rather more desperate itinerant players, they were obliged to seek out aristocratic patrons for guarantees of social protection. However, it was precisely their anomalous position as

both protected servants of powerful nobles and as freelancing entrepreneurs in an underground economy that created new possibilities
for the organization of cultural production in sixteenth-century
London.

It is impossible to say whether or not the decision to stake one's
future in a risk-intensive enterprise like a repertory company or to
invest assets in the construction of a specialized building for stage
plays was prompted by anyone's sexual anxieties, or for that matter
by anyone's desire for artistic freedom and integrity. Cultural meanings of this kind simply do not appear in any of the very sketchy
documents on which we must base our knowledge of these historical
developments. There is, however, evidence that the appearance of
a rudimentary theater business is an instance of strategic economic
activity on the part of artisans, yeomen, and well-placed servants of
the royal household to profit from the redeployment of their limited
stock of surplus capital. Litigation over products like playing cards
and services such as costume rental suggests that there was already a
rapidly expanding market for cultural goods of this kind. These
early traders in cultural production were engaged in the assertion
of an extended property right. They sought redress in the courts
for claims to enjoy residual benefits accruing from the exercise of
their more limited franchise to practice a trade. The early theatrical
proprietors also used their limited assets to build playhouses which
offered a more profitable alternative to the more closely regulated
opportunities available within the framework of the livery companies to which they belonged. Once they had achieved a degree of
financial independence as a result of their profits from theater
ownership, they could afford to allow their membership in the traditional companies to lapse. The theaters then are a striking example
of technical innovation in the sphere of finance as well as in the
sphere of mechanical specialization. In their shift of accumulated
capital resources and in their recruitment of labor from the established trades to a completely new market in cultural goods, they
represent a deliberate strategy of economic diversification.

The strategy of diversification was possible because there was a
considerable volume of discretionary or *ad hoc* economic activity
within the interstices of the much more closely regulated guild
system. The existence of an underground economy in this context is
a consequence of the relatively de-racinated character of early
modern urban life. By the end of the sixteenth century there were
many people in London whose daily interactions were not closely

organized by guilds or other corporations. People newly arrived from rural villages and manors were no longer deeply embedded in a traditional community. Under these circumstances the seasonal rhythms of rural life gave way to an alternation of commercial activity with free time or leisure. The success of the professional theaters was based on its ability to define and to exploit this new leisure market.

In order to consolidate its social and economic gains, however, the new entertainment industry had to bargain for a more secure position within the official economy. This required protracted negotiations with the authority both of the Crown and of the livery companies themselves. In May 1603 Shakespeare's company, The Lord Chamberlain's Men, was reincorporated by letters patent as The King's Men. In this document the Crown undertakes to

> license and authorise these our servants Lawrence Fletcher, William Shakespeare, Richard Burbage, Augustine Phillips, John Heninges, Henry Condell, William Sly, Robert Armyn, Richard Cowly and the rest of their associates freely to use and exercise the Art and faculty of playing Comedies Tragedies histories Interludes moralls pastoralls Stageplays and such others like as they have already studied or hereafter shall use or study as well for the recreation of our loving Subjects as for our Solace and pleasure when we shall think good to see them.
>
> (Schoenbaum 1975: 95)

This document, which follows the pattern of earlier licenses for London repertory companies, authorizes Shakespeare and his associates to engage in playing as a profession as well as a trade. Although they were nominally the King's servants, the sharers in The King's Men had, with the issuing of the letters patent, achieved a status roughly equivalent to that of the traditional guilds in the sense that they had a franchise to practice the 'Arte and faculty of playinge'.

The position of theater has been analyzed in terms of its complicity with state power as well as its capacity for the subversion of a dominant order. However, long before the issuing of the letters patent by King James, it is clear that those who invented the theater had specific interests of their own, most notably an interest in economic survival. In the light of those interests it is not unlikely that many, if not all the principals in these enterprises were entirely indifferent to the possibility either of subversion of state power or of its affirmation. The political outlook of the shareholders was more likely to be linked to a preoccupation with their right to enjoy the profits of their own labor. At the same time, however, it seems evident that they also aspired to a fully acknowledged professional status. The letters patent affirm the specialized competence of theater as an art and a faculty with a distinctive social purpose that goes beyond commercial profit. The complex of motivations created by this situation might have suggested to many workers in the theater business a way to expand their purview to opportunities presented by an expanding market for printed books.

GETTING INTO PRINT

The professional repertory companies of early modern England represent an innovative form of cultural production marked by professional specialization and by the radical separation of dramatic performances from the traditions of communal life. Early modern theatrical entrepreneurs were engaged in a brisk commercial exchange in cultural goods and services. They were either theater owners and managers like James Burbage and Phillip Henslowe or sharers in repertory companies like John Heminge and Henry Condell. The most successful, William Shakespeare, Richard and Cuthbert Burbage, were both. This success is directly linked to the anonymity of a large consuming public and to the impersonal character of communicative interactions within the public space of the professional theater. The consequence of this situation on the supply side of cultural production is that the interest of dramatic works must become more catholic in its appeal. The exigencies of the cultural market tend to discourage anything which depends too heavily on the specialized background knowledge of privileged insiders that typify the patronage system or the structure of the livery companies.

Private patronage retains its importance throughout the eighteenth century and, in the form of corporate foundations, it continues to function today as an alternative to the cultural market. Nevertheless, the owners and operators of the public playhouses, either by choice or compulsion, did not choose to anchor their financial prospects in the vagaries of a patronage system. Instead they helped to invent the cultural consumer as a way to hedge their economic survival. Ironically, however, some members of the theatrical community then found that they actually despised their own social invention. Ben Jonson's resentment of the exigencies of the market and his general view of consumers as a kind of cultural rabble is well documented in the actual prologues to some of his plays. In *The Gull's Hornbook* Dekker complains that the commercial theater degrades poets to merchants. Beaumont and Fletcher's *Knight of the Burning Pestle* shows vividly how theater can actually exploit invidious social distinctions within its audience for the express purpose of entertaining that audience. What these examples suggest is a growing tension between the rival institutional regimes of popular culture as constituted by means of a newly formed show business industry and of literature as constituted by means of a newly formed print industry.

The production of dramatic works for the early modern cultural market in London falls under two distinct jurisdictions, the Master of the Revels and the Stationers Company. The interests of the repertory companies were tied most closely to the Revels Office, since it exercised control over all theatrical performances (Dutton 1991). The office was established as a permanent agency in 1545, initially to co-ordinate and supervise official Court revels, which traditionally extended throughout the festive season from All-Saints Day until the beginning of Lent. The scope of the office was gradually extended, however, and the Master assumed much broader powers to license production in the public theaters. The office of Master of the Revels was a desirable posting since its occupant was close to the centers of power and exercised considerable secular authority. It was also an increasingly lucrative position, deriving income not only from the regular salary for services rendered to the Court, but also from various licensing fees, gratuities, and other perquisites derived from the activities of an expanding and generally profitable show business.

Since responsibility for the Court Revels was one of the many diverse functions of the Lord Chamberlain's Office, the players were governed directly by an official member of the royal household. In effect their activities were part of the private and personal life of the Court. This by no means implies, however, that the players would have been on familiar terms with highly placed court officials in their leisure hours or even in the conduct of their business. Various players may have been directly acquainted with the Master of the Revels, but it is likely that most of their contacts were routine encounters with the clerks and yeomen who carried out the day-to-day management of the Revels Office. The livelihood of the professional companies depended on maintaining cordial relations with the officials of the Revels Office, which controlled their license to conduct business. In this narrowly restricted sense then, the economic interests of the players would be identified with the centralizing authority of the Crown.

The Revels Office provided a legal umbrella under which players could earn a living by staging performances of plays, subject to the oversight of the Master. This legal authorization did not, however, give players a right to residual reproduction of their work in the form of printed books. Although selling copies of the works performed in the commercial theaters would undoubtedly have been a profitable sideline for the players, they were in fact legally prevented from engaging in this type of auxiliary trade. The Stationers Company held the royal charter to control all aspects of printing and bookselling, including the publication of plays. Printers who were able to obtain copies of these works could produce them as books without compensating the companies and without seeking either the permission or the co-operation of their authors.

The Stationers Company was officially incorporated in 1557, although it was based on a much older organization. The company maintained a monopoly on the printing industry for the entire nation of England. This was a powerful guild with extensive *de jure* authority over a complex and far-reaching industrial sector comprised of print shops and booksellers. The guild also exercised indirect control over the segmented modes of production that found a lucrative and in some cases an indispensable outlet for their products in the printing trade. Print shops were a primary market for a substantial volume of upstream economic activity. Through their demand for basic materials they helped to co-ordinate the rapidly expanding manufacture of paper, ink, and other industrial products. They were the exclusive market for the highly specialized type foundries, and for the builders of presses. And of course printers and booksellers were a principal outlet for an emerging cadre of professional writers. Finally, the print shops also introduced a new system for the organization of labor, bringing together the skilled manual disciplines of pressmen and typesetters with the more intellectual trades of editors and correctors.

The Stationers Company also exercised control downstream over the circulation of finished products. Printing shops manufactured goods that were distributed and in some cases even commissioned by booksellers. In contrast with the Revels Office, the Stationers Company was clearly part of the market economy. It operated according to a different moral culture from the Revels Office and was oriented to different social purposes. Since it was organized as a traditional craft guild, the Stationers Company was more closely linked to the outlook of plebeian culture than it was to the aristocratic values of the Court. Printing was also one of the most socially as well as technically advanced forms of commodity exchange during the modern period. The exigencies of the market require printers and booksellers to be responsive to the interests of literate commoners as well as to a formally educated elite of aristocrats. As the corporate body representing the printing industry, the Stationers Company had a considerable impact on the intellectual life of early modern England, emerging along with show business as one of the major branches of a prototypical culture industry.

Printing is a striking technological innovation that has had far-reaching social consequences. Printed books make the experience of reading widely accessible through a system of commodity exchange that effectively disempowers traditional forms of surveillance and control for anyone who knows how to read. The mechanical reproduction of the written word makes the experience of reading incrementally less difficult for readers through the introduction of standardized typefaces and improved sharpness of the graphic imprint. The most significant impact of printing, however, comes not from any supposed transformation in the phenomenology of writing or of perception but from the possibility of a much wider circulation of ideas made possible by the new technology (Eisenstein 1983). The real technical innovation here is not the print medium in the abstract but rather the concrete application of printing techniques to the production of books.

The actual form known as the codex is one of the most remarkable and least noted of modern inventions. The mechanical reproduction of the written word in book form produces an object that is relatively cheap and very portable. Generally speaking, books are also sturdy enough to withstand the extensive handling that enables multiple readings. Most important, the codex form is physically organized to provide rapid and convenient random access memory. You could look it up. These are the technical features that really account for the extraordinary historical impact of printing during the early modern period. There are, of course, other techniques for storing and retrieving information, but the printing of books made possible unprecedented economies of scale. The availability of the printed book very rapidly eroded the monopolies of knowledge retained by a traditional elite culture through the techniques of manuscript production and limited coterie circulation.

The technical efficiency of printing is certainly one of the factors that helps to account both for a redefinition of religious authority and for a broad historical redistribution of political power. It would be misleading, however, simply to describe printing as the creation of a new monopoly of knowledge. Of course only a minority could read, and even fewer had access to the resources of a printing press. Nevertheless, detailed historical investigations of printing have shown that by the end of the sixteenth century the social uses of reading had become extremely diverse. Print was a potential resource for controlling people, but it was also a way for people to achieve unprecedented empowerment through the creation of new patterns of political and social affiliation (Davis 1975; Eisenstein 1983).

Any full consideration of the historical impact of printing must also consider the way in which the circulation of printed books makes possible and even encourages certain kinds of social behavior. The reading of books facilitates a significant degree of disengagement from the oral traditions typical of everyday social life with its many face-to-face encounters. Because books offer rich and intense communicative interactions, however, the reading subject does not experience this disengagement as loss or deprivation; on the contrary, reading provides greatly augmented possibilities for engagement beyond the parochial borders of oral culture. The expanded social horizons created by the medium of the printed book are clearly a salient feature of Bakhtin's description of the great work of art.

Literature assumes its present institutional shape of a bookish community of writers and readers as one of the many important social effects of printing technology during the early modern period. However, not everything that came off the presses was destined to be sanctioned by the literary community. There is a marked contrast between the function of broadsheets within popular culture and the function of costly editions of the works of Virgil within the culture of humanist scholars and their clientele. The publication of relatively inexpensive editions of plays in quarto formats suggests an even greater differentiation of the reading public.

Sixteenth- and early seventeenth-century play quartos have been studied extensively for the purpose of establishing reliable texts of the works of valued authors. Questions related to the sociology of reception for these products, however, have not received very much attention. It is difficult to say exactly who the printers and booksellers had in mind as the intended purchasers of this merchandise. The cost of a play in quarto form probably put it beyond the reach of many readers who nevertheless might be able to afford a copy of the latest ballad. Despite this, however, there is some evidence to suggest that individual play texts were intended primarily for the lower end of the market for printed books. Although some printers were more conscientious than others about the quality of the books they produced, plays in quarto were often carelessly printed. In contrast to better quality editions of classical authors, they have only at best a rudimentary apparatus to assist the reader. Title pages, which serve as advertisements for prospective purchasers, often call attention to their interest as records of performances. All this suggests that individual play texts were produced mainly for a rapidly changing short-term market for cultural goods.

As cultural merchandise, individual plays in quarto offer the appeal of immediate currency and do not lay claim to any permanent literary value. The most important qualities about these products for the cultural consumer would have been their novelty and topical interest. In publishing relatively inexpensive editions of plays, the early printers and booksellers must have assumed that there would be at least a transitory market for these commodities as a kind of spin-off from the popularity of the works in performance. For the printers, care and attention to textual accuracy, details of format, and quality of workmanship would be secondary to speed and timeliness of publication. The immediate concern was to capture an ephemeral market, not to prepare texts for inclusion in a permanent cultural archive. Certainly the early plays in quarto do not seem to have been intended for the libraries of wealthy book collectors, although ironically that would eventually be the ultimate fate of those copies which survived.

The transitory character of play texts is noted in Thomas Bodley's letter to Thomas James, which provides for the acquisitions policy of the Bodleian Library. Plays, along with ballads and almanacs, are to be discarded as unworthy of long-term preservation.

I can see no good reason to alter my opinion, for excluding such books, as almanacs, plays, & an infinite number, that are daily printed, of very unworthy matters and handling, such as, methinks, both the keeper & underkeeper should disdain to seek out, to deliver unto any man. Haply some plays may be worthy the keeping: but hardly one in forty. For it is not alike in English play, & others of other nations: because they are most esteemed, for learning the languages & many of them compiled, by men of great fame, for wisdom & learning, which is seldom or never seen among us. Were it so again, that some little profit might be reaped (which God knows is very little) out of some of our play-books, the benefit thereof will nothing near countervail the harm that the scandal will bring unto the Library, when it shall be given out, that we stuff it full of baggage books.

(Bodley 1926: 221)

The interdiction of plays here is not linked in any obvious way to early modern anti-theatricalism. Bodley's judgement is related to his assessment of the social provenance of this material. Because they are not written by 'men of great learning' they have no lasting value for the larger agenda of humanist learning. Plays have a fleeting topical interest, primarily for what we would now describe as a mass audience. Their purely recreational value does not warrant inclusion among the valued works of the Bodleian collection.

Notwithstanding Thomas Bodley's strictures, Shakespeare's importance for the interests of an emerging culture industry was already apparent to printers and booksellers in London during his own lifetime. What these early publishers grasped was that Shakespeare's popularity in the emerging commercial theaters could be profitably exploited within the diverse markets of an emerging book culture. The situation was particularly advantageous in that the printers had no legal obligation to compensate individual creators of play scripts for the use of their work. What must have been particularly irksome for the players in this situation was that the printers based their marketing strategies on the popular success of the plays in production. The title pages, blurbs, and other promotional materials that accompany the early printed editions suggest how the appeal of texts is referred back to and thus depends on the spectacles of which they are not so much a literary source as a mechanically reproduced record. The early editions offer intended purchasers repeated access to a dramatic spectacle 'as it was lately performed' and access to a faithful record of the poet's unique achievement before it was coarsened by public performance. The point of these advertisements is to exploit the chronic tension between the culture of spectacle and the culture of the printed book by working both sides of the street.

One of the striking proofs of the business acumen of John Heminge and Henry Condell, senior partners in The King's Men, was their decision to gain a foothold in this lucrative market by co-operating in the publication of the collected works of their fellow shareholder, William Shakespeare. The project was evidently conceived by the printing firm of William and Isaac Jaggard some time after Shakespeare's death. It's not really clear why this initiative was delayed for so long or what Shakespeare's pragmatic intentions might have been with respect to the publication of this material. In any case, Heminge and Condell found themselves in a position to claim residual property rights over play scripts by Shakespeare held in their possession. In order to derive financial benefit from these resources, however, they had to defend their financial interest against the printers and booksellers who legally owed them nothing.

Heminge and Condell did not, of course, openly contest the monopoly of the Stationers Company over all aspects of the book trade. They didn't have to. The project went forward as the result of complex business negotiations apparently initiated not by Heminge and Condell but rather by the Jaggards. Heminge and Condell had two important assets to trade with. First, they owned the physical copies of Shakespeare's works, including many that had never been printed. The Jaggards had already published a number of the plays in quarto and evidently believed that a collected edition would be a profitable venture (Williams 1985: 95–97). Second, they had a powerful contact in William Herbert, Earl of Pembroke, who was then Lord Chamberlain. Pembroke wrote a letter to the Stationers Company, instructing them that plays belonging to The King's Men could not be published without obtaining the permission of Heminge and Condell (Bentley 1961: 185–186). The creativity required for conceiving and executing this plan has not, perhaps, been sufficiently appreciated in recent scholarly literature. Nevertheless, the publication of the first folio is clearly an event of considerable significance in the early history of commercial cultural production in the way it establishes a precedent for lucrative co-operation between the competing institutional regimes of show business and print culture. It is also, and not incidentally, a crucial episode in the institutional history of literature.

Seen in the context of an early and prototypical culture industry, the first folio is important as an assertion of the players' property rights and a shrewd device for capturing a share of what was already a profitable market for works by Shakespeare. More specifically, the first folio of Shakespeare's works is an effort to capture a portion of the up-scale market for printed books. In both its physical design and in its much quoted advertisement, the folio seeks to approximate the typical format in which other valued literary authors were marketed. The editors' stress on their good-faith efforts to restore an accurate transcript of the author's textual intentions mimics the humanist philological project for classical authors. It also claims a place for the works of Shakespeare within the cultural archive defined by wealthier and better educated sectors of the reading public. I have argued elsewhere that Shakespeare's subsequent authority flows from this assertion of claims to canonical status and to membership in the archive of high culture (Bristol 1989). Such a judgement may, however, overestimate the relative importance of literature as the institutional agency through which secular authority is sustained.

Shakespeare's activity as a writer unfolds against a complex background of competing performance and print cultures. His works were created not as autonomous works of literary or even dramatic art as we now understand such notions, but rather as a set of practical solutions to the exigencies of a heterogeneous cultural market. The body of works we refer to as Shakespeare was initially composed, performed, and appreciated as merchandise for an emerging market in leisure and cultural services. The secular authority of those works is, practically speaking, entirely independent of the institutions of high literature, since it continues to operate very effectively through the alternative channels of the culture industry.

'TIS NO SIN FOR A MAN TO LABOR IN HIS VOCATION

With the publication of the first folio in 1623, Shakespeare, in the sense of a well-defined body of works, was advantageously situated in the primary sectors of the cultural marketplace. Shakespeare's position is confirmed first in the setting of an emerging show business characterized by differentiated cultural publics. His versatility in managing to cross over between the broad, heterogeneous commercial audience of the public theaters and the upscale market of the private playhouses has been discussed extensively. An important but perhaps unanticipated consequence of this initial show business success is that Shakespeare also becomes established as a significant figure within the competing regime of print culture, first as a primarily topical, mass market phenomenon and second as serious literature destined for a more select clientele. This record of extraordinary achievement is, of course, accomplished through the historical labor of many different individuals. It no longer seems plausible to explain all of this as a natural consequence of individual genius. How then are we to describe Shakespeare's individual activity as a writer and the question of authorship against this complex institutional background?

One way to understand Shakespeare's 'genius' would be to interpret his long-term success as a mostly unintended result of an opportunistic sense of how to exploit the medium in which he worked. The 'universality' of his plays would then be a loose way to characterize historically specific social relations that come into existence with the appearance of the cultural consumer and the circulation of cultural goods in commodity form. Audiences in the popular theaters were a shifting and anonymous public rather than a community, and there was considerable social distance between its various discrete elements and the members of the playing companies. These conditions of anonymity and social distance apply even more accurately to 'the great variety of readers' for printed versions of play scripts.

Shakespeare has been censured repeatedly for indiscriminate pandering to the vulgar taste of the groundlings. He has also been denounced for complicity with patriarchy, oppressive state power, and class domination. It might make more sense, however, to follow the lead of Samuel Johnson in condemning Shakespeare as morally unprincipled and opportunistic. The complexity of the plays might then be described not as an artistic achievement but rather as a shrewd strategy to curry favour with as many sectors as possible within a complex multi-cultural market. This would suggest that a Shakespearean work is in effect an industrial rather than an individual product and that its specific form of appearance is in some fundamental way motivated and sanctioned by an ethos of business success. Shakespeare would then be seen as something more like a modern corporate logo or trademark rather than the specific name of an exceptional individual or creative genius. Such a view would, of course, be radically antithetical to the traditional account of Shakespearean authorship.

The standard picture of Shakespeare as the author of the works that bear his name is initially proposed by textual editors in the early eighteenth century and is built up over time with increasing technical and theoretical sophistication. Central to this picture is the figure of the individual artist committed to the formal perfection of a body of unique works of art that fully represent his complex intentions. The achievement of this sovereign artistic identity is, however, constantly under threat from other social agents with whom it must perforce come into contact in the process of self-realization. The artist's real work is delivered to its public only after brutal mishandling by players, printers, and even by the very editors whose task was to restore the works in their original form.

Belief in the ethical priority of the author's original intentions over any concrete material embodiment of particular works led to the development of an increasingly complex set of hypotheses about the historical transmission of those works. The textual scholars who argued for this description of Shakespeare as an author were certainly not ignorant of the practical and institutional context in which the works were produced. On the contrary, their knowledge of the historical practices of early modern theater companies and print shops was certainly greater in the vast majority of cases than that of their recent post-structuralist critics. The problem with the standard account is not a lack of reliable information about the way the extant texts came into being. It is rather in the explanatory models which were used to interpret that information and to generate a misleading, though perhaps not altogether misguided, account of the role of individual creativity in the production of Shakespeare's plays.

The most responsible and informative critique of the standard account has come from a group of textual editors led by Michael Warren and Paul Werstine. These scholars have shown that in their determination to save the appearance of Shakespearean authorship in its classical, individualized form, editors were forced to develop an unwieldy system of auxiliary hypotheses based on the most tenuous historical evidence. For example, Paul Werstine has shown that the author's 'foul papers', which are assigned a crucial and privileged position in the actual lineage of extant printed texts, are

largely the product of wishful thinking on the part of modern
editors, who need a way to imagine the author's perfected work in
concrete form (Werstine 1990: 68ff.). Unfortunately the critical
rethinking of textual and editorial questions does not actually get us
any closer to a clear or reliable understanding of how these works
were actually created. Conjectures about Shakespeare's revision of
his own plays, or about the collaborative nature of their composition
are not supported by newly discovered historical evidence. These
new theories are simply more cautious interpretations of the
fragmentary evidence with the undoubted virtue of relinquishing
the *ad hoc* explanations required to sustain the older narratives.
In effect the critique of critical editorial practice does very little
except to change the valences of the standard account. The participation of collaborators, revisers and other secondary creative agents
was already well understood in traditional textual scholarship. The
textual revisionists argue that singular creative agency cannot be
disentangled from derivative forms of participation in artistic production and that the social dignity of these complex practices must
be acknowledged.

The broader context for understanding Shakespeare's activity
as a writer has been very thoroughly studied in the professional
literature over the past decade. It is now clear, I think, that some
cherished assumptions about Shakespeare's genius that have survived from eighteenth- and nineteenth-century criticism will have
to be re-examined and perhaps modified. We understand much
better now that the composition of Shakespeare's plays was made
possible within the specific technological and commercial infrastructure of the early London theaters. We also understand that the
publication of his plays in book form was made possible by a quite
different technological and commercial infrastructure in the early
printing industry. The romantic valorization of literary authorship
as an embattled practice of solitary creativity is almost certainly
inaccurate, at least for the early modern period. For some critics this
revision of the practical history of authorship has been interpreted
as support for the far more radical doctrines of the abolition and
death of the author.

In the recent post-structuralist critique of authorship the specific
artifacts known as Shakespeare's works are described not as the
creation of individual authors, but rather as a local manifestation of
larger discursive formations. The idea of a discursive formation has
had undeniable heuristic importance in recent criticism. First of all

this notion draws attention to the undeniable (but perhaps in the end trivial) insight that the existence of works of verbal art is only possible given the prior existence of a human language as well as a community of speakers who use that language in specific ways to accomplish particular social tasks. This of course undercuts faulty conceptions of artistic autonomy or expressive freedom by insisting that language determines what gets said and what gets recognized as worth saying. The idea of a discursive formation also reminds us of the derivative character of even the most original work.

The argument that works are the manifestation of discursive formations correctly insists that the institutional background against which artistic activity takes place must be specified in any historically cogent account of human creativity. However, if taken literally this idea is misleading. The flat statement that works are actually *produced* by discursive formations substitutes the vague operations of a ghostly metaphysical entity for more literal-minded notions of singular agency and purposive verbal activity. The romantic idea of authorship as sovereign and fully self-possessed creative originality is faulty or incomplete as an explanation for the appearance of specific works, but the blanket denial of the author is simply a dogmatic assertion that no explanation is required. To believe literally the claim that works are produced by discursive formations isn't really much different from believing literally in the inspiration of a muse, in the operation of a poetic *daemon*, or in active interventions of the Holy Ghost.

One obstacle to discussing this problem results from basic semantic confusion about the specific way in which the term 'author' is being used in the post-structuralist critique. In a broad sense, the expression simply denotes the specific agent or agents whose skilled and intentional engagement with the already existing resources of verbal expression is a proximate cause for the appearance of a specific work. Publius Vergilius Maro, Geoffrey Chaucer, William Shakespeare, Jane Austen, and Virginia Woolf are all authors in this general and inclusive sense, even though the social arrangements in which they worked were radically different in every case. Here it should be stipulated that the singularity of these agents does not refer to isolated, sovereign, and self-contained individuality. It simply designates the general case of causality that exists between a particular person and a specific verbal artifact. The radical insistence that works do not have authors even in this sense of a broad class of specialized and deliberate forms of activity by singular agents is simply not a plausible alternative to the more conventional hypothesis that the intentional intervention of specific agents is a necessary though perhaps not a sufficient element to explain the actual existence of specific works.

The real cogency of the post-structuralist critique of authorship emerges in relation to questions about the ethical character of the author's *métier*. Do verbal artifacts issue from the distinctive moral vocation of specific agents, or are these artifacts more accurately thought to be under the category of commodity? The guiding intuition of the traditional hypothesis is that singular agents are responsible, both as cause and ethical sponsor, for the salient features of verbal artifacts. Works possess authority because they are sanctioned by their authors' commitment to the activity of verbal expression as well as to a community of social addressees. The death-of-the-author hypothesis, by contrast, answers this question by default on the side of commodity. Works appear, without ethical sponsorship, as local disturbances within the anonymous field of textuality. The abolition of the author is a doctrine that certainly describes contemporary expressive activity such as advertising and, more broadly, those practices of the culture industry where no one in particular is speaking and nothing in particular is being said. Its application to the archive known as Shakespeare's Works would suggest that these objects are motivated not by ethical or craft standards, but rather by expediency and hope for financial success.

In the decades between 1590 and 1610, roughly speaking, William Shakespeare was identified in the records of the Revels Office as the poet or maker of a number of plays licensed for performance in various theaters in London. In the broader sense that I have outlined above, Shakespeare was undoubtedly the author of these works. It is far from certain, however, that any narrower, more contemporary sense of literary authorship was active in his own self-understanding. Although the concept and practice of literary authorship at this time was very different from what it is today, there is no doubt that the category of the author was well known and widely understood. To suggest that an ascription of authorship to vernacular literary works would have been inconceivable at this time is clearly wrong. Certainly a number of Shakespeare's contemporaries, notably Ben Jonson, Edmund Spenser, and Michael Drayton, went to considerable lengths to establish their identity as literary authors through the medium of

printed works. It is not clear, however, whether William Shakespeare did or did not aspire to the status of author in this narrower
and more restrictive sense.

Shakespeare was not particularly scrupulous about preserving his
works for posterity. Reliable information about his apparent lack of
interest in this task is not available, though it is certainly relevant to
observe that playwrights typically alienated their proprietary rights
in their works when they supplied a copy to the companies for performance. As a sharer in the assets and in the cash flow of a major
company, however, Shakespeare would have retained at least a portion of those proprietary interests. What was the ethical character of
Shakespeare's activity as a writer in this context? In exactly what
sense did he 'labor in his vocation?' G. E. Bentley has suggested that
'by profession Shakespeare was a man of the theater, and the most
complete man of the theater of his time' (1961: 119). In Bentley's
usage the notion of 'profession' means something rather different
from just getting paid for what one does. Profession here retains its
fundamentally religious sense of active commitment to the values of
a particular craft. However, the idea of a vocation or profession
already had the diminished contemporary sense of a way to make
money in Shakespeare's time. It is important, therefore, not to overlook commodity as a defining element in his calling.

The companies of players were speculative business ventures
whose owners and operators were freemen of established livery companies (Ingram 1992: 92–119). Although Shakespeare himself was
not a member of any London guild, his social origins were with the
same middling sort in Stratford. What would have prompted these
early proprietors to give up the advantages of a relatively secure
social position and take on the manifold hazards of a career in show
business? Clearly, financial participation in these novel enterprises
proved rewarding. Furthermore, the making of plays in this economic and practical environment would have been relatively more
open to innovation and experimentation than would any of the
established craft traditions. Players and playwrights would have
enjoyed a remarkable measure of freedom because they would have
been free to create their own standards of good playing, and those
standards could be worked out primarily in terms of success in the
cultural marketplace.

The basic facts of Shakespeare's financial success are not in dispute and in fact the surviving documentary record traces a clearer
and more detailed picture of a man of business than of a theatrical

artist. Although many of the most pertinent details are lacking, the overall trajectory of Shakespeare's professional career certainly lends itself to the construction of a conventional success story. Shakespeare started out from modest, although certainly not impoverished circumstances, and ended up as a gentleman of means with a large house, a family coat of arms, and a complicated estate (Schoenbaum 1975: 161–195). He did not, of course, become spectacularly wealthy or powerful, but there is no doubt sufficient upward mobility here for his biography to be structured as a fairly typical success narrative. To many of his scholarly biographers these feats of entrepreneurship are basically secondary to his achievements as a playwright, modest recompense for the gifts of his genius. However, it is perhaps more illuminating to consider a mixed account in which Shakespeare's love of the theater co-existed with an interest in the financial opportunities afforded him by the medium in which he worked.

As a primary shareholder in one of the more profitable of these new enterprises, Shakespeare participated in its risks and rewards, collaborated in its decision making, and benefitted from its success. In the end his personal fortune was the result of the business acumen of the shareholders and of his own shrewdness as an investor rather than a consequence of the artistic quality of his works. Just as today, the early modern culture industry was a high-risk, high-reward occupation. Despite its many perils, it offered the chance of rapid social and economic upward mobility. Shakespeare initially prospered from his ability to capitalize on the resources of a somewhat shady and certainly novel medium of entertainment in both the private and popular theaters of London. However, theater as a trade did not operate in the context of unregulated and unopposed capitalism. The orienting purposes of Shakespeare and his associates, their aspirations and frameworks of evaluation, were determined not only in terms of commodity but also against a social background defined by a more traditional moral and economic dispensation.

Recognition of success in the sense of unfettered personal achievement and unrestricted private commodity becomes an evaluative orientation for human activity only within those institutional formations most characteristic of modern Western individualism in its most isolated and aggressive forms. Success does not appear in either the classical or the Christian table of the virtues. Nor does it figure prominently within the moral culture of any of the important social groupings in Shakespeare's historical milieu. In the modern sense of free and unfettered acquisitiveness and self-assertion, success figures prominently in Aristotle's account of the good life not as a virtue but as a notable vice (MacIntyre 1984: 136).

For traditional Christianity, of course, the pursuit of worldly success strictly for its own sake would be accounted a sin. Even the Protestant ethic, supposedly more comfortable with capitalist accumulation, requires that private wealth be acquired through devotion to a calling and dedicated to the service of spiritual ends. For the governing elites the proper use of wealth and power was defined by an ideal of magnanimity, expressed in traditional practices, hospitality, and *noblesse oblige*. The popular culture of the early modern period has its own distinctive interpretations of these norms based on an ethic of reciprocity and mutual aid. In all these frameworks, agents would be enjoined to regulate their desire for personal advantage and to orient their actions to bring them into conformity with the larger order of things. Within a moral horizon of this kind the pursuit of economic success and private commodity could never be an ethically justifiable pattern of motives, intentions, and actions. Notwithstanding the existence of a durable evaluative framework that would have discouraged the open pursuit of economic success for its own sake, however, Shakespeare and his contemporaries nevertheless organized institutions that constitute the ancestry of the modern culture industry. The unavoidable conclusion would seem to be that the notion of commodity would be necessary, but almost certainly not sufficient, as an explanatory description of Shakespeare's vocation.

Questions of authorship are certainly germane to the discussion of cultural authority. The pragmatic initiatives that lead to the creation of verbal objects are integral elements in the temporally extended dialogue which constitutes the historical life of such artifacts. Unfortunately there is little in the way of reliable evidence that could be used to reconstruct a historical description of Shakespeare's actual practice of writing or of his engagement with particular social addressees. The necessary information is lost, most likely forever, and there is no amount of editorial labor or theoretical ingenuity that can restore or reconstruct that information. Such a deficiency of information does not, however, constitute reliable evidence to support a theory that requires the complete abolition of the concept of the author. It only means that we don't know what we need to know about Shakespeare as an author. As a consequence, his works have been actualized and given finished form through other types of social activity. In this sense Shakespeare's works retain something of those traditional forms of collective authority of which contemporary show business is the alienated form.

Authorship need not be understood as a sovereign and proprietary relationship to specific utterances. It is perhaps more fully theorized in terms of dialogue and ethical sponsorship. The author is both debtor and trustee of meaning rather than sole proprietor; authority is always ministerial rather than magisterial. Shakespeare labored in his vocation at the selection, composition, and verbal articulation of scripts intended for production in the theater. But Shakespeare did not work in conditions of sovereign independence and artistic isolation. As an active poet, Shakespeare would have been oriented to the diverse social addressees defined by the institution of the Revels Office as well as by the public theater. He was in continual dialogue with other writers, including both his literary sources and his immediate contemporaries. More important, perhaps, he engaged in discussions with his associates to work out detailed strategies for their company. Shakespeare's vocation can thus be interpreted both as the practice of a craft and as the production of a commodity in the context of a nascent show business. However, neither craft nor commodity require play scripts to be finished literary forms. Since theater is in many important respects primarily topical in its interests, there would be no advantage to companies in limiting the appeal of a performance by requiring it to conform to the pre-existing template of a finished literary text. The unfinished and provisional character of textual artifacts was to prove highly advantageous in the later development of the supply side of culture.

Chapter 3

Shakespearean technologies

If you build it, they will come.

(*Shoeless Joe*, Thomas Kinsella)

No matter what happens, the telephone company makes money.

(Ziff's Law)

The production of cultural goods and services in the sixteenth century unfolds in a political context of 'representative publicness' (Habermas 1992: 5–14). Power and authority are represented in public space by the body of the monarch, and also by various figures in a complex hierarchy of lesser sovereignties and lordships, both secular and ecclesiastical. The political authority so represented was itself derived from something incomparably greater and more excellent than the ruler's contingent historical person. Rulers, however, were enjoined to manifest this power through the public display of magnificence. Private individuals of ordinary or common social position take no active role in this representation of publicness. They are simply called upon to witness the public display of higher excellence made visible in the sovereign body of the ruler. Sovereign authority in this context is less concerned with obtaining the consent of the governed than with securing the obedience of its subjects, with or without their consent.

Shakespeare's plays were initially produced against a background in which political authority is manifested through public representation and spectacle. The letters patent granted to The King's Men authorizes Shakespeare and his fellows to perform for the solace of the King and the recreation of his 'loving subjects'. Limited royal authority is thus delegated to Shakespeare's company and in a *de jure* sense performances of plays were an extension of the spectacles of the court. Unlike the official spectacles of royal power such as progresses and processions, however, the 'recreation' of the King's subjects is made available in the public theaters as a commodity. The existence of a commercial trade in such an elusive and ambiguous commodity, however, fundamentally alters the character of the representative publicness of which it is the expression. The theatrical representation of power tends to reveal the tenuous theatricality of power itself. One of the unintended consequences of the licensing of profit-making theatrical enterprises is that the theater becomes a space of alternatives in which cultural consumers may come to redefine their own public standing.

When he was still alive, the *de facto* authority of William Shakespeare was reallocated from *de jure* delegations of the Crown to the institutional regimes of show business and print culture. In fact, that authority acquires its significant long-term social dimension only by virtue of this institutional uptake. As a consequence of this reallocation of authority, Shakespeare's works acquire a durable public character not evident in genres such as the court masque. This public character will be developed and enhanced in the even more far-reaching reallocation of Shakespeare's authority that takes place over the course of the eighteenth century. The activities of the public theaters and the printing shops of the sixteenth century anticipate on a small scale the much more extensive development of a public sphere after the restoration of the monarchy in 1660.

The re-positioning of Shakespeare's works as a line of products and services in the eighteenth-century culture market requires extensive modification of the way these goods are presented to the consuming public. The most fundamental of these changes is, of course, that Shakespeare's authority is no longer in any meaningful sense even partially derived from the Crown. That authority comes instead from the social desire of cultural consumers as Shakespeare's works address the public through increasing trade in cultural goods. Re-situated in the public sphere, Shakespeare's works are taken to be salient interventions in a practice of inquiry into the nature of the good life. Literary discussion and critical debate were valued as social experience by many of the individuals who attended performances of Shakespeare's plays and who purchased copies of the new editions created by the house of Jacob Tonson.

Without the enabling devices created in the eighteenth century, Shakespeare as a body of works would have become increasingly

remote and inaccessible, available only to a tiny coterie of anti-
quarian book collectors. The entertainment industry initially takes
the lead here in creating widespread public demand for Shakespeare's plays in performance. This in turn opens up a market niche
for printed editions of Shakespeare's works. Interaction between
these sectors of the culture industry generates accelerating demand
and this in turn promotes an even greater diversification of
Shakespearean products. To some observers this aggressive promotion of Shakespeare is part of the integration of literature into the
ideological state apparatus (De Grazia 1991; Dobson 1992). However, this market spiral is both more and less than an ideological
deception foisted upon a credulous public.

The elaboration of the various technologies for the reproduction
of Shakespeare is linked to the creation of a public culture.
Obviously the common culture promoted in the bluestocking salons
and the coffee houses is inconceivable without access to shared texts
and public performances, along with protocols for their interpretation. Only an active market in cultural goods and services can
supply the necessary products for such a public culture, even though
the articulation of a common culture is in many ways tangential to
the interests of the suppliers themselves. Desire for commercial
profit motivates the supply side of culture, but this desire can only
be satisfied by constituting a large and diverse literary public.

RESTORING SHAKESPEARE

Shakespeare's unfinished, textually dispersed works provided a
convenient substructure for extensive derivative creativity in
Restoration and early eighteenth-century theaters. To a significant
degree, the *longue durée* of Shakespeare's cultural authority is the
product of interactions between a body of incompletely determined
works and a resourceful theatrical ingenuity. Shakespeare's works
are themselves an important instance of derivative creativity highly
responsive to its own moment of contemporaneity. This market
sensitivity is fundamental to the institutions of theater for which
Shakespeare originally wrote, and it has been one of the most conspicuous features of show business ever since.

In devising specific means for the restoration of Shakespeare in
the new social context of a restored monarchy and a restored legitimate theater after 1660, Sir William Davenant is a pivotal figure.
Davenant's career as courtier and show business entrepreneur is a

remarkable narrative of upward social mobility. Like Shakespeare, he began from very modest circumstances and became an eminently successful man of the theater (Harbage 1935: 24ff.). The social trajectory of his success was even more spectacular than Shakespeare's, and he was eventually knighted for his various services to the Crown in 1643. Davenant had been active as a dramatist as early as the 1630s and was therefore well acquainted with the practices of the pre-Restoration theater. In effect he is the primary trustee and also the main beneficiary of the theatrical tradition that survived the closing of the theaters in 1642.

Davenant would have seen how members of Shakespeare's company performed certain roles, and this knowledge would later prove to be of some significance in his post-Restoration revivals of *Hamlet* and *Macbeth*. He would also have learned just how flexible that tradition was by observing how the company modified scripts in response to the changing expectations of their audiences (Edmond 1987: 141). His shrewdness in exploiting the commercial potential of this cultural market is evident in his patent of 1639 for a new playhouse. The playhouse, which was to be constructed in Fleet Street, would have contained state-of-the-art theater technology, with elaborate provision for naturalistic scenery and special effects, including music. This structure would house a company whose performances would be managed and directed by Davenant (Edmond 1987: 75ff.). These plans were not carried out, however, and in 1642 stage-playing was outlawed for eighteen years under the revolutionary government.

Although he often lacked financial resources, Sir William demonstrated extraordinary survival skills during this period. He fought ably on the Royalist side, and was captured and imprisoned in 1650. Shortly after his release he sought permission for the private performances of operas as a way to get around the prohibition of stage plays. Despite his Royalist connections, he was actively engaged in re-establishing the basis for theatrical performances in London as early as 1655. The production of his 'opera', *The Siege of Rhodes*, successfully eluded the surveillance of a government which militantly opposed the staging of plays. More important, perhaps, it was a most encouraging financial success. The public's response to these deliberately equivocal shows must have convinced Davenant that the 1639 project was not only still viable, but potentially a very lucrative undertaking (Harbage 1935: 243–250; Edmond 1987: 159–165).

Almost immediately after the triumphal entry of Charles II in May 1660, Davenant took the initiative to move towards the realization of his plans. In partnership with Thomas Killigrew, he obtained a royal grant that not only authorized his ambitious scheme but also provided the partners with an effective monopoly over stage plays in London. Killigrew formed a company that performed as The King's Men. Davenant's company was organized under the patronage of the Duke of York. Once the company was established in its new theater, an agreement specifying a set of innovative business arrangements took effect (Edmond 1987: 140–159). The principal players, as junior partners, were to share roughly one-third of the company's profits. The remaining two-thirds was retained by Davenant to cover the costs of house rents, the construction of scenery, and the hiring of actresses to play the women's parts. The introduction of actresses has been widely discussed in theater histories; perhaps here it is worthwhile to note that women entered the theater under the regime of wage labor. Although the company was nominally a partnership or joint-stock venture, Davenant himself was in fact 'master and superior' or chief executive officer. This organizational structure, consisting of a specialized manager directing the activities of segmented hired labor, represents a thorough and radical transformation of the practices of the early acting companies. Stage-playing no longer resembled the activities of a guild; it had become much more like an industry.

The theater building in which this company was to be housed was a costly undertaking. Davenant had some independent means, but the project was financed through a private sale of shares in the enterprise to a number of his friends and acquaintances. This marks a further shift in the economics of cultural production from patronage to entrepreneurship. Davenant's company was far more successful than Killigrew's, and it eventually took over the resources of its competitor.

In addition to his skills at finance and administration, Davenant had two assets: first, a theatrical apparatus capable of producing richly detailed scenic backgrounds for stage performances, along with other special effects, and second, Thomas Betterton, the leading actor of the day. This combination of powerful illusionistic effects and the charismatic allure of well-publicized star performers is constitutive of the basic technology for modern cultural markets. The specialized techniques required to produce such richly detailed representations are simply beyond the means of private individuals.

Complex spectacles of the sort offered in Davenant's new theaters require economies of scale that depend on increased capital investment and on cash flow from expanding public demand.

Davenant controlled one additional asset in promoting the interests of his theatrical enterprise during the 1660s. His longstanding loyalty to the Royalist cause and his friendship with the restored monarch gave him a powerful advantage over his competitors in negotiating patents for his theater. That friendship also helped Davenant find a receptive audience for his shows. Charles II was, among other things, a leader of taste and opinion in Restoration London. By orienting his productions to Charles' sensibility, Davenant was able to capitalize on the King's initial popularity with the fashionable public in Restoration London. The fact that two of Davenant's actresses later became royal mistresses suggests the important role of seductive and highly visible heterosexuality in the formation of this cultural technology.

Among the various properties Davenant held when his company was formed were rights to present nine plays that had belonged to the old King's Men, including seven by Shakespeare (Edmond 1987: 168–169). When he turned to the production of Shakespeare's *Hamlet* in 1661, there was nothing in Davenant's experience that would have prompted him to consider any archaizing 'fidelity to the original' as an orienting aim. The initial selection of *Hamlet* was governed primarily by considerations of the play's timeliness and its attractive potential for reinforcing Royalist ideology. *Hamlet* dramatizes the issue of royal succession after the murder of an anointed king. Davenant's cuts eliminate both grotesque imagery and politically offensive language. The reference to worms feasting on the body of a dead king is only one of the improprieties deleted in the Davenant text. More important, it introduces subtle alterations in the depiction of kingship that correspond much more closely to the changed realities of royal authority after the Restoration (Bachorik 1977: 183–199).

Davenant's *Hamlet* treats Claudius and Hamlet more simply as rivals for the throne rather than as contrasting models of moral and political authority. The focus on factional strife and the social derangement that follows from the murder of a lawful monarch is motivated by the intention to reaffirm the legitimacy of the restored monarchy. That ideological agenda is even more vividly dramatized in the 1664 revival of *Macbeth*. As with *Hamlet*, Davenant introduced extensive revisions to Shakespeare's language. He also expanded the role of the witches by adding songs, dancing, and additional scenes. The production was notable for its radically innovative, operatic staging. New stage machinery permitted the witches to fly about the stage, and the production was much admired for its instrumental music and for the finery of its sets and costumes (Bachorik 1977: 199–221). The ideological payload of this spectacle was similar to that of the earlier *Hamlet* production, but Davenant made sure that the Royalist message would not be dull.

Davenant's productions of *Hamlet* and *Macbeth* have often been criticized for their distortion and degradation of Shakespeare's art. Similar condemnations have been directed at the adaptations of Dryden, Tate, and Cibber. However, it is precisely these accommodations of Shakespeare to altered social and institutional conditions that promote wide public interest in his plays. The practice of derivative creativity helps to account for the *longue durée* of Shakespeare's works. Even with flying vaudevillian witches, Davenant's show is still recognizably Shakespeare's *Macbeth*. For all practical purposes it simply is *Macbeth* for a significant percentage of the Restoration audience. Shakespeare's own company routinely engaged in the various forms of derivative creativity; as a former member of that same company Davenant certainly felt that his elaborate theatrical pastiche was fully authorized by this earlier practice.

Restoration and eighteenth-century theater cannot be fully understood without considering its role in the formation of a larger ideological state apparatus. Paula Backscheider has analyzed the role of theatrical spectacle in promoting competing interpretations of the monarchy during the regime of Charles II. Charles' sponsorship of Davenant's company was intended to advance his own conception of royal authority, but, as Backscheider has shown, the theater was too unstable an institution to function as a reliable instrument of social control (Backscheider 1993: 22ff.). Increasingly the métier of theater would lie in the formation of public opinion rather than in the celebration and assertion of royal power. Public opinion was, however, as much concerned with the articulation of standards for private life as it was with questions of the nation's constitution. The drama of the period thus served to codify ideals of gender difference, domestic relations, and everyday social relations. The nation's affairs were to be reviewed from the perspective of well-regulated private lives and Shakespeare would figure prominently in both of these agendas.

According to Michael Dobson in his *The Making of the National Poet*, Shakespeare is canonized as England's national poet as part of the larger ideological apparatus.

> The mid-eighteenth century . . . marks both Shakespeare's offi-
> cial canonization as an august British Worthy and his widespread
> acceptance (particularly through Garrick's extraordinarily
> successful self-representation as his truly begotten son) as a writer
> of unimpeachable respectability. From the 1730's onward, treat-
> ments of Shakespeare's texts, both on and off the stage, are
> profoundly conditioned by their author's newly achieved status
> as a national poet and his simultaneous representation as a
> patron of bourgeois morality.
>
> (Dobson 1992: 184)

The examples discussed in Dobson's account confirm Paula Backscheider's broader hypothesis about ideological links between national politics and middle-class domestic life. Dobson insists throughout his study that Shakespeare is 'normatively constitutive of British national identity' (p. 7). However, this identity is con-tinually shifting. Although the plays are nominally recruited in the service of a controlling ideology of English imperial domination, Dobson shows how that recruitment was mobile and chronically divisive (p. 12).

Shakespeare's authority is not permanently linked to a substan-tive ideological program. As a national figure, Shakespeare is ambiguous and even contradictory, responding to the needs of an increasingly segmented cultural market. Dobson's 'national poet' is perhaps more accurately described as a 'Whig poet'. The most important figures in performing and publishing Shakespeare's plays were all connected with influential Whig circles. Practically speaking, Shakespeare participates in the public sphere under Whig sponsorship. However, the Whigs were a shifting coalition of politi-cal interest groups mainly preoccupied with maintaining a stake in the practical direction of England's national policy rather than a coherent political movement. The 'dominant' ideology in such a context is likely to reflect the need for compromise and for tempor-ary political accommodations. Shakespeare's value for the Whigs was not the presence of any specific picture of desirable social order but rather his undeniable but extremely vague and mobile generic Englishness.

Shakespeare's constituency cannot be described simply in terms of his partisan political affiliations, at least not in the usual sense. It is through Shakespeare that groups of women begin to demand access to the institutions of cultural production and thus indirectly to the public sphere. In 1736 the Shakespeare Ladies Club, an association of socially prominent London women, began to exert pressure on the proprietors of both Drury Lane and Covent Garden for expanded offerings of Shakespearean revivals (Avery 1956: 153–158). This important cultural initiative was prompted by two distinct motives. Shakespeare was the indigenous and homely alternative to the extravagances of foreign opera. More important, Shakespeare could help articulate an alternative standard of domestic morality against the libertine indecencies of Restoration comedy.

The importance of the Shakespeare Ladies Club was recognized by contemporaries, some of whom praised the club's public spirit. The motives of the organization were to receive much fuller articulation in a number of influential publications by women writers, including Eliza Haywood's *The Female Spectator* (1755), Elizabeth Montagu's *An Essay on the Writings and Genius of Shakespeare, Compared with the Greek and French Dramatic Poets with some Remarks upon the Misrepresentations of Mons. de Voltaire* (1769), and Elizabeth Griffith's *The Morality of Shakespeare's Drama Illustrated* (1775). Michael Dobson has argued that the Ladies Club's aim of promoting decency and inspiring virtue served primarily to codify the interests of an increasingly secure commercial bourgeoisie. However, the emergence of upper- and middle-class women as a distinct segment of the cultural market complicates this analysis in two important ways. First, women began to emerge as a distinct social constituency using the cultural leverage provided by Shakespeare as their instrument. Second, as opinion leaders these women challenged the prevailing ideology of the public sphere by affirming the social dignity of everyday life and the household.

During the Restoration, Shakespeare had been enlisted in the service of a Royalist agenda. This required extremely careful disciplinary regulation both of poetic diction and dramatic form. Beginning in the eighteenth century, such features of Shakespeare's dramaturgy as heterogeneity in language and social decorum, clowning, the mixing of genres, and the general failure to observe classical rules of composition gradually come to be interpreted as evidence of his responsiveness to the cultural diversity of his audience. At the same time a deliberate strategy of cross-over becomes evident in the way Shakespeare is taken up by an emerging culture industry. The full market potential of Shakespeare's work could only be realized by abandoning narrowly programmatic ideological commitments in favor of a more ingratiating blend of market-worthy elements.

No one responded to the possibilities for cross-over with greater alacrity than David Garrick, the most brilliantly opportunistic of actors and theater managers in the eighteenth century. Garrick was more successful than any of his contemporaries in responding to the emerging markets represented by the Shakespeare Ladies Club and other new constituencies. However, although Garrick acknowledged his debt to the Ladies Club for its role in expanding demand for Shakespeare, his success was by no means dependent on the support of a single market sector. On the contrary, Garrick's strategies as a theater manager and even more strikingly as an actor were governed by the logic of the box office. The basic axiom here is that ticket sales are ideologically neutral. What matters is the number of tickets sold, not the political opinions of the buyers. In order to accomplish this aim the elements of novelty, sensation, and variety are far more important than any programmatic agenda. Garrick's productions tended to avoid anything like an action-orienting ideology. In the end it mattered far less what audiences thought about political issues than what they thought about Garrick as a performer and celebrity.

David Garrick was already a popular actor on the London stage when he performed in his first Shakespearean role as Macbeth in 1744. In preparing for this production, Garrick rejected Davenant's popular but heavily adapted script in favor of the text 'as Shakespeare wrote it'. He might have been more candid if he had acknowledged that Theobald's edition was his actual working copy, emended by suggestions from Samuel Johnson and William Warburton, as well as by his own sense of what would work best for him as an actor (Dircks 1985: 84). Garrick's decision to use the more reliable texts of Shakespeare's works produced by the publishing house of Jacob Tonson rather than relying on established theatrical tradition was an important element in his remarkable success. His productions had the strong market appeal of novelty, offering an alternative to the familiar standard versions of Davenant, Tate, and Cibber. At the same time Garrick's productions could be advertised as the real thing, rescuing the genuine

Shakespearean article from the shabby compromises of the earlier adaptors. This exploitation of the new scholarly editions did not, however, prevent Garrick from altering the text to conform with his own appraisal of his audience's preferences. Nor did he attempt to restore Elizabethan dramaturgy in the design and staging of his productions. Garrick's productions, like those of his predecessors, were a sophisticated pastiche of Shakespeare's poetry fused with contemporary performance techniques.

In all his productions of Shakespeare, Garrick understood that how performers interpreted their roles was in many ways less important than what they were wearing. Productions were frequently advertised as 'new dress'd' (Burnim 1961:75). Historical accuracy was not, however, his primary consideration. Although he was also well aware of the dramatic interest of period dress, his productions were more often governed by contemporary fashion and the vanity of star actors and actresses. The visual appearance of his performers was of course greatly enhanced by the use of increasingly sophisticated lighting and scene design. Garrick was not himself a stage designer, but he nevertheless saw extraordinary possibilities for the visual elaboration of Shakespeare's otherwise bare scripts. He was shrewd enough to realize that his ideas required the services of highly specialized artists and designers.

Although the technical resources of this theater were crucial in securing Garrick's cash flow, the use of scenes and machines was not his most important contribution to the technology of cultural production. The most powerful expression of Garrick's extraordinary creativity was in the elaboration of the modern star system. David Garrick's greatest creation was undoubtedly David Garrick the celebrity. His career builds on the venerable precedent established by Kemp and Burbage as well as on the more recent example of Betterton:

> those who watched Garrick derived their pleasure not only from appreciating the skill of the performer but also from recognising that his entire approach was founded on a style which, quite apart from his own excellence, could be savoured and defined in and for itself.
>
> (Nicoll 1980: 9)

Although he frequently played tragic roles, Garrick also had a gift for low comedy. This versatility enabled him to expand the base of his popularity. Even more important perhaps was the empathy he felt for the characters he portrayed, and his ability to evoke a similar empathy in his audience. Unlike the more austere Betterton, Garrick was perfectly ready to act out the varied emotional experience of his audiences. This willingness to reflect personal feelings helped to secure a bond between the performer and his public.

The program of cultural Bonapartism pursued throughout Garrick's career could not be fully achieved solely through his efforts as an actor. The demands of big-time celebrity require both an extensive network of personal affiliation with powerful opinion makers and a high level of popular visibility. Garrick was extremely well-connected with the most influential circles in the London salons and coffee houses. He was also an indefatigable socializer. A portion of his rapidly growing income was diverted to maintaining a high standard of hospitality. By 1775 he was in a position to build an opulent mansion where he could entertain his powerful friends and associates in proper surroundings. Because he was not indebted to the generosity of wealthy patrons for his ability to participate in these influential circles, Garrick was able almost single-handedly to raise the social status of the theatrical profession to a position of considerable prestige and influence.

As his financial resources increased, Garrick began to acquire Shakespearean memorabilia, and increasingly sought a kind of fusion of his own identity with that of the national poet in the public perception of his career. This odd identification was perhaps intended to contribute an element of *gravitas* to his profile as a celebrity. However, Garrick's celebrity did not depend exclusively on his repertoire of Shakespearean roles any more than his financial success did on the narrowly exclusive segment of the cultural market he invited to his own home. His theater did not confine itself to a steady diet of high culture, but offered instead an eclectic mix of Shakespeare, contemporary drama, and various forms of popular entertainment. This strategy enabled Garrick to expand the reach of his celebrity far beyond the tight circles of social privilege that guaranteed his position as a cultural force to be reckoned with. Garrick's covenant with this wider public is perhaps most vividly manifested in the extraordinary media event known as the Stratford Jubilee of 1769.

The Jubilee was planned as an elaborate carnivalesque pastiche of tableaux, recitations, and song, all intended to affirm an attitude of national veneration for the figure of Shakespeare. Shakespeare's works were nowhere in evidence, but the use of such material would have been beside the point. The purpose of the event was simply to acknowledge and to celebrate his position in the popular imagination. Garrick acted both as master of ceremonies and as a living surrogate for the national poet. This amalgamation of Garrick's public personality with the historical playwright helped to sever the links between the image of Shakespeare as a source of cultural authority and the determinate body of works that bear his name. The Jubilee has been effectively analyzed in terms of its explicit ideological payloads. However, the larger significance of this event is not to be found in substantive agendas of national self-congratulation or the affirmation of bourgeois morality. The real point of media events like the Jubilee is in their capacity to define what it is to have a cultural experience for a diffuse public and in the way they demonstrate the importance of controlling the technology by which that experience is produced.

THE HOUSE OF TONSON

The rewriting of the plays by Davenant, Dryden, Tate, and Cibber to satisfy the expectations of eighteenth-century audiences has been treated as a particularly egregious scandal of the period. But it was also in the eighteenth century that textual and philological restoration of Shakespeare's works in their 'original' form was undertaken for the first time, prompted in large part by the entrepreneurial shrewdness of the publisher Jacob Tonson and his heirs. David Garrick is often cited as the key figure in establishing Shakespeare's position in the early culture industry. In their succession of Shakespeare editions, however, the printing and publishing dynasty founded by Jacob Tonson demonstrated an even more astute grasp of the dynamics of the cultural marketplace. Each one of his editors set out to create a new and improved Shakespeare product in response to a new cultural market of educated middle-class men and socially influential women for whom the idea of a restoration of the author's original intentions had taken on increasing prestige.

David Garrick clearly understood the importance of spectacle and publicity for the entertainment industry. Jacob Tonson, on the other hand, saw in the printed book, with its relative permanence, low cost, and convenience, even greater potential for the saturation of a complex cultural market. The idea of a reliable text of Shakespeare would assure, at least in theory, a standard referential background for the co-ordination of discourse across the institutional spaces that comprised the public sphere. More important, perhaps, the book, as a compact form of personal property made it possible for Shakespeare to inhabit the domestic sphere. However, it would be a mistake to suggest that the conscientiously edited texts produced by Jacob Tonson were somehow in competition with the theatrical popularizations of Davenant, Tate, and Garrick. The popularity of these productions created the demand for the Shakespeare produced by Tonson.

The history of Shakespeare's textual reproduction in the eighteenth century has usually been told as a story of the achievements of editors from Nicholas Rowe through Edmond Malone. This narrative plots the development of a systematic method for reconstructing Shakespeare's original intentions as a poet. It is perhaps not surprising that literary scholars should focus their attention on the progress of their own field of specialization. What these accounts overlook is the decisive role played by Jacob Tonson and his nephews, both in conceiving these editorial projects and in supervising the production of Shakespeare's works for cultural consumers. The house of Tonson published virtually all the eighteenth-century editions, from Rowe in 1709 through Johnson, Steevens, and Capell, all published in the 1760s. More important, initiative for these ventures came, not from the individual editors, but from the Tonson firm itself. The editors were experts hired to produce a commodity to the general specifications of the publisher. It may well be that a scholarly method for textual scholarship evolved through the work of the various editors, but that result would have been a decidedly secondary consequence of Tonson's more general aim of reproducing Shakespeare as cultural merchandise.

Jacob Tonson was born in London in about 1656. Following his elder brother Richard, he was apprenticed to a stationer in 1670 and admitted as a freeman of that company in 1677. His mother's family were well-established booksellers and publishers, and it is likely that both Tonson brothers were provided with a decent education with a view to their possible succession into the family business (Geduld 1969: 3–27; Lynch 1961: 1–17). Jacob Tonson certainly had notable literary interests, even as a young man; as an apprentice he was taken to visit the residence of John Milton, who had recently died, in the hope of seeing the poet's library. The intended call ended in disappointment, as no one was at home to admit the visitors. Tonson was a great admirer of *Paradise Lost*, and he would eventually acquire Milton's corrected manuscript and a share in the copyright as part of a business agreement which eventually led to the publication of a lavish folio edition in 1688.

Tonson's interest in Milton was connected with a larger and more diffuse plan to publish a line of contemporary British authors. He began a long association with John Dryden with the publication in 1679 of *Troilus and Cressida* and eventually published most of Dryden's major works (Lynch 1961: 17ff.). He purchased copies of Dryden's early writings from Henry Herringman, who also owned a major portion of Shakespeare's plays. Early in his career he also published the work of Congreve and Rochester. The Tonson line would eventually include Pope, Gay, Addison, Cibber, and a number of less well-know writers. For the most part, the authors published by the house of Tonson had Whig affiliations. He did not publish anything by Swift, and he was less interested in more popular or sensational writers such as Bunyan or Defoe. The house of Tonson also stayed away from works of a primarily religious interest.

In addition to this line of contemporary authors, the Tonsons also undertook the publication of earlier writers, including Spenser, Beaumont and Fletcher, and perhaps most notably Milton and Shakespeare (Geduld 1969: 135ff.). This is recognizably the canon of English literature as we now know it, though it is not often acknowledged how much of this canon corresponds to the output of a single publishing firm. Tonson did more than provide reprints of scarce or unobtainable works. His editions reproduced both living and dead writers as private men of letters whose works addressed the public sphere. The effect of all this was the creation of a unified republic of letters to which all readers might have access through the medium of printed books. It's not clear that this was the result of any conscious plan on Tonson's part. On the other hand Tonson was certainly no political innocent, and his close association with many of the most powerful and influential Whig politicians of the period has been well documented. One of the most valuable assets of the Tonson firm was a government contract giving them the exclusive right to print and to distribute the papers of the War Office and several other agencies. Another asset, painstakingly acquired over a period of years, was the right to publish the works of William Shakespeare.

Although Nicholas Rowe is often credited with producing the first modern critical edition of Shakespeare's works, initiative for this ambitious and innovative project actually came from Jacob Tonson the elder. By 1707 the Tonson firm had purchased exclusive rights to publish Shakespeare's works from Henry Herringman and the other copyholders. When the project was conceived, the most recent complete edition of Shakespeare's works available to the reading public was the fourth folio of 1685. This cumbersome volume was to all intents and purposes out of print at the time Tonson commissioned Nicholas Rowe and John Hughes to prepare a 'very neat and correct edition of Mr William Shakespeare's works'. In the absence of any competition, Tonson felt confident that his edition would be an immediate financial success. He did not, of course, have any reliable information to the effect that there was a large potential readership for Shakespeare's plays in a modern edition. On the other hand, his prior experience with other English authors had certainly amply demonstrated that there was a considerable market for new literary products.

Compared with the unwieldy bulk of the fourth folio, Rowe's edition was certainly neat and extremely convenient. It is not clear, however, in exactly what sense it was 'very correct'. Rowe's corrected text was itself based on the fourth folio, and it therefore could not be judged accurate even by the rudimentary standards proposed by Theobald a few decades later. However, the Tonsons were concerned not so much with fidelity to some early and definitive state of the text as they were with intelligibility for contemporary readers. Rowe's task was to explain and where necessary to emend obscure passages. He corrected typographical errors, regularized spelling and punctuation, and changed archaic expressions to accord with contemporary usage. Although his readings were often based on inspired guesswork rather than on reliable textual authority, many of his silent emendations are now accepted as standard in the editorial tradition. Obviously his edition could not resolve the tense contradictions between a scholar's demand for scrupulous accuracy and the general reader's more lenient standard of intelligibility. Nevertheless, Rowe's edition set a crucial precedent for the kind of realistic editorial compromise that responds to the needs of cultural consumers.

Tonson's plan to add Shakespeare to his line of authors was prompted by the popularity of the plays in performance. With this in view, he instructed Rowe to furnish supplementary information that would assist readers in following the dramatic action. Rowe provided the plays with act and scene divisions, following a uniform five-act convention. He added stage directions, including exits and entrances. In addition, Rowe, assisted by Thomas Betterton, composed a life of Shakespeare as a context for the reading of his works. Important as these editorial innovations were, however, they should not overshadow what may have been the most important element in Tonson's plan, namely the physical design of the books. In place of an oversize and awkward folio, Tonson's new edition offered consumers a convenient matched set of octavo volumes with a contemporary look and feel. The clean impression and attractive packaging of Shakespeare's works in Rowe's edition may help to account for its marketplace appeal.

Tonson's edition had to supply not only a text of Shakespeare's works, but also an apparatus that would facilitate reading within a limited schedule of increasingly valued leisure moments. Readers were enabled to make sense of Shakespeare's plays without having to engage in tedious literary scholarship or use their own imagination to reconstruct the shape of a dramatic narrative from the speeches of the different characters. Understanding Tonson's solution to the contemporary problem of cultural technology is far more important in the long-term history of Shakespeare's reception than any quibbling over the precision of Rowe's textual scholarship. Those standards were, in any case, as good as they could have been; more important, they were as good as they needed to be in relation to the cultural market that the house of Tonson intended to supply.

The rapid commercial success of Nicholas Rowe's edition of Shakespeare's works encouraged the Tonsons to pursue an ambitious and comprehensive long-term marketing strategy. Both the initial print run of the 1709 edition and the second impression were quickly sold out. Encouraged by demand for the 1709 version, the Tonsons released a less costly version of Rowe's Shakespeare in 1714 which targeted a larger but less affluent segment of the reading public. In addition to the complete editions, they also supplied individual editions of many of the more popular plays. The Tonsons received invaluable free advertising for these products from the popularity of the plays in performance. Furthermore, Rowe's editions allowed the Tonsons an even more complete saturation of the cultural market by making Shakespeare available in geographically remote regions and among economically marginal classes where frequent attendance at theatrical performances was simply not feasible. Tonson's firm thus benefitted from the wide publicity for Shakespeare created by the commercial theaters, but was not in the end completely dependent on it. The pioneering editions of Rowe supplied the basic infrastructure for a bookish appreciation of Shakespeare's works.

The production of Rowe's Shakespeare in various price ranges facilitated extensive market coverage for the Tonsons. But the larger marketing strategy for Shakespeare quickly developed beyond repackaging of Rowe. The passage of significant copyright legislation in 1710 allowed the Tonson firm to secure its claims to proprietary interest in Shakespeare's works through much of the eighteenth century (De Grazia 1991: 184–202). This advantage was exploited not through successive reprints of the 1709 edition, but through a line of new editions issued at more or less regular intervals throughout much of the eighteenth century. Since they had a virtual monopoly on Shakespeare, it is not immediately apparent why the Tonsons would have any compelling reason to take on the potential headaches of producing new editions. The shrewdness of their strategy can perhaps best be seen in the controversy between Alexander Pope and Lewis Theobald.

In May of 1721 Pope signed a memorandum of agreement with the Tonson firm to produce the apparatus for a new edition of Shakespeare's works. The contract is a model of simplicity.

> I do agree to Pay Mr Alexander Pope one hundred pounds for correcting and writing a Preface and making notes and explaining the obscure passages in the Works of Mr William Shakespeare and the said Alexander Pope doth agree to publish the said works of Mr William Shakespeare in the manner before mentioned within two years from the date hereof.
>
> (from Tonson correspondence)

Jacob Tonson the elder took an active role in assuring the success of this new edition, first by selecting Pope, who was already an influential literary figure, and second by hiring a team of subordinate editors to carry out routine tasks. Pope submitted his work directly to Tonson, who made numerous suggestions for its improvement. Tonson obtained copies of early quarto texts for Pope to consult. Pope's edition contained many readings from the early quartos, but he developed no systematic method for collating the variants and based his own text for the most part on the work of his predecessor, Rowe. Despite having access to early quarto and folio materials, however, Pope was less concerned with fidelity to his author's original intentions than with adapting this raw material to conform with his own standards of metrical regularity and linguistic decorum.

Despite its idiosyncratic character, Pope's edition does realize some incremental progress in the methods and techniques of textual scholarship. Pope did, after all, recognize the importance of comparing the early quartos with the first folio, even though he had no rigorous principles to guide emendation. However, the Tonsons did not enter into their contract with Pope based on any appreciation of his editorial scruples. The costs of this venture, which included expenses above and beyond the payment to Pope, could only be justified by the prospect of a substantial return on investment. In deciding on a new edition, the Tonsons demonstrated an astute grasp of the importance of obsolescence and novelty in the sale of cultural goods.

At the time Tonson and Pope signed their memorandum of agreement, Rowe's Shakespeare had been on the market for about twelve years. Even without market surveys, Tonson realized that sales would diminish as more and more households obtained their copy of the Rowe edition. Prospects for the sale of replacement copies would be unpromising; books, especially eighteenth-century books, simply do not wear out. On the other hand, books can become *culturally* obsolescent. Nicholas Rowe had died in 1718, and his reputation as a poet and dramatist was already in decline. Pope, on the other hand, was one of the most vivid celebrities in London's social and cultural milieu. What Tonson got for his investment of £100 was the latent economic potential of Pope's expanding literary reputation.

The combination of Pope's Preface and Notes, together with modest editorial innovation and the updated design of the volumes, created a product with significant market appeal. Part of that appeal was simply that the new edition made Rowe seem dated and unfashionable, even though the new edition was in many ways nothing more than a repackaging of its predecessor. Most readers would never for a moment consider the purchase of a duplicate copy of Rowe, but if Rowe were obsolete they might well be moved to invest in a new and improved version of Shakespeare's plays. But Tonson had discovered that the unsatisfactory condition of Shakespeare's text could be exploited most profitably. His purpose in committing his firm to a new edition was to notify consumers that

Shakespeare was a changing and evolving cultural product, subject to the dynamic of progress.

Despite its market appeal, it soon became apparent that Pope's Shakespeare was vulnerable to attack by prospective competitors. In 1726, shortly after the release of the final volumes of Pope's edition, Lewis Theobald published his *Shakespeare Restored, or a Specimen of the many Errors as well Committed as Unamended by Mr Pope in his late edition of this Poet*. In this work Pope is attacked for his lack of editorial principles and for his failure to restore the true reading of Shakespeare. Despite the cogency of Theobald's objections, Pope took violent exception to the tone of *Shakespeare Restored*, and interpreted the whole affair as a massive and intolerable personal insult. The ensuing controversy rapidly escalated into one of the most notorious scandals in English literary history. Pope retaliated by portraying Theobald as the King of Dullness in the first edition of his *Dunciad* in 1728. Theobald replied to this personal attack on his reputation with a proposal for a more systematic work on the principles of editing and correcting Shakespeare. He also signalled his intention to produce an edition based on these principles.

Theobald's critique of Pope's edition may have been bad news for Pope, but it was definitely good news for the Tonsons though this was not immediately apparent at the time. In a letter to Jacob Tonson, Junior of November 1731, Pope complains of the rumored plan for a rival edition.

> I learn from an Article published in a late Daily Journal that Thibbald is to have the *Text* of Shakespeare, together with his remarks, published by *You*. As I have heard nothing of this from you, I presume it is not so: at least that you, with whom I have lived ever upon amicable terms, will not be the publisher of any impertinencies relating anyway to my character.
>
> (from Tonson correspondence)

Tonson attempts as diplomatically as possible to inform Pope of the unwelcome reality.

> The truth is this, other Persons being concerned in the Text of Shakespeare with myself, Mr Theobald treated with them to print it and as I found the work would go on by the other parties concerned (though I had not come into the agreement) so I could not avoid being concerned in the edition. This is the truth. I am sensible of the many instances of your Friendship and shall never

do any act to forfeit your opinion of me and since Mr Theobald's Shakespeare must come out I cannot think you will like it the worse that a friend of yours is one of the printers.

(from Tonson correspondence)

There were actually substantive issues at play in the dispute, but they do not seem to have affected the preparation of the editions.

Pope sneered at Theobald and Theobald sneered at Pope. At the same time, Pope copied without acknowledgment from Theobald and Theobald copied without acknowledgment from Pope. The incident is paradigmatic of subsequent cultural hostilities. What occupies public attention is the question of whose reputation has been damaged, whose feelings have been hurt, and who ends up the winner. It's worth noting here that the original imbroglio hasn't completely faded into history. Both Theobald as the better scholar and Pope as the superior literary figure continue to find champions among historians and critics of these events. And in many ways the current state of the art in textual scholarship is a potential Dunciad waiting for a new Alexander Pope to memorialize it. In the mean-time, the Pope–Theobald incident is an oddly premonitory instance of Ziff's law, quoted as the epigraph to this chapter. The house of Tonson had so successfully hedged its position that it stood to profit from every new development in the debate. The residual advantages that accrued from the dispute would all belong to the Tonsons.

EDMOND MALONE AND THE ORIGINS OF SHAKESPEARE SCHOLARSHIP

The last of the Tonson Shakespeares was a ten-volume set in octavo edited by Edward Capell, which appeared in 1767. Tonson's dominance of the publication of Shakespeare ended soon after that date when the firm was liquidated upon the death of Jacob Tonson III. Wide circulation of the Tonson editions had assured that Shakespeare's works were fully integrated into the literary public sphere towards the end of the eighteenth century. Even with-out printed texts, however, theatrical performances of the plays helped make Shakespeare a topic of literary conversation in salons and coffee houses. The extensive availability of Tonson's editions also made the critical essay on Shakespeare feasible as a discursive genre in the literary journals. These conversations, both oral and

written, encouraged further expansion of Shakespeare's authority
through the development of a larger infrastructure of secondary
cultural production.

The Tonson editions themselves had supplied concise though not
altogether reliable information on Shakespeare's life in the form of
Rowe's biographical essay. The editors also contributed prefatory
essays, notes, and commentary, typically following models already
established for presenting the work of classical authors. Gradually,
however, the scope of Shakespeare study is augmented by the
growth of a number of auxiliary sciences. The broader historical
context in which Shakespeare actually worked was investigated in
Thomas Warton's *Observations on* The Faerie Queene *of Spenser*
(1754) and in Richard Hurd's *Letters on Chivalry and Romance* (1762).
Thomas Percy's *Reliques of Ancient English Poetry* (1765) provided
more specific background on Elizabethan drama. Richard Farmer's
An Essay on the Learning of Shakespeare (1767/1821) demonstrated
that Shakespeare could have been well acquainted with the most
important classical authors through the many translations available
in the sixteenth century. Elizabeth Montagu's *An Essay on the
Writings and Genius of Shakespeare, Compared with the Greek and French
Dramatic Poets with Some Remarks upon the Misrepresentations of Mons.
de Voltaire* (1769) established the format for the extended controversial essay on Shakespeare. These scattered and idiosyncratic
initiatives would eventually be co-ordinated in the magisterial 1790
edition of *The Plays and Poems of William Shakespeare* of Edmond
Malone.

Malone's edition is the focus for Margreta De Grazia's scrupu-
lously detailed and theoretically ambitious critique both of the
modern practice of textual editing and of the larger normative
framework in which modern editorial and interpretive practices are
oriented. *Shakespeare Verbatim: The Reproduction of Authenticity and the
1790 Apparatus* argues that the modern paradigm for the study of
Shakespeare is codified for the first time in the work of Malone.
The research agenda followed in this edition takes up a range of
problems that include 'authentic texts of his works, historical
accounts defining his period, facts about his life, chartings of his
artistic and psychological development, and determination of his
meaning' (De Grazia 1991: 1). Malone's apparatus is a detailed and
explicit statement of the ethical norms of authenticity that constitute the orienting framework for all subsequent appreciation
of Shakespeare. These norms privilege the idea of singular and

sovereign individuality as the moral basis for Shakespeare's secular authority. Malone's edition systematized the research agenda and codified the methods for literary scholarship based on that model of authorship. To this day to be a 'real Shakespearean' means to be trained to carry out the activities mandated by Malone's edition.

According to De Grazia, the significance of Malone's edition is its inscription of Shakespeare within this historically overdetermined model of literary authorship. Malone's notion of authenticity privileges unified and singular creative agency as the moral sponsor of valued cultural artifacts. That same notion, however, effaces the contribution of other interested parties to the creation of literary works. De Grazia's larger project is the deconstruction of ideologically distorted attitudes and beliefs that have been completely naturalized within the culture of modernity. *Shakespeare Verbatim* is in many ways an exemplary instance of deconstruction understood not as an unreflective habit of linguistic scepticism but rather as a conscientious scholarly rethinking of a particular archive.

Throughout her discussion, De Grazia demands a shift of attention away from a misguided concern with the essence of the author and his works in favor of a more rigorous consideration of the social being of certain durable cultural artifacts. In these terms De Grazia's project is invaluable, especially in its admirably detailed scrutiny of a wide range of historical evidence. However, I do intend to take issue with several of the larger theoretical inferences that emerge from this study. My criticism of De Grazia flows not from any disagreement about the aims of her scholarship, but rather from differing assessments of the cogency and value of the theories of Michel Foucault for understanding the significance of that scholarship.

De Grazia is candid in linking her discussion of Malone's achievement to Foucault's ideas. Malone's edition of Shakespeare, on her account, is an important instance of the aggressive promotion of unified and autonomous subjectivity characteristic of Western modernity.

> It is such a sovereign subject or consciousness, centered on its own subjective self-reflexivity, that Michel Foucault saw as the late eighteenth century's 'invention of man', an invention sheltered by a massive reorganization of knowledge into anthropological and humanistic disciplines.
>
> (De Grazia 1991: 9)

Readers convinced of the value of Foucault's treatment of these topics may prefer De Grazia's account of Malone's achievement to the brief discussion offered here. My own account does not propose such a dramatic unmasking, nor does it envision a sudden 'invention of man' as the basis for a critique of Malone.

Edmond Malone was born in Dublin in 1741 to a moderately prosperous middle-class family. He was educated at Trinity College Dublin and in 1763 came to London to study law at the Inner Temple. In 1767 he returned to Ireland where he practised law briefly, but his prospects in that profession were not good. He then turned to literature as an alternative, and eventually published an edition of the works of Goldsmith in 1780. It is in a way remarkable that Malone considered his financial prospects as a freelance literary scholar without the security of a modern tenurable academic post better than his prospects as a lawyer. However, after the death of his father, Malone had a moderate independent income, and thus did not have to depend entirely on the vagaries of the literary market for his livelihood. In 1777 he moved to London where he was quickly accepted into the most influential circles. Malone formed important friendships with Samuel Johnson, Sir Joshua Reynolds, and with fellow Irishman and former lawyer Edmund Burke. He also became very close friends with James Boswell and helped him complete the revisions of the *Life of Samuel Johnson*.

In 1778, shortly after he moved to London, Malone published an essay entitled 'An Attempt to Ascertain the Order in which the Plays of Shakespeare were Written'. This essay was part of a much more ambitious project, never completed, to compile a historically accurate biography of Shakespeare. At this time Malone met George Steevens, who had recently collaborated with Samuel Johnson on the 1773 edition of Shakespeare. Malone must have made a favorable impression on Steevens, who presented him with a collection of old plays. In London Malone also met Bishop Percy, and read *Reliques of Ancient English Poetry*, which had appeared in 1765. In 1780 he published a two-volume supplement to Johnson's edition, which included a history of the English stage. The year 1783 saw the announcement of a new edition which was to contain select notes from all earlier commentators.

During this period of more than ten years Malone also carried out extensive original research. The acknowledgements that conclude his Preface suggest he had the opportunity to examine the office book of Sir Henry Herbert, Master of the Revels. He also had access to 'manuscripts relative to one of our ancient theatres', evidently the records and diaries of Alleyn and Henslowe. Malone visited Stratford to study parish registers. His approach to editing and commentary privileges legal documents, municipal records, and similar materials over vernacular memory, legend, and local tradition. The underlying conviction here is that close scrutiny of written documents is a more reliable way to arrive at the truth than hermeneutic ingenuity or aesthetic intuition. And for Malone, getting at the truth of the matter of Shakespeare meant above all the restoration of an authentic text of his works.

In Malone's self-understanding as textual editor, biographer, lexicographer, and interpreter he assigns himself a strictly ministerial function with respect to Shakespeare's authority. Malone is the executor of an incomparably greater authority bodied forth in Shakespeare's works. This position of self-effacement has been an ethical disclaimer required of all delegates and representatives of Shakespeare at least since the time of Malone. But of course even this ministerial authority is not derived exclusively from Malone's decision to retain himself as Shakespeare's solicitor and fiduciary. Like his predecessors and also his successors through to the end of the nineteenth century Malone addressed his efforts directly to the literary public.

Malone's situation differs in important ways from that of the Tonsons and their roster of Shakespeare editors. Although Jacob Tonson the elder was himself a man of letters, the Tonson firm was also a primary supplier of cultural commodities for the market. Production of the Tonson editions was governed by market considerations of timeliness and efficiency. Malone on the other hand presented himself as a private man of letters acting on behalf of the literary public sphere. He was less concerned with economic calculation than with creating optimal conditions for dialogue between a valued author and a community of readers. This morally privileged stance was, of course, only possible because by 1790 the infrastructure for a comfortable literary career was already in place. Nevertheless, the authority of Malone's edition is enhanced because he is not in it just for the money. Towards the end of the nineteenth century the vocation of scholarship will shift its social location from the unaffiliated gentleman amateur to the university professor. Implicit in the standard of authenticity throughout this history is the conviction that a scholar's labor is not available for hire.

Every edition of Shakespeare is the result of a compromise between fidelity to the author's intentions and intelligibility for contemporary readers. Malone understood the need for compromise in an edition of Shakespeare's plays. The guiding purpose of his new edition was to resolve this compromise on the side of accuracy. In order to accomplish this aim, he insisted that the textual editing of Shakespeare should proceed from careful scrutiny of the earliest printed texts rather than from the work of the most recent editors. This principle represents a radical break from earlier editorial practice, and it has become established as the uncontested standard for all modern textual scholarship. The idea did not, however, originate with Malone and in fact his adherence to this principle must be described as equivocal at best. Edward Capell, in the Tonson edition of 1767, had in fact based his scholarship directly on the early editions. Malone's text was not the result of an exhaustive independent review of the early editions; it simply reproduced the more recent work of Capell. The important point here is not, however, that Malone was disingenuous about his claims on behalf of the new edition's authenticity. Malone certainly believed in the authority of the early editions, even though he had adopted someone else's labor in the implementation of his plan. The most significant contribution of Malone is not in his achievements as an editor, but in the elaboration of a larger context for the practice of textual scholarship.

Before considering that larger context, I want to look very briefly at a further ambiguity in Malone's claims to have produced the first authentic edition of Shakespeare's works. To begin with, Malone's edition was radically unlike anything that a contemporary of Shakespeare might have handled or read, because the craft of book production had developed so extensively since the sixteenth century. Technical standards of paper-making, typesetting, inking and impression had all evolved in the direction of greater visual regularity and clarity. The design of typefaces and page layout contributed to the fundamentally different look of an eighteenth-century edition. In addition to these purely physical differences, Malone's edition follows the standard eighteenth-century practice of regularizing and modernizing the spelling of early editions. In his Preface Malone considers and then rejects Thomas Tyrwhitt's argument that a truly accurate edition of Shakespeare would reproduce the eccentricities of the original spelling. It is not necessary to examine Malone's reasons for rejecting Tyrwhitt to see that his central notion of authenticity is not to be equated with anything like mere physical similarity to the early editions. This is even more fully apparent in Malone's complex and elaborate scholarly apparatus.

In the sixteenth century the only 'apparatus' to accompany play texts was the background knowledge readers had about the idiomatic sense of individual words and phrases. Malone's formal apparatus of notes and commentary was designed to compensate readers for deficits in this background knowledge and thus to make Shakespeare's work more accessible in a historically distant context. For Malone this compensatory apparatus was not incompatible with the central aim of authenticity. Making good the deficits in his readers' background knowledge was a basic condition for the possibility of authenticity. Despite his insistence on the overriding importance of fidelity to the singular creativity embodied in Shakespeare's works, the apparatus reveals Malone's pragmatic accommodation to the exigencies of reception. What is perhaps most remarkable about this edition is that Malone succeeds in making his massive editorial interventions on behalf of contemporary readers largely invisible.

Despite his remarkable accomplishments, Malone was not an original thinker, nor is the 1790 edition a radically innovative break with earlier practice. Inspired by Foucault's notion of *episteme*, Margreta De Grazia has claimed that Malone's edition represents a paradigm shift in the way Shakespearean authorship is constituted, but this is in many ways misleading. There is no single element in the edition of 1790 that is not already anticipated in the work of earlier scholars and editors. Most important perhaps, the interrelated notions of authenticity and originality are already assigned considerable importance in the first folio, as they are in all the various Tonson editions, most notably those of Theobald and Capell. Malone did not invent a new model of authorship. The importance of the 1790 edition is that it sets out a protocol of professional methods and standards for Shakespeare scholarship. His edition gives substantive content for these standards based on disinterested scrutiny of archival materials and on rigorous adherence to uniform procedures in the examination of those materials.

De Grazia's critique of Malone's edition suggests that the editorial principle of authenticity is both fundamentally misguided and disingenuous. This ideal is a mask for the interests of bourgeois domination and the administrative state. De Grazia cites Edmund Burke's approbation of Malone's edition as evidence that his quest for authentic Shakespeare is the expression of enlightenment ideology. But if Malone's well-documented associations with Burke and with such figures as Samuel Johnson or Sir Joshua Reynolds are taken seriously, it is more accurate to see his project as the expression of counter-enlightenment ideals. Burke himself was in many ways the opponent of enlightenment principles. In *Reflections on the Revolution in France*, which appeared in the same year as Malone's editions, Burke favors traditional authority over the redress of social grievances through an application of enlightenment rationality. Burke's social and political philosophy is much closer to that of Richard Hooker, or even Aristotle, than it is to any of the enlightenment ideologies promoted in centers like Paris, Edinburgh, or Boston. To the extent that Malone follows an explicit political agenda, it seems more likely that he is, like Burke, a cautious and conservative Whig, committed to sustaining traditional institutions. Malone's concern with a programmatically authentic Shakespeare then, may not be at all connected with radical notions of singular individuality. The aim here may well be the more obviously conservative one of stripping away innovation in order to foster a more immediate relationship with the genius of an earlier stage of the culture.

The 1790 edition's apparatus includes, among other things, a laborious reconstruction of the lost meaning of Shakespeare's local and specific vocabulary. This aspect of Malone's project has an obvious family resemblance to the encyclopedia, perhaps the most characteristic enterprise of the enlightenment as an intellectual movement. However, the encyclopedic impulse here is clearly oriented to hermeneutic interests and to the illumination of the present by the past. Although he is motivated by powerful beliefs about the moral importance of Shakespeare's distinctively individual gift, Malone's practice as a lexicographer, based on extensive reading of sixteenth-century texts, acknowledges the larger framework of linguistic practice in which that gift is actualized. Malone's preoccupation with conserving an authentic Shakespeare is in many ways a form of resistance to an enlightenment ethics based on instrumental reason, marginal utility, and commodity exchange.

Authenticity and accuracy have always been one side of the complex dialectic through which Shakespeare's authority has been sustained. The other side is the requirement of accessibility and intelligibility. These demands cannot in principle be reconciled, since truly accurate texts and performances would be unappealing if not downright incomprehensible to audiences in successor cultures. Malone's edition has managed to achieve a more seamless compromise than any of his predecessors, one that purports to favor the side of authenticity over accessibility, although Malone, bound by the same exigencies as any of his predecessors, nevertheless conforms to exacting marketplace demands for convenience and accessibility.

The processing of Shakespeare for consumption by an educated elite has always been challenged by alternative marketing strategies aimed at more popular audiences. As audiences change, moreover, and as new media develop, the culture industry continues to invent new Shakespeare merchandise. Edmond Malone, working from the painstaking researches of earlier editors, produced the first modern edition of Shakespeare, establishing the protocols which continue to influence academic reception of the playwright's works. In responding so effectively to the needs and desires of an emerging professional community, however, Malone's edition helped create a market for a wide range of alternative Shakespeare merchandise.

The expectations of an emerging middle-class, family-oriented market in the early nineteenth century have been met by Bowdler's 'Family Edition' of the plays and by innovative spin-off projects such as Charles and Mary Lamb's *Tales from Shakespeare*, or Mary Cowden-Clarke's *The Girlhood of Shakespeare's Heroines*. And, as Lawrence Levine has shown, the 'inauthentic' Shakespeare of the popular theaters prospered throughout the nineteenth century, cheerfully ignoring the basically humorless imperatives laid down by Malone. Ironically, all these contrastingly motivated types of activity arise from the same set of background interests. The editors and scholars, no less than the theater managers and publishers, attempt to cash in on a diffuse public demand for access to Shakespeare's works. Malone's edition was a success in the sense that it perfected a technology for making literary works of the past into a viable commodity. It was, however, a complete failure in its larger aim of creating an encyclopedic and culturally stable reference for Shakespeare's authority. In Chapter 4 I will argue that the exigencies of commodity exchange and the seductive disburdening appeal of cultural technology have led to an increasing fragmentation and dispersal of Shakespeare's authority in our more recent cultural history.

Chapter 4

Crying all the way to the bank

You can't make money doing Shakespeare.

(Tommy Lee Jones)

Shakespeare, it has been said, is the greatest show business success story of all time. Through many long runs and return engagements, Shakespeare has demonstrated remarkable appeal across a wide spectrum of market sectors. Lawrence Levine, in *Highbrow/Lowbrow* (1988), has shown how Shakespeare's plays were integrated into a broadly based popular culture in the United States during the nineteenth century. Levine compares nineteenth-century popular theaters to mass media such as the movies and television. He describes it as a 'democratic institution presenting a widely varying bill of fare to all classes and socioeconomic groups' (1988: 21). Shakespeare was not the exclusive preference of educated elites, but part of a 'rich shared public culture' (p. 9). This was a common culture that incorporated a wide variety of theatrical forms, including farce, vaudeville, and innumerable parodies of Shakespeare.

Despite the endurance of vernacular Shakespeare, the interpenetration of high and low culture is not the main story Levine has to tell. *Highbrow/Lowbrow* analyzes the pattern of cultural hierarchy that emerged in the United States in the early twentieth century. Specialized publics organized for the consumption of high culture gradually withdrew from contact with the interests and activities of the popular element. In the early decades of the twentieth century this separation became more and more invidious. The split between institutionally sanctioned art and ephemeral popular entertainment interrupted the dialogue between diverging publics. Van Wyck Brooks, writing in *America's Coming of Age* in 1913, points out the division between these mutually unintelligible cultural domains and laments that 'between academic pedantry and pavement slang, there is no community, no genial middle ground' (Brooks 1915: 83).

Lawrence Levine is certainly right to maintain that towards the end of the nineteenth century an emerging taste community of privileged elites adopts a preference for taking Shakespeare seriously, and that this preference entails a strong intolerance for the characteristic forms of vernacular expression. However, Levine's emphasis on exclusionary cultural engineering misses an important dimension of the problem. It may be that rejection of popular Shakespeare was motivated by the exacerbated snobbery of newly wealthy social groups. For modernist critics like Van Wyck Brooks, T. E. Hulme, and T. S. Eliot, however, the preference for complex and difficult art forms was not a supercilious dismissal of traditional popular culture. High modernism was a form of resistance to the encroachment of a commercial mass culture of pulp fiction, film, and recorded music. What's missing from Levine's account of an elite and exclusive Shakespeare is the odd reappearance of a vernacular Shakespeare within the opaque technologies of the culture industry. This omission does not compromise the basic argument about the secession of serious Shakespeare from a widely shared public culture. The accessibility of Shakespeare provided for by the culture industry does not compensate for the problem of secession. The culture industry has no interest in facilitating shared critical discourse. The entertainment business is concerned with market saturation, and this is best achieved through the rapid circulation of basically innocuous cultural goods and services.

Shakespeare is now a familiar figure in contemporary mass media. This commercial Shakespeare is a defector from the serious cultural regime of high-school classrooms, university seminars, and legitimate theaters. In the modern entertainment business, crossover is a strategy that allows artists and performers to expand the market for their work. Celebrities identified with a well-defined sector of the entertainment business cross over from one market to another to generate additional sales in this second market. If the strategy is successful, however, consumers in this second market may be prompted to cross over from their customary cultural habits to explore the performer's initial sector, thus widening the public for this first market and greatly accelerating returns. At the height of her success, the now fading pop idol Madonna pursued an aggressive cross-over strategy, appealing to a wide range of otherwise fragmented publics that included middle-class teenagers and pre-teens, members of marginalized sexual subcultures, and even some academic feminists and culture critics.

Shakespeare has been even more versatile as a cross-over artist than Madonna. *Shakespearean Spinach* is a 1940 cartoon version of *Romeo and Juliet* featuring Popeye and Olive Oyl in the lead roles. In *A Witch's Tangled Hare*, a 1959 Warner Brothers Cartoon, Bugs Bunny and Witch Hazel offer a pastiche of quotations from *Macbeth*, *Romeo and Juliet*, and *Hamlet*. *Kiss Me Kate* and *West Side Story* have been durable favorites on the musical comedy stage. Shakespearean parody has been featured in episodes of *Happy Days*, *Gilligan's Island*, *The Andy Griffith Show*, and *Moonlighting*. Finally, just like Madonna, Shakespeare provides the occasion for public discussion and controversy in newspapers and other mass media publications from the *Portland Press Herald* to the *New York Times*. This remarkably diverse cross-over implies widespread public familiarity with at least some of Shakespeare's works, a familiarity sustained and guaranteed by the culture industry. It does not depend on the prior experience of cultural consumers with the edifying Shakespeare of elite culture.

As a celebrity, Shakespeare has an uncanny ability to thrive in almost any cultural environment. For this reason Shakespeare has been able to cross over not only among the competing branches of a commercial culture industry but also from the culture industry to the equally fundamental but rival institutions of public education and higher learning. The success of these maneuvers depends on Shakespeare's radically disembodied and culturally promiscuous character. As a canonical literary figure however, Shakespeare's value is said to be embodied in concrete textual material that not only possesses genuine dignity and worth of its own but also serves as an evaluative standard for other cultural activity. Paradoxically it is the belief in Shakespeare's transcendent worth that underwrites his currency in popular culture and secures his commercial value.

Success in contemporary show business depends on an ability to generate large aggregate revenues for corporate investors. The market potential for Shakespeare is not limited to the production of quality entertainment for upscale cultural consumers. The cultural capital accumulated in Shakespeare's works can be exploited to generate finance capital in many different ways. But 'quality' all by itself does not sustain a profitable market. Public notoriety is by far the more crucial element for big-time show business success, even though such notoriety does not require any genuinely significant artistic achievement. The big time really only calls for striking and colorful forms of public visibility. Within the contemporary culture industry Shakespeare retains currency because certain aspects of his reputation have perennial interest for provoking journalistic scandal. The transmutation of Shakespeare's value into cash receipts is not a simple matter of putting a quality product on the market. In the discussion which follows I analyze the destiny of cultural capital as it circulates in an institutional regime of advertising, festival theaters, and commercial cinema. I then take up the issue of journalistic scandal and controversy as the characteristic form of public concern for Shakespeare promoted by the culture industry.

LEVERAGING CULTURAL CAPITAL

As cultural capital Shakespeare is fully negotiable in all financial markets. It is simply untrue that 'you can't make money doing Shakespeare'. For an actor like Tommy Lee Jones, who has in fact done some Shakespeare, action films and other standard Hollywood formats do provide much more lucrative opportunities than an ascetic commitment to artistic quality can offer. In these terms, serious Shakespearean performance is just small time. Venues such as university theaters or off-off-Broadway generally offer low-budget productions to small audiences. Still, the same logic that makes it possible to turn a small amount of money into Shakespeare can also be used to turn a small amount of Shakespeare into money. To convert a limited stock of cultural capital into a generous cash flow requires complicated forms of leverage. Shakespeare must be carefully positioned within a complex network of cultural assets and investments.

The leveraging of cultural capital has actually been explained in a widely circulated advertisement that ordains Shakespeare 'the greatest apartment salesman of *our* time'.

> To *most of us, William Shakespeare* is the quintessential playwright. But when the *Ballard Realty Company of Montgomery, Alabama*, needed tenants for a new apartment complex, Mr Shakespeare proved to be a top-notch salesman as well. With every signed lease, Ballard Realty offered free membership subscriptions to the nearby *Alabama Shakespeare Festival*. In no time, over 80% of the company's units were leased, before construction was even completed. Throughout the country, small and medium-sized

businesses, like Ballard Realty, are discovering what blue chippers have known for years: that the arts can help create a positive public image, increase a company's visibility and improve sales. All this while reducing taxable income. If you would like information on how your company – no matter what its size – can benefit through a partnership with the arts, contact the *Business Committee for the Arts Inc., 1775 Broadway, Suite 510, New York, New York 10019, or call (212) 644-0600*. It may just be the factor that decides whether this year's sales goals are to be or not to be. *Business Committee for the Arts, Inc*. This advertisement prepared as a public service by *Ogilvy & Mather*.

The advertisement ran in both full-page and half-page formats for several years in up-market publications like the *New Yorker* and in academic quarterlies such as *Theatre Journal*. It featured Shakespeare's portrait from the frontispiece of the first folio. The copywriters at Ogilvy & Mather introduce us to a Mr Shakespeare who is not the remote and alien 'quintessential playwright' we always thought he was. In reality he is just a neighborly and hard-working real-estate broker. The easy familiarity here is reinforced by witty and self-deprecating use of 'to be or not to be' as a question about meeting 'this year's sales goals'. Shakespeare's most famous poetry is placed at the disposal of middle management to imply sympathy between the educational background of the advertisement's readers and their everyday practical concerns. Shakespeare negotiates the differences between business and the arts.

The provisional economic links between Ballard Realty and its prospective tenants are secured by a network of corporate entities from both the not-for-profit and private sectors, e.g. the Alabama Shakespeare Festival, the Business Committee for Arts, and by Ogilvy & Mather, whose work is donated *pro bono publico*. The nature of that public service is to make people aware of benefits that accrue from a partnership between business and the arts, not least of which is the prospect of a reduction of taxable income. Even more fundamental is the link between the benefits of subscriptions to the Alabama Shakespeare festival and the benefits of home ownership. Shakespeare is one of the amenities of middle-class domestic life. But why not? After all, Shakespeare used his own hard-earned savings to buy real estate in Stratford. It thus seems perfectly appropriate for Shakespeare to be used to accelerate the sale of condos.

The attractiveness of tax write-offs, condominiums, and more broadly of the upwardly mobile lifestyle to which such things pertain are certainly important elements in the composition of this advertisement. But what is actually being sold here? The headline – 'the greatest apartment salesman of all time' – recalls in an odd way the theme of a book called *The Man Nobody Knew*, a best selling publication of the 1920s that described Jesus as the greatest salesman of all time. Jesus, of course, had a great marketing staff in Peter, Paul, and their associates. It seems clear that what's on sale in this advertisement is nothing less than the practice of selling itself. Ballard Realty hires Mr Shakespeare, another man nobody knew, to promote condominium sales. The Business Committee for the Arts hires Ogilvy & Mather to promote corporate sponsorship and its lucrative tax exemptions. Everyone has a share.

The partnership between Ballard Realty and the Alabama Shakespeare Festival suggests how intimately Shakespeare is linked both to a particular sector of the culture industry and to larger economic structures typical of late capitalist society. Shakespeare is a commercial product, especially in upscale markets. At another level, however, Shakespeare is ambiguously positioned *vis-à-vis* the culture industry. For patrons of the festival theaters Shakespeare is a much more satisfying alternative to the routinized cultural fare available in television and commercial cinema. Teachers hope that Shakespeare can be the *antidote* for the debilitating effects of the culture industry. This view is endorsed by anxious parents hoping that school bus trips to the local Shakespeare festival might save their teenage children from the seductions of rock videos. The festival theaters cannot, however, compete with the multinational entertainment corporation. Economies of scale in the culture industry definitively favor Schwarzenegger over Shakespeare. In the present economic climate, the provision of depth and seriousness in cultural experience is only possible through large-scale corporate sponsorship by the multinationals.

Canada's Stratford Festival does a substantial business in group ticket sales each year for high-school and university students. The festival, whose commercial viability is crucial to the local economy of Stratford, Ontario, is a hybrid institution whose public service mission is fundamentally market-driven. The Stratford Festival has the largest operating budget of all the North American Shakespeare festivals. However, although it is clearly an important institution within the Canadian entertainment industry, the festival has never been self-financing. In recent years, moreover, its traditional funding sources have contracted. Public sector support has declined as federal and provincial legislatures turn their attention to deficit reduction. And the festival's audience, at least for Shakespeare, has diminished. Increasingly the festival has had to rely on the kindness of corporate strangers to finance its long-standing commitment to carefully staged productions of Shakespeare's works.

Ticket sales to the general public still account for about 75 per cent of the festival's operating budget. An additional 10 per cent is received from Canada Council and Ontario Arts Council grants, though this seems likely to diminish in the foreseeable future. Although government funding accounts for only a small percentage of the total, that incremental support has made it possible for the festival to include more risky and innovative productions in its season (Drainie 1994: A-13). As government funding declines, support from the private sector becomes increasingly important. The contemporary renewal of a traditional patronage relationship between the theater company and wealthy donors presumably benefits both parties. The capital resources of corporate sponsors obviously go a long way towards alleviating the financial difficulties faced by the Stratford Festival. In return the corporate sponsors gain a certain moral authority as benefactors of public well-being. They also, and not incidentally, receive valuable free publicity.

Season subscribers and friends of the Stratford Festival receive a quarterly publication called *Fanfares*. In the issue for September 1994 the editors acknowledge the generosity of corporate sponsors in sustaining the festival's public mission. All contributors are gracefully commended for their generosity and for their commitment to the 'continuing dream'. Special praise for the largest corporate donors is included with the announcement of each individual play.

> *Hamlet* Sponsored by Liquid Carbonic. One of our newest corporate partners, Liquid Carbonic Inc. joined the Festival in 1993 as sponsor of our production of *King John*. In 1994, our production of *Hamlet* is underwritten by this enthusiastic supporter.

The notion of 'underwriting' Shakespeare is complex and also revealing. To underwrite is to co-sign or endorse, the way a check is endorsed on the back. And of course the check deposited by Liquid Carbonic is what decides whether or not *Hamlet* is to be or not to be.

The corporate signature also validates this production by providing a warrant of quality and social acceptance.

Obviously the festival's directors must be sensitive to the feelings of corporate sponsors, not only in the deferential rhetoric of these acknowledgements, but also in the overall policy orientation for the organization. This situation is not altogether different from what The King's Men faced in dealing with the Revels Office. But Shakespeare's company also had a larger public of cultural consumers accessed through the public playhouses that evidently brought a quite different ideological outlook to the theaters. At Stratford, on the other hand, the sponsoring agencies and the larger consuming public together constitute a more homogeneous taste community. This is an educated and economically secure public with access to a common fund of cultural capital. It is not, however, a highbrow taste community, at least not in the sense suggested by Lawrence Levine. For Levine, highbrow sensibility entails erudition and serious intellectual reflection as well as a genteel etiquette of reception. Stratford productions characteristically maintain a certain standard of refined, middle-class *Gemütlichkeit* in their productions, but they generally demand little in the way of serious learning or critical attention.

Although the Stratford Festival was founded for the purpose of performing Shakespearean drama in repertory, their commitment to what has been traditionally understood as the values of high culture has been quite equivocal. Stratford productions aspire to a certain standard of amenity in design and decor; they have often been visually sumptuous. They also adhere to a high standard of acting, based on the skills of an experienced resident company. Stratford has built its audience over the years by focusing on aesthetically satisfying and sometimes visually innovative productions of the standard repertory. However, these productions have often not been intellectually challenging or particularly risky. They have also been politically innocuous for the most part, affirming a range of conventional attitudes or at least not openly contesting mainstream sympathies. But the taste community that sponsors the festival is very far from controlling its message or dictating any substantive ideological program.

In many ways corporate backers appear relatively indifferent to the ideological payloads of sponsored productions. Of course the festival's directors are not likely to gamble on offending their patrons, but the discretion and prudence required for this position does not necessarily confine the festival to a narrowly restricted ideological menu. Although the educated public that Stratford draws on for its audiences may have a relatively homogeneous outlook, part of that conventional outlook is tolerance for a moderate range of differing viewpoints. In any case the real problems faced by the festival stem from underlying changes in the structure of the cultural market. To begin with, public demand for Shakespeare in live performance appears to be waning. The festival's productions of Gilbert and Sullivan operettas typically outdraw Shakespeare performances, often by a considerable margin. Whatever the public wants, it doesn't need high culture in the form of Shakespeare to get it. The festival could, of course, adjust its programming to adapt to this kind of shift in audience preferences. But an even more ominous tendency has been noted that could seriously erode Stratford's audiences and even threaten the continuity of the festival itself.

A recent survey of Stratford's audience suggests that its constituency is gradually aging (Godfrey 1992: C-1, C-9). The festival's limited, upscale taste community evidently corresponds to a limited age cohort. Apart from its captive audience of bussed in high-school students, most of the festival's steady customers are aged 45 and over. In recent years the festival's organizers have made a conscious effort to attract a new audience of single men and women as well as young families. The emphasis in its recent advertising campaigns has been on showing how a trip to the Stratford Shakespeare Festival fits into the imagined lifestyle of this affluent younger crowd. But the long-term success of this marketing strategy remains uncertain. Classical theater increasingly must compete in a diverse leisure market that offers a wide range of cheaper and more accessible alternatives to the time-consuming demands of attending a live performance, especially in a geographically remote center like Stratford, Ontario. In the final analysis the lifestyle imperatives that typify this leisure market have a greater impact on the festival's decision making than any direct ideological pressure from its wealthy corporate sponsors.

The primary challenge to the kind of cultural experience provided by the festival theaters comes from the newer technologies of cultural production. Alvin Kernan has argued that declining public interest in traditional high culture corresponds to deeper shifts in institutional authority.

film, television and computer screen [are] replacing the printed book as the most efficient and preferred source of entertainment and knowledge. Television, computer database, Xerox, word processor, tape, and VCR are not symbiotic with literature and its value in the way that print was.

(Kernan 1990: 9–10)

The 'death of literature' as a form of close engagement with printed books may not have a significant impact on the long-term survival of Shakespeare. Astute cultural producers like Garrick or Tonson have always found ways to take advantage of competitive cultural markets and to ensure that rival sectors become mutually self-sustaining. Competition between contemporary mass media and traditional high culture in the form of printed books and festival theater productions offers even more abundant opportunities for the leveraging of cultural capital.

The survival of traditional high literary culture in non-print media depends on the relationship between cultural capital and finance capital. This relationship has never been more artfully negotiated than in Kenneth Branagh's recent film version of *Henry V* and in the media event surrounding it. Branagh's professed aim in filming *Henry V* was 'to make it look like a film of today, to take the curse of medievalism off it, so that the *Batman* audiences could conceivably be persuaded to see it' (Fuller 1989: 5–6). In an interview with Michael Billington published in *The New York Times* just before the film's release in the United States he describes his intention 'to make a popular film that will both satisfy the Shakespearean scholar and the punter who likes *Crocodile Dundee*' (Billington 1989: 18–19). Billington interprets this in relation to Branagh's 'complex . . . Anglo-Irish . . . working class' background, and there's no doubt that Branagh himself is the real story here. In any case, to judge by its healthy box-office returns, the movie was certainly popular in the sense that Branagh intended. It has done less well with Shakespearean scholars.

Branagh's *Henry V* has been widely criticized within the academic community, not for its lack of aesthetic interest, but rather because of its ideological message. Chris Fitter, in 'A Tale of Two Branagh's: *Henry V*, Ideology, and the Mekong Agincourt', has argued that the film version simplifies the play into a conventional cinematic adventure story. The adaptation to the conventions of *Batman* and *Crocodile Dundee* 'works to naturalize ideology rather than interrogate and defamiliarize the action' (Fitter 1993: 273). The result is a film that increasingly moves towards untroubled sympathy for the King and for the English cause. In the end Fitter indicts Branagh for doing ordinary people 'an irresponsible political disservice, in white-washing traditional autocracy and the logic of imperialism. What Shakespeare has demystified, Branagh, persuasively, affably, im-morally, has resanctified' (p. 275). Fitter's case rests on a reading of Shakespeare's play that emphasizes its democratic and oppositional valences. That reading is actualized for Fitter in Adrian Noble's 1984 Stratford production of *Henry V* for the Royal Shakespeare Company, a production that also featured Branagh in the leading role.

Chris Fitter is convinced that Adrian Noble's dissident staging is more faithful to Shakespeare's *Henry V* than Branagh's more ingratiating film. He is very much out of countenance with Branagh for failing to bring the lessons learned from Adrian Noble's produc-tion to the film version. Curtis Breight has been even more severe than Fitter in his denunciation of Branagh's complicity with a pro-grammatic conservative ideology. Breight shrewdly analyzes the film as a large media event, placing it in the context not only of popular films like *Rambo* but also of media coverage of events such as the Falklands War and Operation: Desert Storm. For Breight, the film is deplorable not because it is a betrayal of its audience of 'punters who like *Crocodile Dundee*' but because it is an indulgence of that audience's aggressive militarism.

> Divinely endorsed militarism is probably the most potent defence for a culture's unwillingness to acknowledge its complicity in holocaustal slaughter. Thus Branagh's *Henry V* seeks to excuse militarism by manufacturing a Christian context, and modern vile politicians put a Christian gloss on mass murder. Branagh claims that he wanted to create a 'truly popular film', but unless he is thoroughly dense about modern America, he must under-stand that the United States is a culture of violence, in the 1980s especially prone to the revival of military violence. Young American men who constitute a large percentage of cinema audi-ences . . . do not flee in horror from representations of gratuitous butchery. They revel in it.
>
> (Breight 1991: 109–110)

Breight's discussion insists on the film's active complicity with the military adventurism of the Thatcher and Bush governments.

Branagh, by contrast, has consistently maintained that 'there would be no question about the statement this movie was making about war', meaning apparently that war, imperial ambition, and militarism are social evils that his film intends to oppose.

The critical reception of Branagh's *Henry V* in mass media publications has been altogether different from the response in academic journals. In general, newspaper and magazine reviews have been willing to take Branagh at his word, and have generally described the film's depiction of war as grim and unheroic. *The New York Times* gave extensive coverage to the film, with no fewer than three reviews in addition to the Michael Billington feature story. All these reviews take their cue from interviews and publicity materials supplied by Branagh and persist in stressing the film's darker valences. Benedict Nightingale stresses the contrast with the unproblematic patriotism of Olivier's 1944 wartime version and compares the battle sequences to the poetry of Wilfred Owen (Nightingale 1989: 17). Vincent Canby commends the production as 'immensely intelligent' in its avoidance of pomp and spectacle (Canby 1989: 19). And in an op-ed piece for 6 February 1990, Nicholas Wade speaks admiringly of the 'film's reconstruction of the battle of Agincourt [which] powerfully conveys horrors of a medieval killing field [and] gives the impression of terrifying carnage' (Wade 1990: A-28). *The New York Times* coverage stretched over more than a year, and it helped maintain an extraordinary level of favorable publicity for the film with an affluent and influential sector of the cultural market.

The film's anti-war message is conveyed by means of entirely familiar cinematic conventions in filming of the battle sequences. Branagh, because he was obliged to rely throughout on the experience of an industry-trained technical staff, had very little scope for originality in filming the Agincourt scenes and, to judge by the accounts in his diary, very little interest in cinematic innovation. The 'powerful anti-war message' is nothing more than a derivative montage of stunts, hand-to-hand combat, and wide shots of charging cavalry. The film does show that people are killed and injured in wars, and that this cost may not always be absolutely justified. But these are the routine and orthodox sentiments of a certain genre of war films from *A Walk in the Sun* through *M.A.S.H.* to *Platoon*, and *Full Metal Jacket*. Like Branagh's *Henry V*, these films manage to integrate a sense of the destructiveness of military combat with straightforward glorification of male bonding, of physical endurance, of courage and sacrifice in a noble cause.

Henry V is an 'anti-war' film in the sense that it uses a standard cinematic vocabulary to communicate a package of ready-made ideas. It is not an 'anti-war' film in the sense that it actually has something important to say about the topic. Movie reviewers have for the most part overpraised Branagh's achievement, as they do many commercial films. On the other hand the denunciation of Branagh by academic critics makes his film sound more like *Triumph of the Will* than the innocuous historical costume drama it really is. *Henry V* is no more ideologically noxious than *Crocodile Dundee* and it is hardly more interesting as a cinematic achievement. Compared to *Rambo* it is benign.

The real story of Branagh's *Henry V* is the masterful publicity campaign that surrounds his career as a show business entrepreneur. Like Davenant, Garrick, and the great theater managers of the nineteenth century, Branagh has been able to exploit the financial and technical resources of the culture industry. *Henry V* is an example of successful leveraging of Shakespeare's cultural capital into an advantageous financial position within the entertainment industry. It was produced by Renaissance Films, an offshoot of Branagh's own touring theater company, with financing from public and private sources, including a British government program for subsidizing business expansion. In his diary of the film's production Branagh continually stresses his achievements in staying within his budget and adhering to a strict production schedule. Branagh's real audience here is not composed of 'punters who like *Crocodile Dundee*'. The people he hopes to win over are investors and financial executives in the entertainment corporations. The success of *Henry V* established Kenneth Branagh as a big-time film-maker, and he has since directed a number of moderately successful films, including Shakespeare's *Much Ado About Nothing*. As part of its marketing strategy, the Samuel Goldwyn Company previewed the film for the annual meeting of the Shakespeare Association of America in April 1993. A follow-up letter addressed to 'Dear Educator' offered a study guide and a group sale policy. The obvious intent here is to generate more sales, but the Goldwyn Company is also intent on expanding its stock of available cultural capital.

In the final analysis, Branagh's *Henry V* really has no clearly speci-fiable political purpose. Despite his claim that the film will present a serious debate over the nature of kingship, political authority, and war, Branagh does not really select and focus a critical element from among the play's divergent social and political valences. Instead he simply reproduces the most equivocal and opportunistic features of the original (Sinfield 1991: 109–42). Indeed, the evidence of his own diary suggests that he was never seriously committed to a programmatic or even a minimally coherent political agenda. Branagh's openly professed intention was to produce a film that would satisfy Shakespeare scholars and would at the same time appeal to a mass audience. What he ended up with was a film damned by academic critics and praised by their journalistic counterparts. The film's solid commercial success demonstrates the wide institutional authority of mass media publications in the cultural marketplace. It also suggests that the cultural authority of corporate Shakespeare has nothing to do with ideas of any description.

DON'T SCANDALIZE MY NAME

Increasingly in our public media, intellectual issues are addressed only when they can be presented in the journalistic formats of scandal and controversy; Shakespeare is no exception to this rule. News items about Shakespeare make *The New York Times* regularly, usually in connection with fast-breaking stories about the authorship controversy, the discovery of new manuscripts, or events like the recent excavation of the foundations of the Rose Theatre. In light of the institutional and sentimental importance of his plays in the United States, Canada, Australia, and the UK it is not surprising that Shakespeare should emerge as a topic of controversy in our increasingly exacerbated cultural policy debate, not only in professional journals but in mass-circulation publications as well. There is usually very little news content in any of these reports. Instead, Shakespeare appears in print as the focus of a media event for the brief duration of a single news cycle.

One of the perennial sources of public interest in Shakespeare is the seemingly incorrigible fascination among journalists with the question of the real authorship of Shakespeare's works. This is unquestionably the best known Shakespearean topic among the general public and the one scholars are most likely to find themselves discussing if they become embroiled in a casual conversation about their own profession. Contemporary anti-Stratfordians have shown a remarkable ability to capitalize on public infatuation with this supposed mystery. Newspaper coverage of the authorship story in recent years has invariably been prompted by press releases and other initiatives of the Shakespeare Oxford Society, whose leader, Charles Vere, is a descendant of the Earl of Oxford, the putative real author of Shakespeare's works.

Whatever the merits of the Oxford case, there is no doubt that Charles Vere has an extraordinary talent for commanding the attention of reporters and editors. This is partly because Vere, like his mentor, Charlton Ogburn, is himself a moderately interesting news story. Newspaper accounts of the authorship controversy invariably refer to the lifelong devotion and personal sacrifice of the leading Oxfordians in their quixotic campaign against the academic Shakespeare establishment. In itself, however, this would not be sufficient to generate news. There must in addition be an event of some kind to prompt media coverage. Thus in 1987 *The New York Times* carried a notice announcing that 'Three members of the Supreme Court are going to take on one of history's oldest debates: who wrote Shakespeare's plays'. The Shakespeare Oxford Society took the initiative in organizing and promoting this event. The active participation of Supreme Court Justices in the mock trial suggests that Oxfordians are a well-connected and influential group.

The first mock trial was held in Washington, DC on 25 September 1987. There had been some expectation that William Brennan, as 'the leading liberal on the court', might go against the traditional interpretation. At the conclusion of the trial, however, Brennan was joined by justices Blackmun and Stevens in a unanimous ruling that the works were by William Shakespeare. Just over a year later, on 27 November 1988, a similar mock trial was held in London, with three Law Lords presiding. The British trial was organized by Sam Wanamaker, who raised $27,000.00 for his Globe Theatre project. As in the earlier trial, the Law Lords unanimously ruled in favor of William Shakespeare. Predictably, however, nothing was really settled by the seemingly decisive judicial outcome. L. L. Ware, the lawyer for the Oxford side, promised after the trial that 'It's only the beginning. It has aroused more interest in the fact that there is a problem' (*The New York Times*, 28 November 1988: C-21).

Despite the court verdicts against the Earl of Oxford, his supporters have shown remarkable resiliency. In the spring of 1989, the debate was restaged in a television documentary entitled *The Shakespeare Mystery*. The program conformed to the usual journalistic format for the exploration of controversial topics. Advocates for the two positions were each given air time to put forward their arguments, but no serious effort was made to adjudicate the actual merits of the contending sides. It seems clear that the makers of the documentary had no interest in trying to settle the issue.

> Viewers with opinions on the dispute may not have their minds changed, but this vigorous duel demonstrates that the case for Oxford, though largely circumstantial, is by no means implausible. The passion it continues to arouse is seen especially in Mr Ogburn, whose eyes tear as he assumes the role of Horatio to de Vere's Hamlet, carrying out the injunction to 'report me and my cause alike to the unsatisfied'.
>
> (Goodman 1989: C-22)

The real point here is the display of grievance and resentment by Charlton Ogburn, A. L. Rowse, and the other participants. Walter Goodman, writing in *The New York Times*, praises the aspect of confrontational drama for its 'directness and intelligence'. As with similar public affairs programming, however, nothing was actually achieved in *The Shakespeare Mystery* beyond the affirmation of the adversarial format.

The Oxfordians have shown considerable ingenuity in exploiting journalistic responsiveness to media events designed to promote acrimonious contention and the possibility of scandal. On 1 April 1993, the *Atlanta Constitution and Journal* ran a feature on the front page of the 'Living' section with a lead of 'A skirmish of words flares in Atlanta this week, centering on a question of the ages: Did he or didn't he?' (May 1993: E-1). The story begins by informing readers that the annual conference of the Shakespeare Association of America is to be held in Atlanta over the weekend. What makes the event newsworthy, however, is the simultaneous meeting of the Shakespeare Oxford Society. The article rehearses the familiar and predictable arguments of the Oxford side, but without supplying any context that would make it possible to evaluate their claims. It also describes the 'rage' of Charlton Ogburn as he denounces the Shakespeare Association as a 'totalitarian regime' that refuses to 'look at the evidence'. Claims of conspiracy and cover-up are standard themes for newspaper reporters. In the present context they also provide an attractive opportunity to challenge the authority of the academic community.

Newspaper and broadcast coverage of the authorship controversy provides a revealing illustration of the aims, the methods, and the standards of contemporary journalism. It's apparent that the traditional interest in distinguishing truth from error is not the governing purpose behind these reports. Reporters typically do not show much interest in the complexities of scholarly research on the authorship problem. Instead the focus is on the valorization of a certain kind of interminable debate: 'people on both sides of the dispute assert that there's nothing like a good battle to inspire interest in an issue' (May 1993: E-2). In fact, although scholars generally recognize that the details of Shakespearean authorship require further research, they do not believe that the Oxford hypothesis is even minimally plausible. Scholars have no interest in perpetuating the battle with the Shakespeare Oxford Society. Nevertheless, for journalists, the battle is the only story.

It is important to realize that the Oxford–Stratford controversy is most often reported in the entertainment or living sections of the daily newspaper. The topic is assigned to the categories of leisure and lifestyle. Shakespeare is thus a purely discretionary matter, an optional extra whose work belongs to the sphere of personal preference. Cultural consumers are entitled to the kind of choice that a polarized Oxford–Stratford debate provides. Thus Joseph Sobran, a syndicated columnist writing in the *Daily Oklahoman* in April 1989, lines up with the Oxford side as the affirmation of his own contrarian predilections: 'to do your own thinking is always to risk appearing eccentric to people who follow the herd. In this respect, I'd rather be an eccentric than a centric – a person who assumes the conventional must be correct' (Sobran 1989: B-3).

I don't know anything about textual scholarship, but I know what I like. For Sobran, intellectual positions are the expression of personal style and sensibility. The Oxford–Stratford scandal helps to erode the traditional authority of the academic community, which is represented as an entrenched establishment, and at the same time it affirms the sovereignty of choice in the cultural marketplace.

Sobran wrote a follow-up piece in August 1989 defending the view that Shakespeare was really Oxford. A little less than two years later, in June 1991, he was preoccupied with another scandal that would move Shakespeare from the 'Living' section to the op-ed pages of newspapers all over the English-speaking world. Shakespeare has been increasingly brought to the attention of the public because of various outrages committed against his cultural authority by contemporary academics. 'Today, even Shakespeare criticism is hag-ridden by Marxist and feminist faddists. There is no sadder sign of the way contemplative life is being destroyed by "activism"' (Sobran 1991: B-2). It is only in the past several years that coverage of Shakespeare has taken on such strongly political and ideological overtones. This debate reflects the more traditional task of journalism in defining an agenda for discussion within the public sphere.

Recent journalistic coverage of cultural policy debates on literature in general and on Shakespeare in particular has focused on the prominent role of ideology in recent scholarship. Generally speaking, reporters and editorial writers have been unsympathetic to virtually all these new developments in Shakespeare criticism. The editorials and bylined feature articles typically represent the traditional humanistic valorizations of Shakespeare's cultural authority. George Neavoll, in an op-ed piece in celebration of Shakespeare's birthday in the *Portland Press Herald* for 23 April 1993, asks,

> What would the English language be without Shakespeare, a cab driver once asked me. Indeed, it would be the poorer, and more than we might think. The world's greatest playwright has so imbued our life and thought with the imagery of his works that even now, more than four centuries after his birth, his words have a direct effect on the way we say things.
>
> (Neavoll 1993: A-7)

George Neavoll, like Lawrence Levine, sees Shakespeare as part of a 'rich, shared public culture'. Drawing on the work of Alfred Harbage, Neavoll's editorial affirms and celebrates the people's Shakespeare: 'Shakespeare wrote for the common person, with all the human weakness, prejudices and bawdy language one might find in any setting where we faulted human beings gather' (ibid.). A sidebar to this editorial invites the public to a birthday party for Shakespeare in the editorial offices of Portland Newspapers where free cake and punch or coffee will be served. Neavoll's offer of 'cakes and ale' expresses his reconciliatory and convivial interpretation of Shakespeare's authority.

Joseph Sobran's more hostile treatment of 'hag-ridden . . . faddists' also has its intellectual ancestry in a more reconciliatory understanding of scholarly research and interpretation.

Some of the sweetest moments of my teens were spent reading the Shakespearean criticism of A. C. Bradley. This was my introduction to academic thought, and I got the optimistic idea that college would be like four years of reading Bradley. He was astoundingly perceptive, but always completely gentlemanly in his treatment of those he disagreed with. Alas, Bradley's manners were as rare as his intelligence. By the time I reached college, in 1964, the academy was already getting politicized. . . . The old-fashioned scholar, a contemplative soul is being muscled out by the type we call 'the intellectual,' who by nature is a political activist. Unfortunately, the intellectual is available in both right-wing and left-wing versions.

(Sobran, 1991: B-2)

These ruminations appear in a longer op-ed piece lamenting political correctness. Sobran sees this as a deplorable phenomenon at both ends of the contemporary political spectrum. The editorial is clearly prompted by nostalgia for an older and more harmonious standard of discursive ethics.

The same bewildered and diffuse resentment is expressed in an unsigned editorial in *The New York Times* for 3 September 1993. Here, however, there is no evidence of a background in a traditional humanistic understanding of Shakespeare. Unlike George Neavoll and Joseph Sobran, the anonymous editorialist does not cite earlier scholars like Bradley or Harbage as the standard for Shakespeare criticism. The background of institutional resentment here is nostalgia for a disciplinary and coercive pedagogy.

It's a privileged but shrinking group who had at least one play, at least one sonnet drummed into their heads as adolescents. They still go forth and find magic from that source. Maybe one was Gus Van Sant, who used 'Henry IV, Part I' as the basis for his quirky film 'My Own Private Idaho'.

(*The New York Times*, 3 September 1993: A-18)

Academics, who ask whether Shakespeare was a misogynist or an apologist for imperialism, are condemned as self-important, 'a bunch of myopic spoilsports who miss the point entirely'. Exactly what point these misguided academics have missed is not altogether clear. However, the editorial expresses vexation over two extremely contentious points. First, the writer prefers to think of Shakespeare as 'the ruling genius of English literature' rather than to entertain the thought that he might just be an 'optional extra'. Second, he or she is infuriated at the kind of political interpretation that sees *The Tempest* as 'merely an allegory about colonialism'. Academic critics are out to spoil the enjoyment of 'loyal fans, who merely wish . . . to drink in the delights of his spoken lines'.

Such interventions are, of course, part of a larger and more urgent cultural policy debate. The culture wars are not only concerned with the discretionary interests and preferences of cultural consumers. In a feature article written in December 1988 for the *Spectator*, an increasingly influential American right-wing publication, Marvin Hunt describes a Folger Institute seminar on 'New Directions in Shakespeare Criticism'. Hunt, himself an academic, tells a graphic tale about a cabal of ideologically motivated critics, led by a certain Jonathan Dollimore, who are engaged in plotting revolution in the basement of the Folger Library. Hunt evidently wants both to ridicule the radical scholars he encountered for their hypocritical, self-serving vanity and at the same time to denounce them as a serious cultural threat.

For the mainly right-wing readership which Marvin Hunt addresses in the *Spectator*, the ideological seizure of Shakespeare in the interests of a revolutionary conspiracy would hardly be viewed as a joking matter, even if, as Hunt points out, radical scholars have no realistic chance of success with their social agenda. Shakespeare after all is a privileged embodiment of Western values and a fundamental element in the substantive curriculum of Western culture. It is not really clear from Marvin Hunt's article whether the hard right really takes itself seriously about the urgency of culture and curriculum. A literary tradition would seem to have a decidedly marginal utility in fostering the larger purposes of the market economy. Nevertheless, to some observers the management of cultural capital has serious consequences for maintaining social stability.

In a front page article of the *Wall Street Journal* for 5 February 1993, Tony Horwitz writes, 'At William Shakespeare's old school, lessons on the Bard have become such stuff as bad dreams are made on.' The article then goes on to restage a controversial decision by the British government to require that every 14-year-old student pass a test on their knowledge of a set text by Shakespeare. Horwitz recounts some of the positions taken in this dispute, which range from Michael Bogdanov's forthright claim that Shakespeare was an 'anarchist' and a 'subversive' to the equally confident assertion of Brian John that 'he was a man of the political right'. Tony

Horwitz's own account of the situation apparently leans strongly to this latter view:

> The little that is known of Shakespeare's life also offers succor to Tories. After all, he was a glove-maker's son who got rich and bought the second biggest house in Stratford. In London, he became a shareholder in the Globe theater and was invited to the coronation of James I.
>
> (Horwitz 1993: 1)

It's clear from this that Tony Horwitz and the editors of the *Wall Street Journal* are only marginally interested in the question of how Shakespeare is taught to British schoolchildren. The real point of this article is something rather more complex than the obviously facetious claim that Shakespeare was an upwardly mobile Tory.

Horwitz's article is remarkable for the accuracy of its depiction of what amounts to an intellectual food-fight between contending ideological camps. The article is also effective for its concise delineation of complex institutional antagonisms between academics, journalists, and representatives from various sectors of the entertainment industry over the administration of Shakespeare's cultural authority. There are of course real issues at stake in this argument, but the headline for Horwitz's article suggests just how vitiated and coarsened the debate has become: 'Old Guard and Avant-Garde Joust Over Bard's Meaning For Today's 14-Year-Olds.' Pope's *Dunciad* was, of course, occasioned by his quarrel with Theobald over the editing of Shakespere's plays. The Horwitz article also exploits the unseemly vulgarity of a quarrel about Shakespeare's authority. That the editors of the *Wall Street Journal* thought this new Dunciad would be a matter of interest for its readers is perhaps more important than any of the fatuous assertions about Shakespeare reported here.

The real purpose of Horwitz's article is not the affirmation of Shakespeare's alleged Tory sympathies. In a concluding section headed 'Fooling With Timelessness' Horwitz attempts to move beyond the current debate. He refers to the 'many experts' who maintain that Shakespeare's plays contain a plurality of meanings. In support of this view he quotes John Russell Brown, who says that 'Shakespeare's plays, like the great myths, say something timeless about human beings.' This view is not borne out, however, in the response of the 14-year-old students who are the subject of this report. According to Horwitz, 'all this sound and fury seems to signify nothing for students,' who are capable of full enjoyment of the plays despite the maladroit interventions of scholars and intellectuals: 'Shakespeare's appeal will continue to endure, no matter how the works are taught.' The article concludes with an assessment of Shakespeare by Andrew McArthur, a young student attending his first theatrical performance: 'You know . . . it was better than Super-Nintendo.'

Andrew McArthur's intervention in the debate over Shakespeare's cultural authority is quite ambiguous. Shakespeare *is* better than Super-Nintendo, but in exactly what sense? Does seeing a performance of a Shakespeare play make it possible for Andrew McArthur to connect with his own deeper aspirations along the lines suggested by John Russell Brown? Or is Shakespeare simply a well-designed cultural product, better indeed than Super-Nintendo but not fundamentally different in kind? The thought that Shakespeare might be 'better than Super-Nintendo' seems reassuring. Maybe there really is a salutary alternative to the vitiated products of the entertainment industry (Kernan 1990). A less edifying interpretation of Andrew McArthur's critical assessment of Shakespeare, however, would simply be that nothing succeeds like success. Shakespeare's plays are just like Super-Nintendo in being diverting, but basically empty. His work does achieve ideological transcendence, but only in the sense that the marketplace is indifferent to the human content of cultural goods. In this view Shakespeare is not an alternative to the culture industry; he is simply one of its more successful products.

LESSONS OF LIBERACE

In January 1991, the *New York Times* carried a report headlined 'Era Ends as Times Square drops Slashers for Shakespeare'. The article describes a plan by New York State's Urban Development Corporation to replace 'the world's finest concentration of movie theaters devoted to zombies, nymphomaniacs, aliens, chainsaws, surfers, martial artists, cannibals and, of course, women in prison' with venues devoted to the upscale market for high culture (Tierney 1991: B-1). *Romeo and Juliet* was to be the first of many productions designed to stabilize a dangerous area best known for its street hustlers. The real purpose of the initiative was not lost on the established clientele for Times Square's traditional offerings.

> They're looking to move in a new class of people here. . . . They
> want to get rid of the poor folks. Who's going to pay $22 to see
> Shakespeare? I want to pay $5 to see two karate movies – and
> Man, The Deuce had the best karate movies. This is where I saw
> 'Mad Monkey Kung Fu'.
>
> (Tierney 1991: B-1)

Like Prince Hal in his determination to banish Falstaff, the redevelopment planners intended to eliminate a socially undesirable
element from a potentially lucrative reallocation and redesign of
urban space. If the redevelopment plan eventually proves successful,
Shakespeare will once again have demonstrated a marginal utility
in the leveraging of cultural capital into finance capital. Examples
of such 'appropriation' of Shakespeare by the interests of finance
capital can be multiplied *ad nauseam*. But what does anyone expect
and why does it matter? After all, the expression 'crying all the way
to the bank' was initially coined by Liberace in response to critics
troubled by his vulgar exploitation of classical music (Liberace
1978: 44–46).

Liberace's maxim captures such a fundamental truth about the
nature of the culture industry that it has become, like many of
Shakespeare's phrases, a basic idiom. What Liberace actually said
on the air to his audience after reading a particularly unkind review
of his television show was: 'My brother George cried all the way to
the bank.' Liberace smiled in his most ingratiating way as he said
this, and his decision to treat the whole affair as a joke no doubt
gave rise to the more widely circulated misquotation of '*laughing* all
the way to the bank'. This popular revision conveys the indifference
of the entertainment industry to the exacting standards of artistic
performance required for a *succès d'estime*. More generally, the
notion of laughing all the way to the bank suggests that successful
people can violate prevailing social, ethical, or aesthetic norms with
impunity. The idea is roughly equivalent to Andy Warhol's aphorism: 'Art is anything you can get away with.' Liberace's original
insight, however, is both more subtle and more complex.

Brother George Liberace cried because his feelings were hurt;
perhaps he really did aspire to critical recognition for his violin
accompaniments to Liberace's piano music. He may even have
cried in chagrin because he wanted to be a better violinist. In spite
of these brotherly disappointments, however, Liberace himself
understood that the culture industry could provide more than

adequate consolation for the tears of mediocre concert pianists and obscure second fiddles. If his standard of musicianship was low, it nevertheless represented an aesthetic sensibility that he shared with a wide following of television viewers who made him rich and who lavished affection upon him. His televised concerts reached far greater audiences than those of more serious, legitimate contemporaries like Van Cliburn or Glenn Gould. Furthermore, his fans didn't love him in spite of his mediocrity, they loved him and rewarded him *because* of his mediocrity, if that's what it was. Liberace's musical impurity implied a tacit resistance to the exacting standards of high culture, to the arrogance of cultural hierarchy, and to the kind of disciplinary outlook on the fine arts represented by more arduously trained, serious performers.

The music that Liberace performed was a pastiche of familiar excerpts from better-known musical classics, semi-classical selections from operettas and musical comedy, along with various styles of ragtime, boogie-woogie, and contemporary pop music. This repertoire depended, at least in part, on his own and his audience's reverence for the canonically enshrined tradition of Western European music. Liberace's own veneration for this tradition was expressed, perhaps ambiguously, in his elaborate coiffure, which gave vividly concrete form to the expression 'long-hair music'. His signature candelabra and sequined formal wear helped to reinforce the image of his performances as a special kind of intimate ceremonial occasion. If music had any actual importance in Liberace's performances, it was decidedly secondary to the homey glitziness of the televised spectacle, with its stress on the performer's props, the movement of his hands, his facial expressions, and the rhythmic camera movement that tied all these visual elements together.

In one sense, the kitsch and vulgar spectacle served to articulate a tension between the relatively young but already dominant mass-oriented medium of television and a more exclusive culture of educated elites. But Liberace's performances were not simply a parody of the pretensions of classical music and its audience along the lines of Victor Borge. There was a double payoff available in watching Liberace. People could enjoy Rachmaninoff or even Beethoven, without the boring parts of course, and at the same time they could enjoy Liberace's carefree familiarity with this normally sacrosanct material. However, Liberace's audience did not see him as unmasking the pretensions of either classical music in particular or high culture in general. Liberace's cultural mission was to take classical music away from the stuffiness of the conservatory and the concert hall and to make it accessible in the comfort of the viewer's living room. Classical music is no longer something that people listen to; through the magic of television it has become, weirdly and unaccountably, an object of the gaze. Liberace's performances are a strange anticipation of the rock video.

Liberace's integration of classical and popular musical traditions is a form of cross-over typical of the culture industry throughout its history. Elizabethan popular theater has been interpreted as a reconciliation of elite and popular traditions within a single cultural practice (Weimann 1978). The juxtaposition of popular art with elite aesthetic traditions in the nineteenth century has been described as evidence of successful democratization of cultural activity (Levine 1988: 11–83). The example of Liberace, however, does not suggest even to the most sanguine observer anything like such a quasi-utopian hope for significant cultural dialogue. His performances seem closer to the idea of a false reconciliation between antagonistic cultural spheres described by Theodor Adorno in his critique of the culture industry.

For Adorno, the culture industry is fundamentally inimical to any genuine social movement of reconciliation or emancipation. The culture industry

> forces together the spheres of high and low art, separated for thousands of years. The seriousness of high art is destroyed in speculation about its efficacy; the seriousness of the lower perishes with the civilizational constraints imposed on the rebellious resistance inherent within it as long as social control was not yet total.
>
> (Adorno 1991: 85)

Under the domination of instrumental reason, high art is judged and in effect condemned for its low marginal utility. At the same time popular art is uprooted from local communities where it articulated the distinctive values and hopes of common people. What the culture industry provides in the place of these two powerful currents of human expressivity is neither the historical reconciliation of social conflict nor the hope for an expanded freedom, but rather a standardized and essentially meretricious product that offers only tenuous gratification to its consumers.

Adorno's critique is focused on cultural practices and activities that coincide with the rapid acceleration of capitalist production during the early modern period. Popular culture as the spontaneous activity of peasants and artisans is expropriated in the form of standardized, mass-produced entertainment. This radical alienation of socially embedded cultural practices is mirrored in a similar expropriation of high art. The serious artist is freed from dependence on aristocratic or ecclesiastical patronage, but this new freedom amounts to the outright sale of the artist's skills to the market-driven needs of a managerial class.

Although the beginning of these developments can be identified as early as the sixteenth century, Adorno reserves the term 'culture industry' for mechanized forms of cultural production characteristic of technically advanced societies in the twentieth century. Adorno is particularly hostile to cinema, but only perhaps because of his extremely limited exposure to what he would no doubt have considered the even more egregious medium of television (Adorno 1991: 135–151). By concentrating his attention on the most recent and opaque technical advances in cultural production, Adorno is able to anchor his critique in the standard of autonomous art. This art appears in that historical moment after the decline of the various patronage traditions but before the rise to dominance of the culture industry. It culminates in the achievements of high modernism.

Adorno's faith in modernist art and its classical antecedents was severely shaken by his experience of the Holocaust and its aftermath, but the ideal of artistic autonomy remains central to his critique of the culture industry. The idea here is that initiative for creativity arises spontaneously from the expressive potential of certain exceptional individuals. Art achieves autonomy with respect to earlier contexts: the pastoral mission of the church, patronage by wealthy collectors, the instrumental requirements of the state or party apparatus. But what exactly are the enabling conditions for such autonomy? The ethical indifference of commodity exchange creates the material conditions that emancipate artistic work from its socially embedded character and make the practice of art a self-financing specialization within a segmented labor force. Artists are autonomous only in the sense that they can exercise discretion in calculating their response to the exigencies of commodity exchange.

The claim that artists actually enjoy autonomy within any economic dispensation will not stand up to serious historical scrutiny, and in fact, Adorno himself recognizes this. '[Works of art] reflected and internalized the domination of society. If this is kept in mind, it becomes impossible to criticize the culture industry without criticizing art at the same time' (Adorno 1984: 26). The normative standard of an autonomous art does not, even for Adorno, carry conviction as the description of historical reality. Art never exists independently of its economic environment. The real value of Adorno's critique, however, is not its cogency as historical narrative, but its normative force as a moral horizon.

Adorno's sustained antagonism to the mass-production and mass-consumption of culture does not simply express his own personal distaste for the vulgarity and artistic compromise he found typical of jazz, cinema, television, and other contemporary forms of entertainment. His rigidly uncompromising preferences in music and the other arts are well known. But his condemnation of contemporary popular forms and his insistence on rigorous aesthetic standards cannot be reduced to personal disappointment with the poor taste of ordinary people who consume the products of mass culture. Adorno's quarrel with the culture industry is part of a much larger analysis of the organization of capitalist society in the mid-twentieth century. Artistic practice is fatally compromised within such a regime, because the laws of aesthetic order as well as the distinctive social purposes of art are superseded by the lawless and disorderly realities of the market. Under market conditions, quasi-independent cultural practices such as musical performance or narrative representation survive only insofar as they can be made to serve parochial, class-bound ideological interests (Zuidervaart 1991: 77–81).

The most fundamental objection to the culture industry is not its programmed dissemination of ideologically distorted themes and images. The larger point is that cultural production is an apparatus of social regulation and control for the system of industrial capitalism as a whole. The real message of the culture industry is not its highly variable ideological content, however, but rather the more general maxim that *this is what there is*. Despite the variety and apparent conflict within mass culture, it has become impossible to imagine an alternative to the *status quo* (Bernstein 1991: 9). People no longer aspire to a life free of domination, but seek gratification instead in repetitive accumulation (Adorno 1991: 53–84).

In traditional moral language, the state of mind which Adorno identifies with the products of the culture industry would be called despair. Adorno articulates his ideas in a complex vocabulary derived from the tradition of Marxist thought; he avoids using the language of moral inquiry, since this language has itself been compromised by the culture industry. It is clear throughout Adorno's discussion of the culture industry, however, that the ultimate purpose of art is linked to a vision of the good life. What is less clear, of course, is what that vision of the good life actually consists of. Adorno values art for its capacity to represent human suffering. In addition he maintains at various times that art has a potentiality for the affirmation of utopian hopes, though such hopes remain largely inarticulate.

The ethical dimension of Adorno's critique of the culture industry is very powerfully felt throughout his extensive writings, even though the normative terms of his moral framework remain unexplicit. Adorno consistently appeals to ideas of individual happiness and satisfaction as the evaluative standard for his critical appraisal of the culture industry and for the larger system of industrial capitalism. Following in the ethical tradition of Marxist individualism, Adorno bases his idea of personal happiness on interrelated notions of self-actualization and social engagement (Elster 1986: 41–58). In this respect Adorno's critique of the culture industry resembles the more recent philosophical critique of technology worked out by Albert Borgmann in *Technology and the Character of Contemporary Life* (1984).

The central claim in Borgmann's discussion of technology is that contemporary experience is increasingly dominated by the device paradigm. Borgmann challenges the standard ethical claims for technology that have been used historically to defend the machinery and the social arrangements that offer to make goods available without effort or struggle.

> Technology . . . promises to bring the forces of nature and culture under control, to liberate us from misery and toil, and to enrich our lives. . . . Who issues the promise to whom is a question of political responsibility; and who the beneficiaries of the promise are is a question of social justice.
>
> (1984: 41)

Even more fundamental than questions of political responsibility and social justice are the immediate effects of technology on the users of a device. According to Borgmann, the burdens from which we are liberated by technology often entail a skilled and complex engagement with the world. Borgmann uses the example of music to question the benefits of such a technological disburdening. A traditional gathering of people to make music together provides an opportunity both for the pleasurable exercise of a skill and for complex forms of conviviality, even if the standard of musical accomplishment is only moderate. Sound reproduction technology makes a vast repertoire of musical performances available in the home, which can be enjoyed without disciplined study or extensive practice. For Borgmann, the benefit of increased access to good music in the form of mechanically reproduced commodities does not offset the cost in personal satisfaction that comes from direct engagement with the actual making of music. The response of the culture industry to this criticism is to smile through its tears on the way to the bank.

In liberal democratic society it seems impossible to achieve political consensus around a substantive conception of the good life. Indeed, both contemporary neo-liberal theory and post-modern critiques of the liberal tradition specifically forbid any such totalizing project. Borgmann argues, however, that in the absence of a substantive account of the good life, the rule of technology prevails by default. The focal practices that provide orientation and purpose in everyday life give way to shallow distractions made available through the device paradigm. It is clear that, for Borgmann at least, technology cannot provide a basis for people to consider their deeper and fuller aspirations.

In Borgmann's critique of technology, art has the task of directly pointing out the possibilities for more complex human aspirations through the concrete representation of focal concerns and practices. This deictic representation or pointing out, moreover, has what amounts to explanatory force. An art work affirms that there really is some alternative to *what there is*, something not only better but different in kind from Super-Nintendo. Furthermore, the art work's power of deictic representation arises from the substantive conceptions of the good life in which many older works of art are historically embedded. Borgmann is not interested in the dispute over whether or not works of art 'transcend ideology'. The point is that such works transcend the device paradigm and the exigencies of the cultural market.

Shakespeare's durable popularity is one of the striking instances of the success of the culture industry, from the time of its inception in urban centers like London in the latter part of the sixteenth century until the present. It is the activity of the culture industry that puts Shakespeare at the disposal of a wide popular audience. Shakespeare's currency depends on the media of popular entertainment and on cheap, mass-produced editions of his works. Naturally these commodities make money for cultural suppliers, but they also enable cultural consumers to acknowledge concerns and aspirations that lie beyond the distractions provided through the device paradigm.

Obviously works of dramatic literature only 'survive' if they are embodied in the concrete material form of actual performances and texts, and in this sense the suppliers of cultural goods and services have been indispensable in sustaining the long-term cultural authority of Shakespeare. But there is more to this story than the repetitive chronicle of appropriation and return on investment. Shakespeare's plays are not just ephemeral products of the culture industry.

> Works break through the boundaries of their own time, they live in centuries, that is, in *great time* and frequently (with great works, always) their lives there are more intense and fuller than are their lives within their own time. . . . Everything that belongs only to the present dies along with the present.
>
> (Bakhtin 1986: 4)

The device paradigm itself belongs 'only to the present'. Like any product of the culture industry, Shakespeare as a commodity is more often than not trivial and inconsequential. Even in the most vitiated and meretricious presentations, however, the semantic potential of Shakespeare's works can 'break through' to a 'more intense and fuller life'. The possibility of 'breaking through' is what makes Shakespeare essential. Essential Shakespeare is a vital continuation of the past; his work can force even the culture industry to express something beyond crying all the way to the bank.

Part II

The pathos of Western modernity

Chapter 5

Re-introduction: essential Shakespeare

> The Song of the Singer is Neither Solicitation nor Trade.
>
> (Martin Heidegger)

In 1589 Christopher Marlowe meets a mediocre but ambitious young actor named Will Shaxberd at the White Horse Tavern, somewhere near London. Shaxberd's desire is to become a play-wright and to that end he has asked Marlowe for his opinion on his first play. Marlowe is clearly appalled at a particularly lamentable passage invoking 'comets' to 'scourge the bad, revolting stars' (*I Henry VI* 1. 1. 4). He bluntly tells his aspiring younger colleague that although he is undoubtedly competent as an actor, he alto-gether lacks the talent to be a successful poet. Shaxberd, discour-aged at the fading of his dream, laments that his aptitude falls so far short of Marlowe's: 'I would give anything to have your gifts. Or more than anything to give men dreams that would live on long after I am dead. I'd bargain, like your Faustus, for that boon' (Gaiman *et al.* 1990: 13). Also present in the tavern at this moment is Lord Morpheus, King of Dreams, who overhears the conversa-tion. He approaches Will Shaxberd and makes him an offer. As a result of the ensuing discussion, Shaxberd embarks on his wished-for career as the poet of men's enduring dreams.

Neil Gaiman's brilliantly rendered account of this important meeting in D. C. Comics' *The Sandman* confirms the widely held belief that Shakespeare's enduring cultural authority must have been brought into being through the intervention of a supernatural power. The exact nature of this power, and of the specific means by which Shakespeare is endowed with the power to 'create new dreams to spur the minds of men' is not revealed, however. And in fact the deal struck between Will Shaxberd and Lord Morpheus is of only minor importance in Gaiman's larger story. The central narrative of 'Men of Good Fortune' concerns a fourteenth-century peasant named Robert 'Hob' Gadling, who is seen in the opening panels explaining that he sees no point in dying. 'It's rubbish, death. It's stupid. I don't want nothing to do with it' (p. 3). Lord Morpheus listens to this conversation with his sister, Death, who agrees to bestow immortality on Gadling, because 'It might be interesting . . . ?' (p. 4). The narrative is a series of brief encounters between Hob Gadling and Lord Morpheus, who agree to return to 'the tavern of the White Horse' at intervals of exactly one hundred years. At each of these meetings Morpheus asks if Gadling is ready to surrender his immortality. Each time Gadling opts for continued life.

The story of Robert Gadling gradually reveals that individual immortality is indeed a kind of 'pointless luxury' exactly as Freud maintained (1959: 31). Certainly mere deathlessness proves to be not nearly so interesting a phenomenon as Lord Morpheus had hoped it would be. At their meeting in 1889 Gadling confronts Morpheus with his own intuitions about the meaning of his immortality.

> Y'know, I think I know why we meet here, century after century. It's not because you want to see what happens when a man don't die. You've seen what happens. I doubt I'm any wiser than I was five hundred years back. I'm older. . . . Have I learned ought? [sic]
>
> (Gaiman *et al.* 1990: 23)

The real reason for Gadling's immortality is to provide companionship to help alleviate the King of Dreams' interminable loneliness. Morpheus is offended by the suggestion that he needs the friendship of an ordinary human being. But Gadling's intuition is confirmed when his supernatural companion returns for their meeting in 1989 and acknowledges that it is 'impolite to keep one's friends waiting' (p. 24).

'Men of Good Fortune' is a fascinating meditation on the complex and paradoxical relations that subsist between big time and small time, between the *longue durée* of culture and the parochial horizons of everyday life. In this context the example of Shakespeare turns out to be not so tangential after all. At their meeting in 1789 Hob Gadling tells Lord Morpheus that he has seen Mrs Siddons as Goneril in *King Lear*, but that 'the idiots had given it a happy ending' (p. 18). Morpheus assures him 'That will not last. The great stories will always return to their original form' (p. 18). However, the reasons for Shakespeare's particular kind of immortality are not disclosed. When Gadling asks whether Shakespeare gave up his soul in return for his exceptional powers, Morpheus will only reply 'nothing so crude'.

The mysterious contract with the King of Dreams has multiple valences for understanding the authority of Shakespeare's works. For one thing it provides an answer to the tiresome nagging of anti-Stratfordians, who ask how a mediocre actor and provincial *arriviste* could possibly write such great literature. The answer of course is that 'the wind bloweth where it listeth' – there is no simple way to explain by what agency literary gifts are bestowed. More important, perhaps, the story provides an extraordinary metaphor for Shakespeare's 'entry into great time'. The crucial intuition here is that 'great stories always return to their original form'. Of course, literal belief in 'original form' would be roughly equivalent to literal belief in the existence of Morpheus, King of Dreams. Nevertheless, Hob Gadling's example of *King Lear* is a telling instance, one that hints at the power of strong narrative forms to assert their pre-eminence over the ephemeral modifications prompted by cultural technologies created for the supply side of culture. This would suggest that the supply side hypothesis is at best incomplete, and that the story of Shakespeare's cultural endurance can be 'nothing so crude' as an account of commercial practices all by itself, no matter how detailed or how revelatory. A full explanation of Shakespeare's cultural authority also has to consider the specific shape of 'the great stories'. Whatever we may take Lord Morpheus to represent, his interest in the aspirations of Will Shaxberd suggests something beyond the supply side mechanisms of cultural production.

DESIGNING A BETTER VIRUS

Neil Gaiman's 'Men of Good Fortune' gives vernacular expression to Emerson's affirmation that Shakespeare 'wrote the text of modern life' (p. 211). The insights of Morpheus, King of Dreams are worked out in Marjorie Garber's *Shakespeare's Ghost Writers*. This book explores the morbid sway Shakespeare holds in the modern imaginary. Garber is willing to consider the supernatural – or at least the uncanny – dimensions of Shakespeare's cultural authority

through a serious consideration of the colorful theatrical super-
stitions that surround *Macbeth*. The bizarre anecdotes which mark
the theatrical history of this play show that the text has its own
initiatives and resistances, that it is not inert material available for
opportunistic ideological appropriation. Garber's larger conceit in
this study of ghosts and haunting in Shakespeare is that our own
contemporary experience of subjectivity has itself been ghost-
written by Shakespeare, and here Lord Morpheus takes on a weirdly
appropriate relevance. For Garber, Shakespeare's uncanny power is
a capacity for verbal representation of unknown provenance that
vividly objectifies what is repressed and frightening in the modern
psyche.

The idea that the Shakespearean text is internalized as the template and the engine of a radically transformed subjectivity has been
variously elaborated in contemporary scholarship. Catherine Belsey
is representative of those critics who see a prototypical modern self
taking shape on the renaissance stage as the reflection of massive
social change in sixteenth-century Europe (Belsey 1985). Harold
Bloom takes exception to the view that the works reflect historical
change and claims that Shakespeare's characters are the source of
the modern identity.

> I do not think it useful to say that Shakespeare successfully imi-
> tated elements in our characters. Rather, it could be argued that
> he compelled aspects of character to appear that previously were
> concealed, or not available to representation. . . . Shakespearean
> representation has usurped not only our sense of literary charac-
> ter, but our sense of ourselves as characters.
>
> (Bloom 1990a: 7)

Although this is an extreme view of Shakespeare's cultural authority, it is really no more so than that expressed by one of Bloom's own
precursors, Ralph Waldo Emerson. This is not to say that Shakespeare described with superlative accuracy something that already
had an objective existence. In fact he discovered a new way of being
human; as participants in the culture of modernity we are simply
characters written by Shakespeare.

Bloom maintains that certain of Shakespeare's characters, most
notably Falstaff and Hamlet, have 'overdetermined our ideas of
representation ever since he wrote'. The specific form of this Shake-
spearization of consciousness lies in the 'active self-assimilation of
one's own language'.

Most of what we know about how to represent cognition and personality in language was permanently altered by Shakespeare. The principal insight that I've had in teaching and writing about Shakespeare is that there isn't anyone before Shakespeare who actually gives you a representation of characters or human figures speaking out loud, whether to themselves or to others or both, and then brooding out loud, whether to themselves or to others or both, on what they themselves have said. And then, in the course of pondering, undergoing a serious or vital change, they become a different kind of character or personality and even a different kind of mind. We take that utterly for granted in representation. But it doesn't exist before Shakespeare.

(Bloom 1990b: 214)

Shakespeare's particular achievement here is not simply that he developed improved techniques of literary representation. The greatly expanded powers of self-reflection and self-transformation found in Shakespeare's characters, together with their experience of interiority and depth, are crucial to the making of the modern self.

It is on this basis that Bloom has proposed that Shakespeare, not Freud, is the founding father of psychoanalysis. The massively exacerbated self-consciousness described here is nothing less than the psychoanalytic trajectory itself. What Bloom evidently means by 'psychoanalysis' here is neither any particular form of clinical practice nor any particular theory of human desire. Psychoanalysis is a way of being in language characterized by a radical self-narration in which self must assume sovereign authority over the complex functions of author, addressee, artifact, and interpreter. In his more recent reflections on this point, Bloom has subordinated psychoanalysis to the more traditional category of literature.

Just recently, I was sitting down, alas for the first time in several years, reading through Shakespeare's *Troilus and Cressida* at one sitting. I found it to be an astonishing experience, powerful and superb. That hasn't dimmed or diminished. But surely it is a value in itself, a reality in its own right; surely it cannot be reduced or subsumed under some other name. Freud, doubtless, would wish to reduce it to the sexual thought, or rather, the sexual past. But increasingly it seems to me that literature, and particularly Shakespeare, who is literature, is a much more comprehensive mode of cognition than psychoanalysis can be.

(1990b: 200)

Psychoanalysis is a derivative story that flows from the strong poem created by Shakespeare. Or, as Lord Morpheus would have it, the great stories always return to their original form.

Bloom's discussion of psychoanalysis as the derivative form of Shakespeare's work is an extension of his notorious theory of poetic influence. In its narrow, specialized literary form and in its broader anthropological dimensions, the theory of influence is an attempt to account for the *longue durée* of culture. This account privileges the figures of the strong poet and the strong poem as definitive sources of the social imaginary. In his idiosyncratic and often obscure elaboration of this doctrine, influence has a narrow and restricted domain of application. Influence is both an indispensable resource and an occupational hazard confined to a small, and we might be tempted to add, a deeply neurotic lineage of practising poets. However, in the Charles Eliot Norton lectures at Harvard, published as *Ruin the Sacred Truths*, and in other more recent work, Bloom has repeatedly argued that Shakespeare is the source of a more widespread cultural influence that affects the population at large.

Bloom insists that the complex artifacts he calls strong poems have lasting effects on the way a given culture is organized. Poetic influence has real social effects that flow from specific acts of willed literary creation. These effects are not limited to the small group of people who read great poetry. Because an original poem can deeply and permanently affect a culture's customary idiom of representation, it will determine the orientation to self and to others even of those who read no literature. This is the meaning of Lord Morpheus' endowment to Shakespeare, who, as a poet strong enough to ignore the influence of Marlowe and even of Chaucer, acquires a lasting power to give men dreams. Although Bloom does not make this point himself, Shakespeare's pervasive saturation of modern popular culture would actually provide the concrete mechanism by means of which his originality limits and pre-empts self-determination within successor cultures. Unlike many of the humanist critics with whom he shares important orienting beliefs about the centrality of literature, however, Bloom does not claim that the influence of literature is beneficial or even particularly healthy. Influence is inaccessible to self-understanding and highly resistant to any kind of cultural therapy. In its broad anthropological application, influence is the cultural equivalent of influenza, and indeed there are times when Bloom treats these two words as if they were synonymous.

Human influenza is, of course, spread by a virus. In the opinion of some scientists, although their chemistry resembles that of living things, viruses are not in any meaningful sense themselves alive. A virus is a genetic recipe, a piece of genetic code that invades a living cell, overrides the cell's resident programs, and forces it to make copies of the virus. Left unchecked, the virus will spread at exponential rates. On this view a virus is perhaps best characterized as a type of embodied information inimical to the purposes of the host organism.

If a biological virus can be explained as bad information, then the use of this term in the expression 'computer virus' will turn out to be more than just a figure of speech. In fact, a computer virus is a piece of electronically transmitted digital coding that uses a computer's resident programs to generate copies of itself. Like biochemical viruses, computer viruses, though unobservable by ordinary means, are physically embodied things that function according to a principle of obligate parasitism. In other words they can only propagate inside the right kind of host, whether biological organism or system of microchips.

Does the principle of a self-replicating code or informational virus appear in the domain of culture? Bloom's theory of influence suggests that memorable literary works are a complex form of obligate parasitism created by skillful linguistic hackers. On this view the literary artist uses the resources of a natural language to devise a self-replicating code. This is then loaded into human bioware where it makes copies of itself.

> What's in the brain, that ink may character
> Which hath not figur'd to thee my true spirit?
> What's new to speak, what new to register,
> That may express my love, or thy dear merit?
> Nothing, sweet boy; but yet, like prayers divine,
> I must each day say o'er the very same,
> Counting no old thing old, thou mine, I thine,
> Even as when first I hallowed thy fair name.
> So that eternal love in love's fresh case
> Weighs not the dust and injury of age,
> Nor gives to necessary wrinkles place,
> But makes antiquity for aye his page;
>   Finding the first conceit of love there bred,
>   Where time and outward form would show it dead.

Shouldn't we interpret Sonnet 108 as the confession of a hacker? In this verse Shakespeare comes closest to describing exactly how it is that his 'powerful rhyme' can outlive 'marble and the gilded monuments of Princes'. The figures recorded in the poet's brain are 'downloaded' to the mind of the reader where they are replicated. This power of self-replication is the poet's guarantee of transcending his own mortality.

The virus model I have extrapolated from Harold Bloom's theory of influence is an extreme example of the kind of theory that explains the *longue durée* of culture in terms of a deep background that can never be adequately represented. On this view individual subjects are never lucid about their identity, their routine practices, their most fundamental values, all of which are somehow 'always already' given. The idea that a given cultural identity or way of life is sustained over time through processes of the social imaginary is not, on the face of it, implausible. Nor is the idea that these processes act through specific encodings which have a capacity for self-replication within individual imaginations. The originality of a strong poet is ineluctable; it is not freely chosen or refused according to contingent ideological affiliations.

The idea of ineluctable and pervasive influence can be usefully glossed through a comparison with the ideas of Pierre Bourdieu. Bourdieu does not, of course, speak at length of Shakespeare. However, a very interesting and I think useful way to analyze a phenomenon like the cultural *longue durée* of Shakespeare's work is through his notion of *habitus*. The concept of *habitus* is a set of interpretations that enable persons and social groups to make a virtue of necessity (Bourdieu 1984: 170 *et passim*). Everyday social experience is based on cognitive discriminations, intentions, plans, practical reasons, just as it appears to the self-understanding of ordinary people doing ordinary things. But this self-understanding also entails an important misrecognition. The coping skills, practices, tools, and other objects that agents take up are 'objectively harmonized among themselves, without any deliberate pursuit of coherence' (Bourdieu 1984: 172–173). *Habitus* is thus a pre-organized set of everyday objects (*opus operatum*) produced by anonymous social patterns (*modus operandi*). This ensemble of relationships creates the perceptual, evaluative, and classificatory schemata for what Bourdieu calls 'life-styles'. The notion of *habitus* has a family resemblance to ideas such as hegemony or ideology. An alternative sense of the term is usefully articulated by Flip Wilson's transvestite character Geraldine, who explained her lapses in judgement by saying, 'the devil made me do it!'

The concept of *habitus* is intended to cover more than instances of subjective irrationality and thus differs from related notions typical of the modern critique of domination. Unlike the notion of hegemony, *habitus* is not simply the means by which people are somehow coerced by inimical structures of power or deceptively confined to present circumstances. *Habitus* has the sense of cultural constraint and limitation, but it has the further meaning of the enabling condition for coherent and well-formed actions against the background of a community. It is the ground and the basic explanation not only for everything that people actually do, but also and more importantly for everything they believe and desire. According to Bourdieu's account a preference for Shakespeare would be among the tools and techniques constitutive of lifestyles characteristic of Western modernity.

Whether we resort to complex ideas like uncanny causality, poetic influence, hegemony, *habitus*, or simply say 'the devil made me do it!', there seems to be widespread acceptance for the view that Shakespeare is more than a simple amenity or optional extra within the *longue durée* of Western culture. It would, however, be misleading to suggest that these convergences imply anything like a broad consensus as to the significance of this extraordinary cultural longevity. Many recent accounts of Shakespeare's continuing vitality have focused on the apparatus of legitimation and control. Shakespeare has been seen as, at best, in passive complicity and, at worst, in active collusion with various historical projects of deception and domination. This kind of orientation to the cultural work of the strong poem has been denounced by Harold Bloom as the 'school of resentment':

an extraordinary mélange of latest-model feminists, Lacanians, that whole semiotic cackle, latest-model pseudo Marxists, so-called new historicist, and third generation deconstructors, who I believe have no relationship whatever to literary values. It's really a very paltry kind of a phenomenon. But it is pervasive, and it seems to be waxing rather than waning. It is a very rare thing to encounter one critic, academic or otherwise, not just in the English speaking world, but also in France or Italy, who has an authentic commitment to aesthetic values, who reads for the pleasure of reading, and who values poetry or story as such, above all else.

(Bloom 1990b: 209–210)

On the whole, members of the various branches of this 'school' have responded to Bloom's strictures by completely ignoring him. This is in many ways unfortunate, not least because it would be useful to understand more clearly just how Bloom might square his account of ineluctable poetic influence with the strong claims he makes for the recognition of literary value. One way to reconcile the opposing sides here would be to point out that ideological appropriation and commercial exploitation of Shakespeare's plays are possible only because of the uncommon capacity of this material to represent the complex pathos of Western modernity. Bloom's basic intuition here must surely be correct. To read Shakespeare is to experience *historica passio*, in the words of the unemended quarto and folio versions of *King Lear* (Halperin 1991: 215). We remain deeply interested in Shakespeare's characters simply because we recognize what they are going through. Before considering the referential capabilities of particular plays, however, it is important to review the idea of literary value in more detail.

TASTE AND JUDGEMENT

Heuristic models that attempt to explain long-term cultural processes through notions like virus, cultural influenza, *habitus*, hegemony, and the like all imply diminished capacity for the voluntaristic, discretionary, and lucid aspects of human agency. Such models should not be rejected simply because they don't conform to a culturally preferred picture of sovereign individual subjectivity. On the other hand, these models should not be adopted just because they constitute such a massive insult to that same humanistic account of the modern self. Ideas of influence, habit, and lifestyle preference do not explain what kind of satisfactions a Shakespeare play might offer. A traditional humanistic account of this question would stress the lucid response of knowledgeable agents in making such choices. The importance of a great writer like Shakespeare would flow from a collective *recognition* that his works embody significant aesthetic value and quite possibly moral value as well. The collective multiplication of such individual acts of recognition would certify that the aesthetic value is stable, and non-negotiable, unlike the strictly arbitrary values that circulate within the price system. Such judgements thus become crucial for sustaining collective as well as individual identity for a successor culture.

Gregory Currie, the author of *An Ontology of Art* and of other important work in analytic aesthetics, once remarked to me in a private conversation that 'The ten greatest plays in the world were probably *all* written by Shakespeare.' For Currie, a work of art can only be great in accordance with the standards of artistic achievement typical of a specific community. 'Our conception of aesthetic value is essentially bound up with *our* interests, experiences and abilities' (1989: 39). Despite the rigor in his own theory of artistic value he was nevertheless entirely comfortable presenting such a sweeping aesthetic judgement as a straightforward fact. More interesting, when I described my own work on the ideological recruitment of Shakespeare in the United States, the point of that kind of sociologically oriented research into literary works seemed to escape him. Still, I share Currie's gut intuition that Shakespeare's plays really do represent a significant reserve of literary value and I suspect that most Shakespeare scholars, including many of those whom Harold Bloom would consign to the 'school of resentment' have a similar belief. Speaking only for myself, however, I have found it increasingly difficult to come out about this. To begin with, such convictions seem epistemically untrustworthy; it is difficult to give a lucid account of the criteria that one would be using in making any such judgement. Moreover, recent criticism has suggested that such judgements are only invidious social distinctions that are often demeaning or even harmful to others.

The basis for making matter-of-fact aesthetic judgements is difficult to articulate, especially since aesthetics seems to be in a way *defined* as the domain of subjective preference. In order to show just how difficult some of these problems are, I will be looking at the very careful discussion of the issues in David Hume's 'Of the Standard of Taste', first published in his *Four Dissertations* in 1757. Although he is not particularly concerned with Shakespeare in this discussion, the choice of Hume's essay is not altogether adventitious. The 'science' of criticism emerges in eighteenth-century England partly as a response to the problem of reconciling broad public appreciation for Shakespeare with prevailing standards of neoclassical aesthetics. Lord Kames' *Elements of Criticism* (1756) bases its extensive demonstrations on a broad and wide-ranging selection of examples from Shakespeare. Lady Montagu's *An Essay on the*

Writings and Genius of Shakespeare (1769) defends the British taste for Shakespeare against the vigorous polemic of Voltaire. *The Dramatic Censor or Critical Companion* by Francis Gentleman (1770) is a practical compendium of critical judgements and interpretations designed for casual theater-goers and other cultural consumers. Hume's essay concisely articulates the basic terms for these discussions and for much subsequent debate as well.

Hume begins by conceding that the variety of tastes is obvious even to a parochial sensibility (1757: 203). The universal capacity for preference, however, must co-exist somehow with an equally universal capacity for judgement. Hume notes that there are terms in every language that signify both blame and praise (p. 204). Because basic terms of evaluation are used with different meanings in discussions of preference, however, variations in taste are actually greater than they appear to be. On the other hand, matters of opinion in the sciences can often be resolved simply through careful definition of terms. The position of moral inquiry here is uncertain and equivocal: 'Those who found morality on sentiment, more than on reason, are inclined to comprehend ethics under the former observations' (p. 205).

Hume cites the examples of Homer and the 'Alcoran' as salient examples of the way morality appears to fall more under the rubric of cultural preference than of knowledge and rational deliberation. The inclusion of morality within the discussion of aesthetics suggests that something much more important is at stake here than simply a matter of establishing a basis for good taste.

Philosophy and common sense agree that it is useless to argue differences in taste. But there is another species of common sense that opposes the maxim *de gustibus non disputandum est*. When people compare Bunyan to Addison and conclude that Addison is the better writer, they are confident that their opinion is a judgement rather than simply a preference even if they can't be lucid about their reasons. Hume concludes that

> It is very natural for us to seek a *standard of taste*; a rule, by which the various sentiments of men may be recorded, or at least a decision afforded confirming one sentiment and condemning another.
>
> (1757: 207)

The same terms that express a preference are also used to make evaluations. If, in a reflective moment, someone should speculate about just which preferences she should prefer, then the problem of a general standard of taste has been posed as if it could be interpreted as a matter of fact.

Hume concedes that in the case of Bunyan and Addison the apparently matter-of-fact idea of a 'better writer' may reflect nothing more than a momentary fashion. However, this does not resolve the issue of aesthetic judgement versus aesthetic preference, since there are writers whose work is valued in widely differing historical settings.

> The same Homer, who pleased at *Athens* and *Rome* two thousand years ago, is still admired at *Paris* and at *London*. All the changes of climate, government, religion, and language have not been able to obscure his glory. Authority or prejudice may give a temporary vogue to a bad poet or orator; but his reputation will never be durable or general . . . on the contrary, a real genius, the longer his works endure, and the more wide they are spread, the more sincere is the admiration which he meets with.
>
> (Hume 1757: 213)

The weaknesses of this argument will be apparent to anyone familiar with current research on the institutional use of canonical literary texts, but nevertheless I think Hume does have a point in suggesting that you don't have to be a warrior living in archaic Greece to appreciate Homer. Of course, you don't have to be Jewish to love Levy's Rye Bread either, to use a more contemporary example. Individual aesthetic preferences, whatever else they may be, are not exclusively culture-specific.

The example of Homer's cross-over appeal suggests to Hume that aesthetic judgements entail something more than indefensible likes and dislikes. However, he is careful not to base his argument on what he would regard as a faulty metaphysics. Beauty and ugliness, like sweet and bitter, are not properties of objects. These qualities exist in the mind that contemplates them. Furthermore, aesthetic and moral judgements cannot be true or false, because their rules cannot be fixed by reasoning *a priori*. Nevertheless,

> Some particular forms or qualities, from the original structure of the internal fabric, are calculated to please, and others to displease, and if they fail of their effect in any particular instance, it is from some apparent defect or imperfection in the organ.
>
> (Hume 1757: 217)

Objects may not have the qualities of beauty and ugliness, but they nevertheless do have qualities, and our ability to recognize such qualities forms the basis for our ability to make judgements of taste.

Hume elaborates this point by using an incident from *Don Quixote* in which two of Sancho Panza's kinsmen are asked to help evaluate a new hogshead of wine. The first tastes the wine and allows that although he finds it quite good, there is a faint taste of old leather. The second also finds the wine acceptable, but notices a definite trace of iron. The other judges all ridicule these assessments. 'But who laughed in the end? On emptying the hogshead, there was found at the bottom, an old key with a leathern thong tied to it' (Hume 1757: 217). This little parable is the basis for Hume's version of a cautious philosophical realism about aesthetic objects. He concludes that there are qualities naturally suited to produce certain feelings and sensations. These sensations, if properly cultivated, form the basis for knowledgeable aesthetic judgements.

For Hume, the reality of critical judgements is confirmed by what he calls delicacy of taste. This delicacy is achieved through practice and wide experience in a particular field. It is not so much a natural endowment as a carefully developed skill. To the extent that agents are lucid about the skills they exercise in making judgements they will be able to describe general patterns of artistic composition. The production of such rules is like finding the key with the leathern thong.

The assessments of Sancho Panza's relatives about the hogshead of wine were not only true phenomenologically as descriptions of their sensations, they were also true scientifically as descriptions of qualities that were actually in the wine, even though they could only be observed after the wine was drunk and the hogshead emptied. But Hume stops short of endorsing a strong realism in the domain of aesthetics. He is finally committed to a weaker phenomenological position, which relies on consensus as the only reliable standard for aesthetic judgement.

> Strong sense, united to delicate sentiment, improved by practice, perfected by comparison, and cleared of all prejudice, can alone entitle critics to this valuable character; and the joint verdict of such, wherever they are to be found is the true standard of taste and beauty.
>
> (Hume 1757: 229)

The fact of a 'joint verdict' among individuals with comparable skills suggests a genuine recognition of real properties underlying the agreed upon evaluation, even though the actual properties remain unobserved and undescribed. However, the inclusion of a 'no prejudice clause' points to a fatal weakness in Hume's argument.

In the end Hume must admit that his analysis is inconclusive. Despite the appeal of possibly 'finding the iron key', no such aesthetic 'key' has actually been discovered. Hume realizes that there are no viable candidates in criticism corresponding to the iron key in the wine hogshead. His argument peters out in wishful thinking. A critic who is learned, sensitive, and without prejudice would be 'valuable and estimable'. Nevertheless, he concedes that a critic with no prejudices is not likely to turn up, let alone a community of such critics capable of forming a reliable consensus. Notwithstanding various efforts to fix a standard of taste, there would always remain two sources of variation. 'One is the different humours of particular men; the other, the particular manners and opinions of an age and country' (Hume 1757: 232).

Hume's exploration of the problems of a standard of taste is unable to get beyond the relativism of historically conditioned aesthetic preferences. Although there is a theoretical basis for expecting critics to make reliable, matter-of-fact aesthetic judgements there appears to be no way to realize the theory in critical practice. However, Hume may have overlooked one of the more interesting implications of his own arguments. In order to see this we have to go back to Sancho Panza's relatives and the hogshead of wine. Hume was interested in the punch-line of the hogshead story when the key is produced and the judgements of Panza's cousins are vindicated. But the appearance of the key suggests an overly naturalistic account of aesthetic properties. More might have been done with this anecdote if Hume had considered the practical background of Cervantes' story.

Wine-making is a human practice and the achievements of Sancho Panza's relatives only make sense in the context of this practice. I want to adopt here Alasdair McIntyre's sense of the notion of practice in order to suggest another, perhaps more useful way of understanding Hume's 'iron key with the leathern thong'. On McIntyre's account practices are forms of social and cooperative human activity 'through which goods internal to that form of activity are realized in the course of trying to achieve those standards of excellence which are appropriate to, and partially definitive of, that form of activity' (MacIntyre 1984: 187).

This argument lays particular stress on the notion of 'internal goods', or goods specific to a particular practice. Playing baseball might well result in fame or wealth, but these benefits would be external goods. Willie Mays' great catch in center field on a ball hit by Vic Wertz in the 1954 World Series would be an example of an internal good. Practices like playing baseball, making wine, or writing plays are governed by rules and necessarily entail standards of excellence. Such rules and standards are necessarily exclusionary. All practices have histories, however, and therefore standards, rules, and exclusions remain open for discussion and even radical transformation. Nevertheless, to enlist in a practice requires acceptance of the authority of what has already been achieved. The basic requirement for confirming aesthetic judgements is knowledgeability of a particular craft sufficient to specify correctly those goods internal to the practice, to understand the means by which these goods may be achieved, and to recognize both the authority of earlier achievements and the force of radical innovation within the practice.

McIntyre's analysis does not produce anything like a universally binding solution to the problem of the 'iron key with the leathern thong'. As with Hume, there is no naturalistic, transcendental, or rationally defensible basis for aesthetic judgements. Critical evaluations are socially and historically contingent. This does not, however, mean that aesthetic verdicts are arbitrary and capricious social preferences. Critical judgements are authorized by a strong social ontology of collective human practices oriented to the realization of well-specified internal goods. So you don't have to be Jewish to love Levy's – but you do have to know what bread is.

The idea that critical judgements presuppose knowledge of specific practices confirms their reality. However, the very matter-of-factness of these judgements should suggest an important limitation in the notion of aesthetic value. Aesthetic judgement is specialized and parochial. The fact that I can make sound judgements about good violin-playing or good cooking does not certify that I can accurately appraise good play-writing or good baseball. Ability to make aesthetic judgements does not establish the political importance or the moral dignity of the practice in question; there is no reliable way to adjudicate the value of one practice as opposed to another. It's possible to defend the claim that Shakespeare's *Hamlet* is better than Kyd's *A Spanish Tragedy* or Shaw's *The Devil's Disciple*.

It's not clear why anyone would want to defend the claim that any of these plays is better than a good baseball game.

Harold Bloom is a fan of the New York Yankees, of rock videos, and of Sophia Loren. He is also an eloquent champion of the principle of literary value, which he defends against the 'resentment' expressed from both right and left on the political spectrum. Bloom insists that literature matters only because of the complex pleasure and satisfaction it can offer readers. He vigorously opposes any reduction of literary works to their ideological functions, and denies that they have any real impact on politics. Literary criticism is, for Bloom, 'agonistic', which means that it is always concerned with the question 'more, equal to, or less than?' (Bloom 1990b: 225). This has been most provocative and controversial in his *ex cathedra* assessments of contemporary figures, praising Philip Roth, condemning John Updike, ironically equivocating over Norman Mailer, to cite only a few of the more notable examples. On the face of it these magisterial assessments simply reflect the kind of skilled and experienced reading that Hume prescribed as the only reliable standard of taste. And for the most part Bloom is consistent with his own principle of the separateness of literature, as he confines his evaluations to what appear to be purely literary matters. However, in his response to Shakespeare's *The Merchant of Venice* it becomes apparent that even for Bloom the idea of literary value is more complex and problematic than might at first appear.

The Merchant of Venice is, for Bloom, a derivative and therefore a disappointing work, one that simply rehearses what he has called 'the ancient Christian slander against the Jews'. Shylock, in this account, is a far less striking invention than his precursor in Marlowe's Barrabas, and *The Jew of Malta* is thus a better and more satisfying play. The idea of the play's diminished literary value seems explicitly tied to its deep complicity with traditional anti-Semitism. Bloom has in fact argued that an honest production of this play, one that faithfully transmits the work's original intentions, would be unbearable and intolerable in a post-Holocaust context. Here it is abundantly clear that Bloom speaks as a concrete situated subject, a Jewish son of immigrant parents who still remembers fighting street battles to defend himself against persecution by Irish gangs in the Bronx during the 1930s (Bloom 1990b: 197).

The point here is not to suggest that Bloom is disingenuous in his polemic with 'the school of resentment', though it is perhaps worth remarking that if one of Shakespeare's works can lack 'originality' for the way it portrays Jews, the same principle ought to apply for the portrayal of women or of Moors. The more important argument here is that literary value can never be reduced to a narrowly conceived aesthetic value as if it were like a mathematical abstraction. Fictions make at least indirect reference to real selves, and literary value is thus never uniquely apprehended through disinterested contemplation of a work's formal properties. The judgement of literary value, as Hume recognized as early as his 1757 essay, can never in practice be separated from a literary work's moral character.

In his more recent statements Bloom concedes that *The Jew of Malta* offers only easier pleasures. The more difficult pleasure of *The Merchant of Venice* requires a greater effort of imagination. 'I'm well aware . . . that my trouble in achieving any pleasure in reading or viewing Shylock is because other factors are getting in the way of apprehending the Shakespearean sublime' (1990b: 225). In making this point, however, Bloom acknowledges the crucial point that has been made over and over again by the 'resenters', namely that literary works are always received against the resistances and the grievances of their actual but unforeseen addressees. Criticism really is 'agonistic'; to do it successfully requires the achievement not of critical objectivity, but of a 'deep subjectivity' (1990b: 219). The idea of deep subjectivity here suggests that great literary works are not altogether like dreams, as Will Shaxberd imagined in his dealings with Lord Morpheus. They are instead more like complex and difficult memories that trouble the waking life of successor cultures.

SOCIAL MEMORY AND HISTORICAL GRIEVANCE

Taste, as eighteenth-century aesthetics understood, may simply reflect the vagaries of prejudice and of fashion. In contemporary terms we are more likely to say that cultural preferences are subject to the operations of ideology and of the market. The idea of literary value, on the other hand, is an intuition about what things matter, and an interest in exploring how and why they are important. But there is no straightforward or uncontroversial way to resolve the issue of Shakespeare's literary or artistic value, partly because the question is too imprecisely specified. What criticism attempts to grasp and to articulate is why Shakespeare matters, and whether we think his work should continue to matter. But this question is only meaningful if we can first answer with some precision the question 'who cares?' In other words, research into this problem has to be specifically oriented as a set of questions about the purpose of reading in the historically specific social context of successor cultures.

For Harold Bloom the purpose of reading is in the end nothing more than consolation for and deferral of one's own death. On this view literature speaks most powerfully to private fears and private sorrows. This intuition is probably an accurate description for the larger part of any vernacular readership. Bloom sees reading as a strictly palliative measure, and denies that literature can have genuine therapeutic efficacy as more traditionally inspired humanists have believed. The various critics and polemicists of cultural *ressentiment* have seen reading in less intimate and personal terms. For oppositional critics of the left, the purposes of reading must be emancipatory. Literature offers the possibility for mobilized resistance to entrenched structures of domination, including domination by the institutional tyranny of the great works themselves. Conservative advocates of traditional canon and curriculum, by contrast, see the reading of set texts as crucial for sustaining social cohesion.

There are many conservative culture critics who are altogether disingenuous in their advocacy of the great books, but, as I suggested earlier (see p. 30–31), the conservative agenda is in touch with something much more compelling than coercive valorization of 'dead white guys' or the merely cynical promotion of the interests of heterosexual white males. The great works of Western literary culture are recommended as the educational remedy for widespread social fragmentation, disorder, and anomie. This may be wrongheaded, not least because education cannot provide a diagnosis, to say nothing of a cure, for the very real social ills addressed, but the basic intuition here needs to be taken seriously. The conservative program for canon and curriculum strikes a powerful chord with a broad social constituency because it acknowledges anxieties provoked by increasing cultural disorientation (Borgmann 1992: 2–20).

The basic confusion in the conservative response to this widespread problem of disorientation is not in its reading lists or in its principles of exclusion or inclusion, though these matters continue to exacerbate the public controversy. The real problem here, as with the similar programs sponsored by oppositional critics, is in the failure to articulate honestly and candidly exactly what the point of reading is supposed to be. Without a clear sense of what reading is actually good for, aggressive publicizing of lists, and programmatic agendas is simply fatuous:

there are systematically different and incompatible ways of reading and appropriating such texts and . . . until the problems of
how they are to be read have received an answer, such lists do not
rise to the status of a concrete proposal.

(MacIntyre 1990: 228)

The various reading lists and other proposals for the entrenchment
of a common curriculum all entail an overly simplified understanding of the cultural inheritance of which readers are the putative
legatees. As Alasdair MacIntyre points out, however, readers within
the successor culture are themselves embroiled in precisely those
conflicts present in the various objects that constitute the archive of
great works.

The problem of what to read is not simply a matter of negotiating
substantive conflicts that flow from antagonistic and competing traditions which define successor cultures. MacIntyre points out that
there is a deeper and more intractable conflict over exactly what it
is to interpret the past. He distinguishes 'three rival traditions' that
correspond to the encyclopedic enterprise of the enlightenment, to
the genealogical modes of Nietzsche and his followers, and to the
dialectical program initially worked out by Thomas Aquinas. The
possibilities for this third alternative have been rejected in an
increasingly acrimonious contention between the other two movements. The contemporary culture wars are a deplorably vulgarized
and increasingly vitiated contest, not over what should be read, but
over what reading is for. The stark alternatives of affirmation and
resistance leave no room for mature and realistic assessment of traditions or for the achievement of a 'deep subjectivity' that would
enable the inheritors of Western modernity to understand their complex situatedness as fully as possible.

Shakespeare's works remain as conspicuous landmarks in the
modern cultural terrain. In order to discover how we can best be
oriented to these remarkable features of our cultural landscape, it is
imperative to consider how we regard our historical past. The possibility for 'deep subjectivity' and for a well-oriented social position
depends on how intelligently we interpret the cultural traditions
that define us as members of a particular community. The verbal
artifacts that embody these traditions are not transparent or uncon-
taminated springs for reliable intuitions about our predicament,
though it would be fatuous to deny that the reading of literary
works has enabled many people to discover something about their

own deeper needs and aspirations. At the same time great literary works are more coherent than dreams. In my view the best way to interpret both the cognitive and the social status of these objects is through the category of memory. The idea of memory here can help to elucidate exactly how Shakespeare's works enable readers within successor cultures to be informed by as well as about their own complex traditions.

Memory is a type of mental representation. Remembering is the manifestation in the present of a past event, and in this sense entails at least a partial overcoming of temporality, the irrevocable pastness of the past. Of course what is manifested for us here and now is not the thing itself but merely its representative, and for this reason some theorists of memory have wanted to emphasize links between memory and fantasy. In this view, memory, as representation, is best understood as image or as text, the manifestation not of anything like the *truth* of the past, but rather of present feelings, wishes, embarrassment, or anger. It is certainly true that the past is not available in full and vivid immediacy, and to make matters worse the veracity of memory is not to be trusted. But before memory is abandoned to the abyss of textuality, it's important to draw attention to cognitive aspects of memory, and its relationship to knowledge.

Memory figures prominently at the level of practical consciousness, and in fact a reliable memory is indispensable for planning and co-ordination of our activities. Everyone appreciates the importance of keeping promises, meeting commitments, and carrying out scheduled tasks. To guarantee the performance of these duties, various *aide-mémoires* may be useful, whether in written or electronic form. Related to this is the way memory sustains co-presence or relatedness, especially against spatial and temporal separation. Notwithstanding an extended geographical distance of over three thousand miles and lengthy temporal separations, I vividly remember my own daughter, I recognize her when I see her, and this remembering entails not only a comprehensive ensemble of determinate facts, but also a complex of affective and evaluative states. These states are both inside – I remember how I feel about this co-presence – and outside – I remember *how it feels* to experience this co-presence. Finally, there are forms of memory that help people to specify themselves as socialized subjects or members of larger, corporate identities. A simple illustration of this facet of memory would be remembering the words to *God Save the Queen* or *My Country*

'Tis of Thee. As with the previous case, this entails affective and evaluative states along with specific factual recall.

All these dimensions of memory are necessary to the coherence of personal identity over time, and to the co-ordination of actions. Memory is partly constitutive of the contingent, private self and is also a necessary condition for personal autonomy. Radical failure of memory, as in pathologies such as Korsakoff's syndrome, are catastrophically destructive of personhood. Patients don't remember who they are, because they are unable to identify any of the figures who populate their world. The forms of reliable and coherent remembering are aspects of what Mikhail Bakhtin calls 'exotopy' or outsideness. A memory is not an *ingredient* of consciousness but a *transgredient* element, external to the subject but nevertheless 'crucial to its completion and totalization'. A basic capacity for memory must be somehow hard-wired in human subjects. Exotopy refers to the semantic content of memory as something we receive from others. This reception of memory from or by means of others is best interpreted as a type of gift exchange.

Gift exchange rather than monetary circulation is one of the central categories necessary for an understanding of Shakespeare's plays both at a thematic level and at the level of their historical reception. The gift economy is also powerfully operative in the cultural *longue durée*; that is, in the relations of cultural reproduction that augment and amplify the value of the Shakespearean *oeuvre*. Unlike a commodity, a gift – the collected works of Shakespeare, for example – entails a bond between giver and recipient. These relationships typically involve both differentiated status *and* solidarity within a community. In this sense every instance of gift exchange has an enduring impact on the micro-organization of a community, in that it extends complex patterns of honor, prestige, and deference among individual subjects.

Giving increases the authority of the donor; reception obligates or binds the recipient. There is deep ambivalence in the binding character of the gift. We can stress communal solidarity, and interpret the gift as a medium of socially distributed *eros*. Alternatively, we can focus on hierarchy, deference, and obligation and interpret it as a medium of repression. In either case, the gift is 'unfinished business'. Reception is not always, and indeed not usually, voluntary.

As I indicated earlier, cultural memory as gift or 'transgredient' combines affective and evaluative states with knowledgeability. To the extent that these affective/evaluative states predominate, the

gift may be redefined as an heirloom or memento, and its importance is primarily in its ability to conserve a sense of relatedness.
I still keep my father's watch, even though it hasn't worked for the
last seventeen years. But a gift can also provoke a sense of unresolved
grievance. Harold Bloom, reading *The Merchant of Venice*, cannot
forget the aggressive assault on his personal identity committed by
the anti-Semitic street gangs of his boyhood. To deny such memories
would be a repudiation of personhood amounting to social death.

Literary works are enjoyed by real persons with their own complex personal memories and their own relationship with history.
The experience of culture cannot be modelled on the abstraction of
a judicious common reader any more than the experience of politics
can be reduced to abstract bearers of rights that inhabit both neo-
liberal and neo-conservative theory. The achievement of reflective
subjectivity requires candid self-recognition and self-acknowledge-
ment. And, as Charles Taylor has pointed out, this necessarily
means the specific recognition of concrete situatedness in terms
of age, gender, ethnicity, and historical background (C. Taylor
1992: 25–28). Literary artifacts have value for us in the way they
help us to remember who we are in precisely this concrete sense.
Here it is important to stipulate that such objects are not an alien
and hostile exteriority. Nor are they purely discretionary choices
encountered in an impersonal cultural market. The great works
of literature are taken up in the more personal way suggested by
Bakhtin's notion of transgredience as memories external to the self,
but necessary for its completion even when the message it bears is
hurtful and inimical.

The Merchant of Venice is a play that denies full and genuine recognition of personhood to its Jewish characters. For a reader like
Harold Bloom to respond to this play with serenity demands candid
acknowledgement of the deep and very personal enmity expressed
towards its Jewish readers. Such acknowledgement would entail
a firm refusal of the consolation suggested by the thought that
Shakespeare intended the play to be an affirmation of Shylock's
human dignity. Bloom has argued, rightly in my opinion, that such
a view cannot be reconciled with the play's comic resolution, where
Portia's retribution against Shylock is necessary to a joyous affirmation of the Venetian community. To recognize the enmity expressed
by a great literary work, however, need not be to react in sullen
resentment and withdrawal. Bloom's idea of 'difficult pleasure'

requires full and candid acceptance of the pathos of literary works and of the cultural traditions they express.

The ideas of ineluctable influence and of literary value make sense only on the condition that the economy of literary works is seen in terms of gifts rather than of commodities (Hyde 1983). Bloom is right to insist that the artifacts which comprise a literary tradition are not optional extras that circulate in the marketplace, though his own complicity with that cultural market is perhaps evident in the recent publication of his list of the all-time great works (Bloom 1994). As gifts, great literary works entail particularly complex and onerous obligations. The principle of reciprocity requires that gifts be returned (Becker 1990; Cheal 1989; Mauss 1967). Gifts received from the past under the dispensation of tradition entail non-voluntary obligations. Even though they haven't been asked for, they are nevertheless binding encumbrances on the recipients.

Charles Taylor, following Bakhtin, has argued that every person's individual identity is necessarily dialogical (C. Taylor 1992: 32–35). This dialogicality of the self implies that individuals are always embedded in a framework of 'strong evaluations' (C. Taylor 1989: 20).

> We become full human agents, capable of understanding ourselves, and hence of defining our identity, through our acquisition of rich human languages of expression . . . including the 'languages' of art, of gesture, of love, and the like.
>
> (C. Taylor 1992: 32)

Individual human agents come to understand and recognize themselves as concretely situated within a specific cultural, ethnic, religious community (Benhabib 1992: 148). Although languages provide discretionary and instrumental capacity to social agents, those agents are nevertheless defined in dialogue or in struggle with significant others. An agent's basic competence to identify and to enjoy the range of social goods is not punctually acquired at some moment in time and then freely deployed for whatever purposes that agent may hit upon. Dialogue with significant others is continuous; membership in or identification with some form of common life is not simply one among many competing goods. It is that, but more fundamentally it is the condition of possibility for the enjoyment of any other specific goods.

The public and collective goods that take the form of literary works are durable over time, and their movement is governed by the principle of serial reciprocity. In other words, there is no form of compensation by which the objects of a tradition are rendered back directly to the giver. Gifts of this kind can only be 'returned' in the sense that they are bestowed on successor generations. In these inter- actions cultural resources 'typically move in a serial flow from each generation to its successors' (Cheal 1989: 59). Serial reciprocity is necessary for intergenerational dialogue and the affirmation of com- munal solidarity. But there is a fundamental pathos to the principle of serial reciprocity, and not simply because cultural endowments entail non-voluntary obligations. The pathos of a tradition, however, is that gifts are not always benefits. As the example of *The Merchant of Venice* ought to suggest, the gifts of a tradition can be inimical and even injurious to members of a successor culture. The past bestows goods on all members of a successor culture in the sense that language, institutions, and cultural practices are the funda- mental enabling conditions for social life. Neither the benefits nor the costs of Western modernity have been equally distributed how- ever. And in some ways this civilization – like all civilizations – has been harmful even to its most fortunate beneficiaries.

The broad argument proposed in the ensuing chapters is that Shakespeare's plays represent the pathos of tradition with extra- ordinary force and clarity. In each of these chapters I try to articu- late Shakespeare's own contradictory understanding of the social and cultural past, often through identification of elements of the carnivalesque in the structure of his dramatic fictions. I begin with *The Winter's Tale* because it is in this play that Shakespeare sets out most fully his own complex model of social time. The structure of the play is based on the traditional festive calendar and the rhythms of seasonal alteration. But the play is also about the transmission of value over time, and about the ambiguous gifts that the various characters receive from the past. In my discussion of *Othello* I will broaden the scope of the analysis to consider the historical reception of the play and the way latent semantic potentialities come to be realized within successor cultures. *Othello* is based on the popular ritual of charivari, a noisy and abusive protest against a socially unwanted marriage. This play, I suggest, is not just an important social memory; in an important sense it reflects the bad conscience of Western society. Finally, in the concluding chapter I consider the figure of Hamlet as the 'speculative genius' of Western modernity, and I try to suggest just how powerfully this play continues to speak to our own predicament.

Chapter 6

Social time in *The Winter's Tale*

Time is number and tale, numbering and telling, in all things
that are numbered and told . . . nothing is more uncertain than
time, nothing is more unperceptible nor more unknown of itself,
for as Isidore sayeth, time is not known by it self, but only by
works and deeds of men.

(*Batman uppon Bartholome*)

Time reveals itself above all in nature: the movement of the sun
and stars, the crowing of roosters, sensory and visual signs of the
time of the year. All these are inseparably linked to corresponding moments in human life, existence, and activity (labor) – the
cycles of time that are marked by degrees of intensity of labor.
The growth of trees and livestock, the age of people are visible
signs of longer periods.

(Bakhtin, 'The Bildungsroman and its Significance in the History
of Realism')

In a pivotal scene in Shakespeare's *The Winter's Tale*, a baby is
abandoned in the middle of a storm, and the man responsible for
this deed is pursued and soon after devoured by a bear. This bizarre
episode supposedly takes place in 'The deserts of Bohemia'. The
play's haphazard geography is compounded by an equally chaotic
temporality apparent, for example, in the play's many well-known
anachronisms (Ewbank 1964: 83ff.; Salingar 1966: 3–11). *The
Winter's Tale* is equally notorious for the abrupt temporal hiatus or
'wide gap of time' that marks its formal organization (Blisset 1971:
52–57; Krier 1982: 341ff.). These oddly conspicuous features in the
play's structure in fact correspond to a complex model of social

time. The play links two seasonal narratives based on traditional festive cycles of winter and spring. The story of family violence that connects these two narratives suggests how social benefits and grievances are held in trust over time.

SPATIO-TEMPORAL DERANGEMENT AND THE GENRE OF *THE WINTER'S TALE*

Although distortion, compression, and discontinuity in the time-scale are by no means uncommon in Shakespeare's plays, *The Winter's Tale* is unusual in that the gap in time is deliberately and ostentatiously foregrounded.

> TIME: Impute it not a crime
> To me or my swift passage that I slide
> O'er sixteen years and leave the growth untried
> Of that wide gap, since it is in my power
> To o'erthrow law and in one self-born hour
> To plant and o'erwhelm custom.
>
> (4.1.3–9)

The chorus openly admits here that the passage of time is not only without duration in the ordinary meaning of that concept, but also without content. Sixteen years are missing, and to all intents and purposes they are empty. The temporal deficit or 'untried growth' is the actual content or 'fullness' of time in that sixteen-year hiatus (Trousdale 1976: 30ff.) The brute fact of change is dramatically foregrounded, but ideas of growth or lived experience or of any sequence of developmental steps or incremental stages are repressed.

These surface features draw attention to a derangement of space and time at an even more fundamental level. The action of *The Winter's Tale* unfolds within a temporality that is both classical and contemporary in its semantic and social content. Viewed as a whole, moreover, the play seems equivocally situated between the narrative space times of 'here and now' and of 'once upon a time'. Do these anomalies suggest that the play is best understood as timeless, as many of its interpreters maintain? Or should these mistakes alert us to the presence of a topical agenda of some kind (Marcus 1988)? This difficulty is no longer addressed as a problem of representation or of 'making nature afraid'. Nor is it any longer a matter of defending Shakespeare's failure to observe the classical unities.

The spatio-temporal heterogeneity of this play is now most often understood as a question of genre.

The presence of anachronistic and anatopical surface features and the deeper structural peculiarities manifested in the play's temporal deficits have often been explained as a privilege of representation within certain genres (Frey 1980: 114ff.). *The Winter's Tale* is a tale of romance, and this amounts to a general warrant for the suspension of all norms of accurate history and geography, not to mention logical or psychological consistency. Anachronism and careless geography are neither mistakes nor transgressions, since they are fully authorized in the purely imaginary space–time of fabulous narrative – or so the argument goes. This move explains the derangement of space and time by ruling the question out of order. But why should such sweeping artistic license be demanded, and why should a reader grant any text such sweeping indulgence? It is perfectly true that the spatio-temporal peculiarities of this play are features of its ontological status as a 'salient world', but this should not be construed as mere 'atmosphere' or as the expression of some sort of artistic whim requiring no explanation (Pavel 1986: 43–73).

Although *The Winter's Tale* is derived from a prose romance, it simply won't do to blame the 'deserts of Bohemia' on the supposed laxities of this genre. For one thing, although it diverges markedly from the spatio-temporal norms of the empirical or non-fictional world, romance as a genre is not especially permissive. More specifically, spatio-temporal heterogeneity is not definitive of romance worlds. Many romance narratives display considerable rigor and precision in the representation of space and time, not only in the case of purely imaginary worlds such as Tolkien's Shire, but also in the 'mixed' environment of Shakespeare's magical island in *The Tempest*. The problem of *The Winter's Tale* is not that everything happens 'there' in *a* world of delphic oracles, tragic losses, and miraculous recoveries, but that some of it happens also 'here' in *the* world of ballad-mongers, thieves, and country feasts.

The main narrative of *The Winter's Tale* is a dramatized revision of a story derived from a Greek Romance (Gesner 1970; Mowat 1976). In his essay 'Forms of Time and of the Chronotope in the Novel', Bakhtin identifies a specific 'chronotope' or space-time as typical of this genre. Bakhtin calls this form of spatio-temporal organization 'adventure time', a time composed of isolated narrative contingencies and moments of crisis and also a time that lacks any sense of causality, development, or duration (Bakhtin

1981: 86–110). In the world of adventure time there are distinct and vividly intense events and in these events space and time may be richly concretized. The movement of the adventure novel, however, takes place primarily in abrupt and unmotivated leaps.

In these terms, the adventure-time chronotope of Greek Romance is implicated in the notion of 'untried Growth' that Time, in *The Winter's Tale* wants to have de-criminalized. Action is motivated here not by growth or development but simply by a desire that remains absolutely opaque.

> There is a boy and a girl of *marriageable* age. Their lineage is *unknown, mysterious*. . . . They are remarkable for their *exceptional beauty*. They are also exceptionally *chaste*. They meet each other *unexpectedly*, usually during some festive *holiday*. A *sudden* and *instantaneous* passion flares up between them that is as irresistible as fate, like an incurable disease. However, the marriage cannot take place straightway. They are confronted with obstacles that *retard* and delay their union.
>
> (Bakhtin 1981: 87)

Bakhtin's general account of adventure time clearly subsumes the events of the second half of *The Winter's Tale*. Romance itself in this description consists of a more or less indefinitely protracted erotic ordeal. The individual agents who occupy this 'adventure time', however, display a remarkable immunity to change and to the 'cyclicity of daily life'. All the emphasis here is on the trials of the hero, and the genre is in fact a genre of testing. But the individual tested in this *mise-en-scène* has nothing of the familiar or the everyday. In the world of the Greek romance and its generic descendants, the human figure is isolated and private. Such a figure has no 'internal content' and therefore cannot be made to reveal anything we might recognize as a motivation.

According to Bakhtin, the usual scale of human time and space expressed in mundane temporal forms such as the calendar is suppressed in Greek romance. Instead, time and space are abstract, arbitrary, and vaguely delineated.

> [It is] an abstract alien world, and furthermore one utterly and exclusively other, since the native world from which the author came and from which he is now watching is nowhere to be found in it.
>
> (Bakhtin 1981: 101)

The Winter's Tale, as I have already suggested, is actually quite full of rich and diverse content belonging to the 'native world from which the author came'. Even the archaic and stylized characters who inhabit Greek romance themselves have become familiar items for popular literary consumption in the world from which the author and his audience are watching.

In order to fully understand the spatio-temporal peculiarities of *The Winter's Tale* it is useful to recall Bakhtin's cryptic statement to the effect that what we call 'content' is always new and that what we call 'form' is stereotyped, congealed, old (familiar) content. 'Form serves as a necessary bridge to new, still unknown content' (Bakhtin 1986: 165). In *The Winter's Tale* a 'familiar and generally understood congealed world view' is performed by a cast of characters transplanted from the genre of Greek romance. The chronotope of this genre sticks to the surface of the characters and defines their subjectivity. But even though some of the characters seem to live their own subjectivity as an ordeal narrative, the play as a whole is not dominated by an abstract or empty time. Despite its temporal deficits, this is in fact a play full of richly concretized time. Indeed, a part of the uncanny and melancholy effect of this lies in the contrast between the empty and atemporal internal content of certain characters, and the abundantly concretized spatio-temporal environment that they inhabit. In general *The Winter's Tale* exhibits a deliberately constructed spatio-temporal heterogeneity which demands a much fuller account of its chronotope, one that goes beyond consideration of its genre.

It is sometimes argued that Shakespeare is writing in a moment of transition between mythical or poetic conceptions of time and space and more rigorously 'scientific' ideas of historical discourse. These accounts generally concede that explanation rather than mere description is called for in relation to the problems of spatio-temporal form in the play. But in the schematic form just summarized this seems rather skimpy as the explanation of the play's mingling of obviously archaic strata with an equally obvious and very local contemporaneity. What is retrospectively interpreted as the unity and coherence of a historical epoch is actually lived as a heterogeneity or bricolage of earlier social formations. These earlier, more or less archaic strata, are differentially sedimented as institutions, customary practices, technologies, and symbolic systems of various kinds. The synchronic co-existence of these disparate strata corresponds to what has been called 'the spectrum of social time' and it could be argued that the 'foreignness' of other cultures is linked in fundamental ways to their modes of spatio-temporal organization (Giddens 1984: 110–161; Muchembled 1985: 44–61). But how 'foreign' is the spatio-temporal ensemble of renaissance culture? Some elements in that society persist within our present culture, even though the totality of that earlier society may have been completely transformed.

Part of the problem with any historical analysis of time and temporality is that our own conceptual vocabulary for telling or interpreting time is relatively impoverished and very abstract. Because we live in the systematically regimented but qualitatively undifferentiated spatio-temporal environment of industrial discipline, we tend to seek out similarly abstract categories for interpreting the space time of earlier cultures. This has led to the widespread orthodoxy that accentuates the contrast between a cyclical time experienced by 'medieval man' and a historical or progressive 'linear' time experienced by 'modern man'. As I hope to show in the next section, however, this over-simplified model requires further elaboration.

SPATIO-TEMPORAL ORDER IN RENAISSANCE SOCIETY

The ability to recognize anachronism depends on a very exact sense of time. Such an exact sense of time emerges over and against exact sense of individual identity, so that the concept of anachronism is specific to the historical regime of well-defined and well-bounded individuality (MacFarlane 1978). Such a regime requires a technological infrastructure of accurate clocks and calendars. These technological developments themselves only follow after deeper, more fundamental changes in society's institutions and in its *episteme* (Foucault 1972; Parkes and Thrift 1980). The characters in *The Winter's Tale* appear to live in an undifferentiated *longue durée* and they are evidently unable to take note of the anachronistic character of their own experiences. This should suggest that these are subjects who do not know who they are, in the sense that knowing who you are entails knowing specifically when and where you are living.

The poorly defined, porous ego boundaries of such characters as Leontes and Hermione should not be construed entirely as lack, deficit, or failure of self-possession. There are, in this text, compensations for not knowing exactly who you are. In his long, celebratory essay 'Freud and the Future', Thomas Mann reflects on the nature of the 'ego of antiquity' and in particular about the shifting and uncertain relationship of that ego to time.

> It was, as it were open behind; it received much from the past and by repeating it gave it presentness again. . . . He searched the past for a pattern into which he might slip like a diving-bell, and being thus at once disguised and protected might rush upon his present problem.
>
> (Mann 1937: 424)

The archaic ego, as Mann imagines it, is deeply preoccupied with a reanimation of myth not as a distanced form of representation but as the immediate practical content of everyday life.

The view of the 'ego of antiquity' set forth here requires a theory of traditional society in which the underlying nature of the social bond is completely opaque. Members of the community live the life of myth unselfconsciously, spontaneously, and in full immediacy. This is an extreme view of pre-industrial consciousness, and it would be extremely difficult to prove that such a state of affairs ever existed, or that it could exist even in principle. Mann provides a more moderate account of the 'ego of antiquity', however, through his notion of the feast.

> The feast is the abrogation of time, an event, a solemn narrative being played out conformably to an immemorial pattern; the events in it take place not for the first time, but ceremonially according to the prototype. It achieves presentness as feasts do, recurring in time with their phases and hours following on each other in time as they did in the original occurrence. In antiquity each feast was essentially a dramatic performance, a mask.
>
> (Mann 1937: 425)

Here the feast constitutes a privileged locus or agential space in which the life of myth is actualized but only as half of the duality of holiday and every day. On this view traditional society would not have to be based on an absolutely opaque social bond. Its members could experience an intensified life of myth through the rhythmic alternation of sacred and profane time (Kristeva 1982).

The duality of holiday and every day, and more generally the duality of a cyclical versus a linear understanding of time, has often been invoked as an explanatory model for interpreting various aspects of the culture of early modern Europe (Quinones 1972). This contrast in ways of interpreting time is often related to large-scale patterns of social change, and specifically to the transition from a medieval subsistence economy to a modern, capitalistic one.

> Money capital and mobile property naturally linked up with the kindred power of time for, seen from that particular point of view, time is money. Time is a great 'liberal' power as opposed to the 'conservative' power of space, the immobile soil. . . . Such an attitude had been unknown in the Middle Ages; to them time was plentiful and there was no need to look upon it as something precious. It became so only when regarded from the point of view of the individual who could think in terms of the time measured out to him. [But in the middle ages] men lived as part of an all-embracing unity and thus life lasted long beyond its natural span. . . . For the Middle Ages knew a hand-to-mouth economy, as was natural in an age of primary production, for agricultural produce will not keep over long periods, and the accumulation of values was thus impossible.
>
> (von Martin 1944: 16ff.)

Although one should be sceptical about historical arguments that privilege the category of transition, this formulation is none the less valuable as a good first-order approximation of how the time experience changes over time. What this account suppresses, however, is the *concreteness* of time in pre-capitalist social formations. The 'abundance' or 'scarcity' of time in this setting was not an abstract abundance in which time is directly comparable to money or to capital, but rather an abundance of concrete temporal forms.

Although in some respects the structure of time does begin to change as European society evolves from a subsistence economy through the various stages of capitalism, the idea of transition *from* cyclical recurrence *to* linear progression does not describe this change very accurately. First of all, the middle ages recognized temporality both as cursus or rhythm *and* as vector or line (Higgins 1989: 29ff.). And in fact the *linear* perspective of temporality is fundamental for Augustinian Christianity. The medieval peasant certainly knew seasonal recurrence both in the labors of the months and in the liturgical calendar, but it was his understanding of a providential and eschatological, that is to say, linear destiny that supposedly distinguished him from the pagans.

In the Renaissance, time is still fundamentally grasped and interpreted by means of both cursus and line, although novel ways of
conceptualizing this dialectic begin to emerge during this period.
Although the liturgical calendar is still carefully followed as a
matter of civil policy, the exact nature of festive observance is
increasingly called into question. The controversy over 'old holiday
pastimes', for example, reveals deep anxieties over the way social
time and social labor are regulated (Marcus 1986). That anxiety is
reflected in another way in the enormous popularity during the
period of printed texts that make available a combination of almanac and prognostication (Capp 1979).

Almanacs are concerned with all the complex recursive aspects of
temporality, and above all with the co-ordination of natural and
liturgical cycles. The almanacs of the period contain a good deal of
practical information about the scheduling of regular feasts or red-
letter days, and about the system of customary practices associated
with these feast days. Here the existence of a 'popular liturgy'
parallel to the 'official liturgy' appears very clearly (Gaignebet and
Florentin 1979). This popular liturgy consecrates the recursive
aspects of agricultural and craft labor by recording, for example,
the system of 'ploughman's feast days' such as Plough Monday or
Harvest Home (Bretnor 1615; Buckmaster 1571; Gray 1591). These
schedules take note of the housewife's obligations as well as the
husbandman's and even suggest suitable menus for the feasting.
Related to this are various folkloric 'calendars' based, for example,
on the flowering of plants. This horticultural calendar, which is
alluded to in Perdita's speeches in 4.4, begins with the snowdrop,
which emerges on 2 February (candlemas) followed by the crocus
on 14 February (St Valentine's Day), ending finally with the
Christmas greens, ivy and holly, which 'appear' on 25 December.
These festive greens are then taken down at the end of the Christmas
cycle, again on 2 February, a rule noted by Herrick and evidently in
the proverbial calendar lore as well.

The orderly tracking of these various sequences through the
annual cycle helps to stabilize a potential underlying disorder in the
recursive structure of time. This structure incorporates and attempts
to integrate the two powerful but fundamentally incommensurable
rhythms of the solar and lunar calendars (Higgins 1989: 234ff.).
It appears that the lunar and solar calendars are correlated with
the idea of the Law and the Gospel, at least in some writers, because
the Jewish year was (and still is) a lunar year. In addition, the

non-coincidence of these two rhythms has both technical and administrative importance. For Bede, accurate calculation of the date of Easter was a relatively straightforward matter of deciding between Celtic and Roman systems of ecclesiastical administration. The Gregorian reforms of 1582 were an attempt to correct inaccuracies in the Julian calendar, but these initiatives could not be separated from questions of power and authority (Gimpel 1976).

Sixteenth-century English almanacs generally do not address the theoretical background to keeping track of time, but concentrate instead on the scheduling of feast days and work days. Here the duality of the year is organized around two great ritual programs: the immoveable (solar) and the moveable (lunar) feasts. The immoveable or solstitial feasts are calculated in accordance with the solar calendar. They recur on the same day of the month, but they 'move around' in respect of the days of the week. The moveable or equinoctial feasts are 'fixed' by a complex calculation of both lunar and solar movement in relation to the days of the week. Easter, the crucial event in this second cycle, must occur on the first sunday on or after the first full moon after the vernal equinox. To refer to these systems as 'solar' and 'lunar' calendars is an obvious over-simplification. The moveable feasts, for example, appear to have a 'lunar' surface structure but a 'solar' deep structure.

The duality of the liturgical year is most often expressed during the period not as an opposition between solar and lunar calculation, but rather as a movement between Christmas-tide and Lenten-tide, each with its own distinctive rites, practices, and systems of meaning. The Christmas season begins very early, with the feast of All-Souls, and it ends some six weeks after Christmas Day with the feast of Candlemas. The Easter season officially begins with Ash Wednesday, the first day of Lent, but of course this is always preceded by the 'disordered' and 'excessive' practices of Carnival or Shrovetide. The core events of the season belong, strictly speaking, to Lent, but, as with Christmas, there is a somewhat protracted aftermath lasting until nearly midsummer and including the pentecostal or Whitsuntide observances and the celebration of Ascension Day.

By consulting their almanacs, the husbandmen and huswives of early modern England would be able to organize and plan for a wide range of activities. But the typical almanacs of the period were also manuals of prognostication. These were used not only to calculate the dates of the moveable feasts, but also to forecast the weather

(I. F. 1598). Other entries provide guidance on the optimum timing of a long list of practices from bleeding and purgation to haircuts and clipping nails (Godfridus 1608). Finally the technique of prognostication could be extended to a forecast of specific events such as the likelihood of someone dying, or abundance of the next harvest (Digges 1605).

These manuals reflect the strategic orientation to time that we are used to associating with a scientific or instrumental rationality. The emphasis is on foresight, planning, and the optimization of the schedule (time–energy budget). Despite its outward resemblance to popular superstition, prognostication has some resemblance to what the engineers and economic planners call the critical path. The *aim* of these manuals is to provide reliable information about weather, market conditions, political events, and so on, all of which have obvious practical importance for the readers of almanacs. The *method*, on the other hand, was obviously faulty, since there is no scientific basis for predicting future weather by basing predictions for the twelve months on observations about the twelve days of Christmas. However, even if the thematic and discursive content of these manuals of prognostication still belongs to the so-called pre-scientific *episteme*, based on resemblance and correspondences, it is obviously not accurate to characterize the readers of these texts as living the life of myth, despite the emphasis given to recursive aspects of temporality.

Almanac and prognostication represent the two fundamental axes of temporality as cursus and line for the sixteenth century. Time is clearly understood and experienced in manifold concrete forms, natural processes, and practical activities such as the growth of flowers, the preparation of food, the care of the body, and in the more abstract, symbolic commemorative elements of the liturgical calendar. *The Winter's Tale* reflects this densely layered awareness of temporality in many of its particular details. More important, as I hope to demonstrate in what follows, the *structure* of *The Winter's Tale* adheres closely to the underlying structure of recursive time represented in the almanac. The first half of the play is dominated by the temporal forms of Christmas-tide. In the second half of the play, the symbolism of Midsummer is augmented by the practical temporality of rural life. In between these two fundamentally solstitial movements, the play turns around a structuring absence or temporal pivot defined by the complex of the bear and the abandoned baby.

CHRISTMAS-TIDE AND THE ECONOMY OF EXPENDITURE

The problems of temporal derangement and temporal deficit that mark the narrative organization of *The Winter's Tale* are also manifested in a deficit or lack of adequate motivation for the jealousy of Leontes from which the action is generated. The opening scenes of *The Winter's Tale* provide no detailed sense of psychological development leading up to Leontes' extreme jealousy. Instead, what we have is a discontinuous sequence of full-blown affective states such as friendship, jealousy, hostility, and so on, without any idea of a graduated sequence or evolution from one of these states to another. The notion of adventure time, and of characters who lack internal content, accounts for this only in part. It is also useful to explore not only why Leontes is jealous but also when he is jealous; that is, to ask what feast or myth his jealousy enacts and commemorates. What I hope to argue here is that his jealousy is a type of spatio-temporal derangement of the ethos of gift, hospitality, and expenditure, mandated by the observances of the Winter Festival or Christmas-tide (Le Roy Ladurie 1979: 278ff.).

Hospitality is the dominant preoccupation of scenes 1 and 2 of *The Winter's Tale*. In the atmosphere of generosity and liberality that seems to prevail as the action begins, Leontes' fantasies of sexual betrayal appear particularly outlandish. Jealousy, by definition, is groundless and unjustified, 'otherwise it is not jealousy' (Felperin 1972: 114). But to speak of jealousy as 'unmotivated' is to raise a different set of questions. Jealousy could be the result of a mistake or deception as it is in *Much Ado About Nothing*, *Othello*, and *Cymbeline*. Or it could be systemic, a fundamental aspect of the relations of reproduction within a given sex–gender system (Erickson 1982: 819ff.; Williamson 1986: 111–123). In its most extreme form, such an argument would explain jealousy as a consequence of the radical ambiguity or *différence* of language itself (Felperin 1985). In all these instances jealousy would be groundless in that there are no objective circumstances to which it is a rational response, but it would by no means be unmotivated. The problem in trying to understand Leontes in these terms is simply that there does not seem to be enough time for any of these forces to act upon him. The violence and intensity of his jealousy emerges full blown, and this suggests that it might be the result not of any external social forces, but rather a sudden outbreak of dream-work processes such as condensation and displacement (Stockholder 1987: 184–196).

It is a fundamental presupposition of every psychoanalytic interpretation that something is missing, and moreover that something is missing specifically from the experience of temporality. In the classical Freudian variant of the psychoanalytic trajectory, the appearance of a complex affect, in this case jealousy, may be construed as a spatio-temporal deficit that must be filled up with an archaic content. In other words the presence of irrational or unmotivated affect is itself a type of spatio-temporal d'erangment or return of the dead. In a 'successful' psychoanalytic explanation the archaic content that makes up or compensates for the gaps and deficits in spatio-temporal continuity is unmasked as a repressed memory or wish that has only been shamming dead. On this view it may be argued that Leontes' jealousy is motivated by a barely conscious fantasy or wish in which he gives his wife to Polixenes for his sexual enjoyment in order to intensify the social bond between the two men (MacCary 1985: 196). Leontes then disowns this perverse and forbidden wish by ascribing it to Polixenes and Hermione. This otherwise implausible conjecture has the undoubted virtue of drawing attention to the centrality of the bond between Leontes and Polixenes in the symbolic economy of this play.

The idea of offering one's own wife to a friend is in fact motivated, though not necessarily sanctioned by the terms of the guest–friend relationship within the dispensation of a gift economy. The affective and ethical complexities of the guest–friend bond are a central preoccupation of the opening scenes. Here the dispute between Sicily and Bohemia over the question of Polixenes' departure must be understood as something much more than a routine exchange of courtesies. The visit has lasted nine months, during which time Polixenes has been separated from his wife and son. These details suggest that in some respects Polixenes is treated more like a hostage than a guest. And indeed Hermione more than hints at this aspect of the relationship as she urges Polixenes to extend his stay.

HERMIONE: Verily,
You shall not go. A lady's 'verily''s
As potent as a lord's. Will you go yet?
Force me to keep you as a prisoner,
Not like a guest; so you shall pay your fees

> When you depart, and save your thanks. How say you.
> My prisoner? Or my guest?
>
> (1.1.48–55)

Hermione's speech proves to be the clinching argument, and some-what reluctantly Polixenes agrees to remain a guest at the Sicilian court for an additional week.

The distinction between a prisoner who must pay fees and a guest who must return thanks is crucial to understanding the negotiations between the two kings. To submit to the position of prisoner, to pay fees and settle accounts, would profoundly dishonor Polixenes, since it would transform the relationship into an impersonal 'exchange of equivalents' or commodity transaction. At the same time, however, in agreeing to remain even longer, Polixenes risks another kind of dishonor in that he may not be able adequately to reciprocate the lavish generosity or magnificence of Leontes. Polixenes' determina-tion to depart entails, among other things, an obligation for Leontes to return the 'visit', so that, in the fullness of time, the imbalances that come to exist between giver and recipient, between host and guest, may be redressed.

Despite their protestations of love and friendship, then, and despite the imagery of the 'twinned lambs', Leontes and Polixenes are in fact engaged in a bitter and potentially deadly struggle for honor and prestige. Leontes does not want to let Polixenes go home, because Leontes does not want to go north where he will be obliged to receive the hospitality offered by Polixenes. The lavish entertain-ment provided for Polixenes is prompted by Leontes' desire to exceed his guest-friend in honor and prestige. The Bohemian courtiers are already somewhat anxious about this, because Leontes' exorbitant generosity may compromise their ability to offer ade-quate compensation. This extraordinarily long entertainment, then, might well be interpreted as a deliberate strategy on Leontes' part of pre-emptive gift-giving. Polixenes' attempt to thwart this plan is what actually prompts the otherwise incomprehensible outburst of the King. On this view the ensuing sacrifice of family members is the final, violent stage of potlatch undertaken by Leontes as a primitive affirmation of honor.

The elements of gift and sacrifice appear in the first half of *The Winter's Tale* as the local enactment of the annual drama of the Winter Solstice. Shakespeare rewrote the story of Robert Greene's *Pandosto* by reversing the positions of the two kingdoms, making

Sicily rather than Bohemia the locus of the initiating action, and by changing the names of the characters. In this new version the King of Sicilia, which is associated with summer, with the south, and also with fertility, is given the name of *Leo*ntes, i.e. Leo, the central zodiacal sign of summer, associated with the sun as its planet. The King of Bohemia is *Poli*xenes, i.e. Polus, the north star. Leontes is certainly Leo-like in his behavior, moving between extremes of heat and cold, proximity and distance, warm affection and paranoid rage, etc. Arguably Polixenes is 'polar'; that is, steady and unmoving. Leontes' refusal to go north to Bohemia and repay the visit would then signify a literally catastrophic derangment of the temporal and cosmological order. There are other encodings of the calendar in this text. Faith Wallis has suggested that the twelve dancers in the second half could signify the four seasons, each consisting of three months. This rather cryptic encoding of time as natural cursus is correlated with the spatio-temporal organization of the gift exchange or guest–host relationship. In other words, the guest–host relationship, like the relationship of the sun and the planets to the fixed stars is one of reciprocity, balance, give and take, but only in the context of *longue durée*. The balance is accomplished by means of complex local imbalances, sacrifices, gifts and their redemption, rather than through an immediate audit or settling of accounts.

In Shakespeare's England, of course, the drama of the sun's return at the Winter Solstice is linked to the celebration of Christmas. The full observance of this system of immoveable feasts, moreover, is not confined to a single day but is extended over many weeks. Many of the festive observances during this period commemorate sorrow and loss rather than the joy of Christ's nativity. The twelve days of Christmas, for example, include not only celebration of the nativity, but also the feast of St Stephen, the first martyr, on 26 December; the Holy Innocents' unwitting martyrdom on 28 December; the circumcision, a feast of fools, on 1 January, and so on. Even the Twelve Days, however, are only the centerpiece of a much longer schedule of Christmas-tide observances or immoveable feasts.

The Winter Festival begins with the feast of All-Hallows or All-Souls on 1 November. This is a propitiary rite or feast of the dead, and it is also the customary time for the arrival of the Lord of Misrule in great households. The onset of winter is the time of 'expenditure' as the governing social movement and this is made concrete in the annual butchering of livestock that usually begins

around the feasts of All-Hallows and St Martin's at the beginning of
November (Tusser 1573: 54).

> At hallontide Slaughter time entereth in
> And then doth the husbandmans feasting begin.
> From thence unto Shrovetide, kill now and then some.
> Their offal for household, the better will come.
>
> (Tusser 1573: 46)

The periodic killing of livestock during the Winter Festival has a
propitiary as well as a practical meaning. Some of this complexity is
expressed in the 'culinary calendar', which mandates the roasting of
fowl or of large 'joints' at this time. The Christmas-tide feasting and
gift exchange mandated here, however, are emphatically not the
private and domestic experience of consumption characteristic of
bourgeois political economy.

The political economy of Christmas-tide is a particularly contentious issue during the Elizabethan and Jacobean periods (Bristol
1985: 82–87). For some, the practices of gift exchange and of festive
abundance are denounced as pagan excess, or as a commercializ-
ation of the birth of Christ. Many of the important social groups in
Elizabethan and Jacobean society, however, continue to affirm the
value of traditional hospitality. Tusser's interpretation of Christmas
is broadly representative of a popular tradition widely disseminated
through almanacs as well as in the various manuals of husbandry
and huswifery.

> At Christmas the day doth begin to take length,
> Of Christmas our faith doth begin to take strength.
> As Christmas is only a figure or trope.
> So only in Christ, is our strength and our hope.
> At Christmas we banquet, the rich with the poor,
> Who then (but the miser) but opeth his door
> At Christmas of Christ, many Carols we sing
> And give many gifts, in the joy of that king.
>
> (Tusser 1573: 55)

Tusser presents the concept of Christmas as a social movement
governed by the idea of the gift as a primary form of economic
exchange. Behind this notion stands the idea of the Nativity, Christ's
Incarnation, which is comparable to a kind of divine potlatch or
lavish expenditure that permanently binds and obligates all who
receive it. For Tusser, this season of expenditure is clearly organized

to renew and to reaffirm certain principles of solidarity and mutual assistance. The economy of expenditure, however, is defined as much by an obligation to receive as it is by an obligation to give, and in fact the custom of gift exchange at Christmas is sanctioned precisely by a prior willingness to *receive* the extraordinary gift of a divine baby born in the depths of winter.

The events of the first half of *The Winter's Tale* take place during a period of time which stretches from All-Hallows, when ghost stories and winter's tales are told, to Candlemas, when the bear emerges from her cave to devour the souls of evil men (Alford 1937: 16–25; Bernheimer 1952: 53ff.; Le Roy Ladurie 1979: 309ff.). In the middle of all this a baby is born, offstage. This does not, however, occasion a joyous celebration of nativity and new birth. In this re-enactment of the nativity, Leontes takes on the role and the demeanor of raging Herod. This is, however, as unmotivated as Leontes' jealousy in the sense that it is not primarily an expression of coherent internal content. The taking on of these grotesque masks of jealousy and rage is part of the decorum of the season. Leontes' character represents the movement of expenditure or emptying out of the spatio-temporal order in its social, cosmological, and providential dimensions. This movement would presumably be completed in a final emptying out; that is, in the death of Leontes. And indeed, in the final scene of the first half of *The Winter's Tale*, we see this closure achieved, not by Leontes himself, but by his representative, Antigonus.

THE CANDLEMAS BEAR

'Exit, pursued by a bear' is one of the relatively few stage directions in Shakespeare authorized by the earliest edition. This bear is not really required for the working out of the fundamental plot moves in *The Winter's Tale*, since Antigonus could more easily be disposed of in a maritime accident that took place offstage. The problem of the bear has been addressed primarily as a practical and contingent question of theater history, an aspect of the play as spectacle (Biggins 1962; Gurr 1983; Randall 1985). Was it a real bear or a man in a bear suit? How does the bear fit into the play's atmosphere and its decor? Was it supposed to be funny, or was it intended to frighten the audience? These questions treat the bear either as a charming divertissement or as yet another instance of bad taste.

By concentrating on how the bear was actually staged, however, rather than on why there is a bear at all, these discussions ignore the manifold symbolic functions of this device and its specific function as a significant marker of spatio-temporal form.

It is Antigonus' destiny not just to die as a substitute for Leontes, but specifically to be devoured or swallowed up by a bear during a late-winter thunderstorm. The reason for condemning Antigonus to this gruesome fate is to be found in the symbolic identification of the bear with the winter season, an identification that seems to be pervasive throughout European folklore (Gaignebet and Florentin 1979: 18–21; Laroque 1982: 25–33). A 'bear', usually a man dressed in furs or animal skins, appears in a variety of popular festive observances, occasionally during the Christmas season, but more often in the later stages of the winter cycle. A 'straw bear' appears as part of the observances of Plough Monday in parts of England. In France a bear or bear-chase is associated with the feast of Candlemas on 2 February and the feast of St Blaise on 3 February, the earliest possible date for Shrove Tuesday. The bear also participates in Shrovetide observances in Bohemia. In all these instances the bear is a rough and hairy, often begrimed man, a scary monster who chases and sometimes catches young women.

Although the actual date of his appearance may vary from one locale to another, the carnivalesque bear-man is connected with a range of practices and observances that mark the end of Christmastide leisure and the beginning of the agricultural work year. Like the groundhog in North America, the bear is a prognosticator who appears on Candlemas, 2 February, to forecast the end of winter weather. When the bear appears during a storm, winter will be shorter, and the arrival of spring earlier than in years when the weather is fine. This appears to hold good for *The Winter's Tale*, at least from the audience's point of view, since the wintry part of the story ends in this scene, and the springtime comedy begins shortly after the intermission.

In addition to its function as a temporal marker, the bear has many further valences in the symbolic economy of early modern European culture. To begin with the bear is proverbially noted for exceptional ferocity and violence. The natural fierceness of the bear is also associated with the violence of secular authority.

Vitoldius, King of Lithuania, kept certain Bears of purpose, to whom he cast all persons which spoke against his tyranny, putting them first of all into a Bears skin, whose cruelty was so great, that if he had commanded any of them to hang themselves, they would rather obey him than endure the terrors of his indignation.

(Topsell 1607: 13)

The bear as symbol of the excessive cruelty of royal tyranny has an ironic resonance in *The Winter's Tale* in that it is Antigonus, the compliant servant, rather than any of the characters who spoke against Leontes, who suffers this extravagant punishment.

The bear is also a symbol of bold and aggressive sexuality. The 'venerous and lustful' character of bears is usually masculine but not exclusively so, for in Topsell's account the she-bear is also characterized by her continual lust and provocation of the male. Furthermore, bears may seek out humans as sexual prey: 'A bear carried a young maid into his den by violence, where in venerous manner he had the carnal use of her body' (Topsell 1607: 37). This story is evidently not reported as part of the bear's natural history, but is rather linked to the bear's folkloric relations with the satyr and the 'wild man'. The bear's immoderate sexuality, like its ferocious cruelty, is linked, though in a more circuitous way, to the character of Leontes, specifically to his fantasy of Polixenes as woman-chaser and violator of chastity. The bear hunt, as an echo of the story of Callisto, further complicates the situation. In this context the bear is specifically linked to the punishment of unchastity and, as the constellation of the Great Bear, to the memorialization of its unwilling victims (Topsell 1607: 42ff.).

Bears are connected with violence, rape, and destruction, but they are equally important as symbols of nurture and creativity. The connection between the bear's hibernation and its patterns of reproduction have rich symbolic associations for renaissance culture. 'The constitution of the body of a Bear is beyond measure Phlegmatic, because he fasteth in winter time so long without meat' (Topsell 1607: 38). The wintry character of the bear, and its ability to survive by a kind of mimicry of death, is connected with certain remarkable and even bizarre aspects of the bear's reproduction. Tiny cubs are born in winter during the hibernation period. These small infants are protected by the she-bear, who 'huggles them to her breast' as a shelter from the winter cold. In both natural science and the folklore of the period these facts are interpreted as a kind of deliberate making. The cubs that emerge from the bear's den in the springtime are not born in the usual way; instead the she-bear licks her whelps into shape from a formless mass of her own bodily secretions. This fantastic notion amounts to a grotesque inversion of the normal birth process. The infant takes shape outside the womb as a purposeful action of a mother who is herself inside the womb or den. Furthermore, this 'phlegmatic' mother, who survives 'without meat', literally makes babies or licks them into shape without the co-operation or the assistance of an inseminating male. From these indications it is possible to suggest that the bear is an ambivalent, carnivalesque image, an androgynous or polymorphous figure of winter and of earth whose den symbolizes both a grave and a womb.

The bear is a figure of boundaries and of transformations, marking both the moment of ending or death and the moment of new beginnings or birth. The appearance of this complex and ambivalent figure at the end of the second half of *The Winter's Tale* is certainly consistent with the thematic content of this scene, where, as the shepherd says to his son,

> Heavy matters! Heavy matters! But look thee here, boy. Now bless thyself. Thou mettest with things dying, I with things new-born. Here's a sight for thee, look thee, a bearing cloth for a squire's child.

> (3.3.114–120)

In parts of Scotland a basket containing a doll is set outside in observance of the feast of St Bridget on 2 February. The appearance of the bear is linked in certain contexts to the feasts of Candlemas and of St Blaise, which take place at the same time. It is extremely appropriate to consider this bear as a Candlemas bear, since Candlemas is the *time* of boundaries and transformations.

Candlemas is the terminal date of the Christmas cycle, the last of the immoveable feasts specifically connected with the nativity. This is the feast of purification, when the Virgin Mary is presented at the temple in accordance with Old Testament law. This event has a doubly paradoxical character. The purification demanded by the law is not, of course, required in the case of the mother of Christ. And of course the miraculous character of the Incarnation marks the end of the dispensation of the law. Candlemas both acknowledges the old dispensation and simultaneously supersedes it. In this respect the feast has providential or historical meaning as the hinge or pivot between the two great epochs. On a more mundane level, Candlemas is a time for taking down the Christmas decorations, for predicting the weather, for manuring the fields, for the beginning of outdoor work prompted by the noticeable lengthening of the day, and so on. This is also traditionally the last day on which candles are used at the vesper services, a practice that begins each year around All-Hallows or Martinmas in early November.

In the years 1610 and 1611 when this play was initially performed, Shrove Tuesday fell on or near its earliest possible date of 3 February. In 1611 Ash Wednesday fell on 4 February, which meant that the gap between Christmas-tide and Lenten-tide is limited to a single day, that is Shrove Tuesday. In those years Candlemas would have been linked very directly to pre-Lenten observances of Shrovetide. But this early date for Ash Wednesday would compress the permissible time for carnivalesque observances almost to nothing. Instead of a fully extended carnival with its license and festive abundance, there is only short shrift. This aborted Shrovetide means that there is *no time* for a transition or accommodation between the typical themes and social behaviors of Christmas-tide or Winter Festival with its focus on expenditure, and those of Lenten-tide with its focus on abstinence, fasting, and repentance.

The condensation amounting to a complete omission of time for carnival is reflected in the structure of *The Winter's Tale*. Although this is a play in which temporality is heavily overcoded, the heightened spatio-temporal alterity of the annual battle of carnival and Lent is conspicuous by its absence. Shrovetide is simply left out, or skipped over. Furthermore, in the first half of the play, the margin of anomie preserved in such carnivalesque features of the Christmas season, festive laughter, misrule, gift exchange, and the communal meal are also suppressed. Both carnival as a liminal *event* and the carnivalesque as liminal *behavior* function within a structuring absence in *The Winter's Tale*. That structuring absence entails a Lenten penitence that lasts for sixteen years. The narrative sequence of the play breaks apart at this point. In the context of an actual performance, of course, this probably corresponds to the intermission, which functions as a kind of liminal space-time in relation to the spatio-temporal reality mandated by the world of the play text. After the interval, Time must take the stage to account for and redress the play's spatio-temporal deficit. That deficit or absence comprises not only the typical activities of Shrove Tuesday, but those of the entire Lenten-tide as well.

SHEEPSHEARING, AND THE ECONOMY OF STRATEGIC CALCULATION

Lenten-tide is not only a season for penitence and fasting in the culture of early modern Europe. It is a busy time of year, leading up to the observance of the vernal equinox and to the liturgical/ providential culmination of the year in the Easter celebrations. Batman upon Bartholome interprets Lent as a time of Christian chivalry and also as the restitution of a heritage that was lost. There is, however, a more specifically seasonal and practical interpretation of Lent:

> Lent is time of quickening, for the earth that seemed as it were dead in Winter time, quickeneth again and waxeth green in Lent. Also Lent is time of renewing for the earth is arrayed and renewed with herbs and flowers, and trees with branches and leaves. Also Lent is time of conceiving. For then the virtue of generation is most strong in beasts, trees, and herbs. . . . Also Lent is the time of making nests and of breeding . . . in Lent seeds be sown upon earth: and grafts be grafted upon trees.
>
> (*Batman uppon Bartholome:* 150–151)

Lenten-tide has enormous practical importance in the chiefly agricultural economy of the period. It is during this period that the cycle of agricultural labor begins, with the annual manuring of the fields. There is also increased activity in the market economy. It is during Lent, for example, that butchers are actively engaged in buying livestock for future delivery (Bristol 1986: 72–88).

When the action of *The Winter's Tale* resumes after the intermission, it is clear that the Lenten movement of time has already been completed. R. C. Hassel links the play specifically to the celebration of Easter, mainly on the grounds of its thematic sympathy with the annual commemoration of Christ's resurrection (Hassel 1979: 143–144). However, except for the cryptic reference to Florizel's absence – 'Sir, it is three days since I saw the Prince' – the play as calendar makes no specific reference either to Easter or to the Lenten-tide activities that normally precede it. And indeed, the Prince's absence has less to do with Easter than it does with the customs of Whitsuntide and going-a'maying.

The season of Pentecost, like the Lenten-tide that precedes it, is marked by sensory and visual signs of the time of the year:

then is the time of all gladness of joy and of mirth for all the
beasts and fowls live in most love . . . hearts be green and woods
burgeon. . . . Also it is the time of good smells and of sweetness . . .
the time of riping.

(*Batman uppon Bartholome:* 152)

Batman also notes that this is the season in which cholera breeds,
especially in very hot, dry seasons. As with other aspects of spatio-
temporal form, however, the cycle of natural transformation is
linked to the system of human labor. During late spring and early
summer agricultural labor reaches a peak of intensity. And of course
it is also a time for 'wakes, fairs and bearbaitings'.

In the second half of *The Winter's Tale*, the patterns of adventure
time and of the time of the Winter Festival are augmented by the
time of agricultural labor and market exchange. This additional
layer of time, however, is much more than the completion of an
annual cursus of liturgical, natural, and practical commemorations.
Spatio-temporality has been changed in fundamental and irreversible ways here. The gift economy which was dominant in the first
half of the play must now co-exist with an active and aggressive
market in commodities and commodity exchange. The popular
festive and customary forms of production such as sheepshearing are
now organized on a large scale that involves considerable strategic
calculation. Finally, the financial windfall that came along with the
abandoned baby has been used with great success as investment
capital, and this has led to an irreversible social mobility.

The figure of Autolycus is linked to the development of the placeless market and to the predominance of the commodity form.
Ballad-mongers were typically small-time entrepreneurs or sub-
contractors who earned their livelihood selling mechanically
reproduced entertainment to a mainly lower-class buying public
(Würzbach 1990: 13–28). Ballads are wares or commodities, and
the ballad-monger is a kind of pitch-man who finds his market at
the edges and interstices of organized economic activity. But of
course Autolycus is a good deal more than a simple ballad-monger.
He is also a versatile economic opportunist who preys upon the
typical consumer psychology of wealthy *arrivistes*. In this respect
Autolycus is definitive of commodity exchange as this is understood
in the placeless market. But as a person with no fixed address and for
that matter no fixed identity, he also represents a dangerous margin

of anomie in relation to the comparatively more stable economy of agricultural production.

The time of agricultural production appears in *The Winter's Tale* as an extended celebration of the sheepshearing festival. It is clear that this sheepshearing is a great deal more than a piece of colorful folklore. The wealthy shepherd who organizes this feast has planned a celebration on a large scale, one that reflects his very considerable economic substance. He is, according to Polixenes, 'a man they say, that from very nothing, and beyond the imagination of his neighbors, is grown into an unspeakable estate' (4.2.43–46). This 'unspeakable estate' raises the contentious issues of surplus, accumulation, and the tension between an ethos of subsistence or redistribution typical of an aristocratic gift economy and an ethos of accumulation and social mobility typical of a market economy.

'You may shear your sheep when elder blossoms peep.' Although sheepshearing is seasonal, like other forms of agricultural labor, the actual time of the sheepshearing festival is governed primarily by strategic calculation rather than by folkloric indications. Although ritual and propitiatory aspects of sheepshearing are noted in the almanacs of the time, economic considerations are in fact paramount. This event must be scheduled in relation both to weather conditions (nature) and to market conditions (culture), and is therefore subject to considerable local variation. A sheepshearing is rather like a 'round-up'. To begin with the sheep do in fact have to be rounded up and provision must be made for washing them. It is also important to allow time for the sheep to dry, which takes a few days, and therefore requires at least a rudimentary skill in weather forecasting. For this reason the sheepshearing cannot be rigidly tied to the annual cursus, but must instead be carefully planned, taking into account a large number of independent factors including not only weather, but also the availability of resources and the current state of wool markets.

When the sheepshearing is done on a large scale, as it is in the world of *The Winter's Tale*, there must be social co-operation on a fairly large scale. A sheepshearing entails a very complex division of labor. First, a labor force has to be assembled. In some contexts this is provided for in the indentures or traditional master–servant agreements. In the sixteenth century these annual contracts are renewed each year at the time of the sheepshearing. On some large estates more straightforward types of hired labor are also used.

Second, sheepshearing requires a co-ordination of husbandry (man's work) with huswifery (women's work). The sheepshearing is one of the cycle of ploughman's feasts mentioned by Tusser, and it is the huswife's duty to make provision for this observance. In the sixteenth and seventeenth centuries this feast no doubt represented a kind of partial payment rather than being a purely ceremonial observance. Here it takes on a kind of heightened importance as a way of masking the open secret of the wage labor relations that define this activity.

The feast planned in *The Winter's Tale* by Perdita suggests that these are unusually prosperous shepherds. The clown or bumpkin who plays the role of Perdita's brother tries to calculate the cash income from 1500 sheep, but finds he cannot perform such a feat of calculation 'without counters'. He then turns to his shopping list. 'Three pound of sugar, five pounds of currants, rice – what will this sister of mine do with rice?' (4.3.37–38). The rice, along with the sugar and the currants, are no doubt intended to be made into a rice pudding, which will be served at the sheepshearing dinner. The other ingredients, primarily milk, cream, eggs, and beef suet, would all be available within the domestic economy of a well-to-do establishment like the old shepherd's (Markham 1986: 72). The brother's question no doubt pertains to the cost of these exotic store-bought ingredients. According to Thomas Tusser, there is an extraordinary range of foodstuffs, and of other products that can be home-grown. Rice is mentioned as one of the very few commodities that could only be found in the market economy. Perdita also wants to use 'store-bought' sugar, instead of the honey widely available in the countryside in early summer. This may suggest that Perdita has a kind of inborn preference for luxury commodities. But it may also express something about her interpretation of the sheepshearing feast in terms of the lavish expenditure typical of gift economies. Her plans for rice pudding hint at a notion of the feast that goes beyond simple cost-benefit analysis.

Perdita interprets her role as 'mistress of the feast' in a way that is consistent with traditional notions of festive abundance and hospitality. Here economic surplus is redistributed in accordance with notions of expenditure and social generosity that define the housewife's role:

Of all other doings, housekeeping is chief
For Daily it helpeth the poor with relief.

The neighbour, the stranger, and all that have need
Which causeth thy doings, the better to speed.

(Tusser 1573: 28)

Traditional hospitality, however, is not easily distinguished here from conspicuous consumption and from the more general aims of upward social mobility. Her own stepfather's fortune has grown 'beyond the imagination' of the neighbors, and the envy this might provoke calls for propitiary strategies on the level of local public relations. But the lavish expenditure she has planned can be viewed as an element in a strategy of social accommodation, for Perdita is of course the primary agency through which social mobility is accomplished *without* any danger of social instability.

As housewife to her widowed father, Perdita has the task of administering a portion of the wealth the old shepherd has accumulated. In her ceremonial and festive role as 'mistress of the feast', she performs this task as a bricolage, or pastiche of disparate elements. She is both Flora and 'The queen of curds and cream' (4.4.160), a classical goddess and a farmer's daughter. In her role in the popular festive observances of the sheepshearing festival, or 'Whitsun pastoral', Perdita links a classical spatio-temporal order to here-and-now, practical contemporaneity. The duplicity of her character, moreover, makes possible a negotiated solution to emerging class tensions between the aristocratic characters and the wealthy shepherds who rise up to be 'tall fellows' as the play draws to a close. 'See you these clothes? Say you see them not and think me still no gentlemen born. You were best say these robes are not gentlemen born' (5.2.150). This extraordinary social transformation reflects local spatio-temporal derangements that make it possible to be 'a gentleman born before my father' (5.2.150). The purchase of the right clothes, however, makes it possible to avoid incipient social violence.

Although there is a certain sentimental appeal in the idea that Perdita is somehow responsible for the reconciliation of latent class antagonisms in this play, there is in fact another, more important factor required for achieving this social result. The basket that the old shepherd found contained not only a baby and a 'squire's bearing cloth', but also a quantity of gold. It is this financial endowment, and not just Perdita's native attractiveness, that provides the conditions for the possibility of social reconciliation here. In this respect Leontes' initial sacrifice takes on the surprising character of a successful long-term investment. Time is, indeed, money here, and it is this element of time as a factor in strategic long-term calculation that redefines the spatio-temporal form of the play as the action draws to a close.

In the first half of the play Leontes loses everything that has value for him. Furthermore, he *knows* the extent of the losses he has sustained and he knows his own responsibility for this calamity. In the fullness of time, however, these losses are made good and even his supposedly dead wife is returned to him. It is usual to argue that Hermione has forgiven Leontes for the misery he has caused, not only to her, but to other people, and to interpret the play's conclusion in terms of reconciliation. This may explain what the forgiveness *means* as an allegory of divine grace. However, it seems unsatisfactory as an account of what might motivate Hermione's action. What these religious interpretations seem to say is that Hermione forgives Leontes 'objectively'. But there is no attempt to describe this forgiveness as something *achieved* or *developed* in the fullness of time, for the very good reason that no such temporally lived process is manifested in the play's organization. In fact, a conscientious effort has been made to exclude the experience of duration as lived *by Hermione* in the 'fullness of time'.

It is not at all clear that Hermione's forgiveness is the result of a choice, or even, at this stage of events, that Hermione possesses that degree of personhood which would make the choice of forgiveness a meaningful one. To put the question as crudely as possible, why does Hermione agree to take Leontes back and why on earth would she want him? The Queen's fidelity and her forgiveness seem as utterly groundless and also as unmotivated as the jealousy of Leontes. However, in the spatio-temporal economy of the play, Hermione's forgiveness makes sense as the result of a strategic calculation on the part of Leontes. This strategy is initially conceived in terms of expenditure within the spatio-temporal realities of a gift economy. It is actually accomplished, however, by means of fiduciaries in the profoundly altered spatio-temporal realities of a market economy. In this setting, the living statue is the ultimate in luxury goods, a lavish promise of consumer satisfaction. Viewed in this way, Leontes' redemption is not brought about by grace and forgiveness but is rather the result of his own bold, risk-taking decisions combined with his patience and enormous capacity for deferral.

In the end, however, Leontes' success appears somewhat equivocal. The simulacrum he has purchased here is not, perhaps, altogether his own possession, for when Hermione actually speaks she says nothing of forgiveness to Leontes, and indeed she does not speak to the King at all.

HERMIONE: You gods, look down,
And from your sacred vials pour your graces
Upon my daughter's head: Tell me, mine own,
Where hast thou been preserved? Where lived? Where found?
Thy father's Court? For thou shalt hear that I,
Knowing by Paulina that the oracle
Gave hope thou wast in being, have preserved
Myself to see the issue.

(5.3.121–127)

Hermione has another story to tell, and there is time enough to tell it. But that telling, like the fullness of time as Hermione has actually lived it, belongs not to the world of *The Winter's Tale*, but to its margins, entailments, and structuring absences. The Queen is linked here to the forms of reproductive time which encompass not only growth, change, and development, but also the inter-subjective or dialogic fullness of time symbolized so powerfully in the gestation of the child in the mother's body. It is that experience of co-presence in time and space that constitutes the untold story that Hermione promises here, a story systematically and violently excluded from the social time and space represented in this play.

The ending of *The Winter's Tale* is ambiguous. Hermione returns to a husband who condemned her to death and who ordered the fatal exposure of her infant daughter. In the closing scene the characters see Hermione embrace Leontes – 'She hangs about his neck' (5.3.112). To describe this as a reconciliation, as so many commentators have done, is simply a form of wishful thinking. Perdita has been found, but all 'that which is lost' has not been recovered. Mamilius 'remains unaccounted for' (Cavell 1987: 193). *The Winter's Tale* may well speak to a social desire for healing and the redress of grievance. But Leontes' murderous folly has had irrevocable consequences not only for himself but for others. It is not altogether clear that the embrace of husband and wife in the final scene can be adequate compensation to Hermione for the loss of her son or for the time that she has spent waiting for the return of Perdita.

Chapter 7

Race and the comedy of abjection in *Othello*

There is something repulsive to my mind in the idea of a beautiful Venetian girl falling in love with an African prince.

(Fannie Ragland)

The Winter's Tale articulates the complexity of social time and the hope for compensation and reconciled wholeness. Taken more literally, however, it is the story of an abusive husband who is rewarded with constant love, even though he had intended the death of his wife. In this sense *The Winter's Tale* belongs to the history of violence against women. To interpret the play in these terms is not just a contingent ideological appropriation. Just as in the case of *The Merchant of Venice*, *The Winter's Tale* must be read and understood by concrete, situated subjects who are equally aware of anti-Semitism and of the prevalence of domestic violence. The difficult pleasure of reading the great stories contained in these plays comes from the way they express the collective bad conscience of our civilization.

The painful difficulty of confronting this bad conscience is even more vividly felt in the case of *Othello*. Harold Bloom has argued that the comic structure of *The Merchant of Venice* only makes sense in terms of the 'ancient Christian slander against the Jews'. The happy ending brought about by Portia's ingenuity affirms the life of a community that takes satisfaction in the humiliation and exclusion of the Jew. Bloom has argued that an accurate staging of the play would be insupportable for anyone who knows the truth about the Holocaust. Anything less than the full truth of the play's intentions would be profoundly dishonest. I intend to make a similar argument here for *Othello*. I read the structure of the play as a comedy of abjection that depends on a background of racial hatred and violence. An honest production of *Othello* would be just as intolerable as an honest production of *The Merchant of Venice*. In fact, as I hope to show, many readers and spectators of *Othello* have indeed refused to tolerate what is expressed so brutally in this play. As with the other plays I have referred to here, we cannot avoid the difficulty by taking refuge in a historicist argument. The abjection of women, of Jews, and of people of color remains a salient and distinctive feature of contemporary experience. How then do viewers of *The Winter's Tale*, *The Merchant of Venice*, and *Othello* actually participate in the social experience represented by these works? What does it mean, to borrow a usage from French, to 'assist' at a performance of this text?

GUILTY CREATURES SEATED AT A PLAY

Ritual and theater have a long history of strained and sometimes openly hostile relations. This conflict between hieratic ceremonies and the meretricious performances of actors is, however, deeply equivocal. The manifest antagonism between the liturgical forms of religion and the dramatic spectacles of the theater are continually haunted by the trace of a hidden complicity. The integrity of religious practice depends to a considerable extent, therefore, on the control of access to redemptive media and to places of sanctity within a given community. Such integrity is, of course, of decisive importance for maintaining the collective life of the believers.

For Emile Durkheim, every rite, both in its ceremonial formality and in the transgression that accompanies it, is a process by which a community reproduces modes of consciousness and social interaction that maintain its solidarity over time (Durkheim 1915: 39). Durkheim argues that ritual depends on misrecognition. A community reaffirms its own well-established social hierarchies which are experienced by the believers as a manifestation of the sacred. The divine presences evoked in ritual may be non-existent; however, contact with the sacred is not, for that reason, some kind of delusionary fantasy, since the communal life so richly experienced in ritual has a concrete and sensuous actuality that does support and sustain the members of the community. Ritual misrecognition always has some element of objective cogency, no matter how fantastical its overt manifestations may be and no matter how fallacious the interpretations of the participants. Moreover, the anomie that appears at the time of the festival is a functional undifferentiation that strengthens the resolution and closure that concludes the rite. Misrecognition is a special kind of mistake, one that somehow seems a necessary condition for the possibility of social continuity.

Those responsible for the management of liturgical practice must always ensure that ritual, despite its spectacular accoutrements, is never linked openly to theater. The ontological claims on which ritual depends are not always easy to sustain, for the very good reason that the practical exigencies of any liturgy are not very different from those of a theatrical performance. The distinction between a priest's vestments and an actor's costume is never an easy one to maintain, and this is especially so in a historical setting such as Elizabethan and Jacobean England, where some theatrical costumes are in fact expropriated vestments transferred from the altar to the *mise-en-scène*.

Contamination of religious authority by illicit contact with theater was a condition that occasioned chronic anxiety during the early modern period and this anxiety has been examined in a number of recent studies (Mullaney 1988; Schechner 1988; Turner 1982). Stephen Greenblatt's important essay on 'Shakespeare and the Exorcists', for example, shows that the scandal of exorcism is precisely its character as a theater that dissembles its own theatricality (1988: 94–128). The evacuation of religious significance from exorcism, the chastisement of its practitioners, and the instruction of the public in the correct allocation of charismatic and juridical authority are all accomplished by means of a thoroughgoing theatricalization of exorcism. This is done in part by the exposure of various theatrical techniques and special effects used by the exorcists on an unsuspecting audience, and in part by the re-staging of the exorcists' performances in a juridical setting. As Greenblatt's essay shows, however, the use of theater as the primary instrument for this evacuation of a vitiated or unauthentic ritual is extremely dangerous. By openly asserting its capacity for dissimulation, theater addresses the element of misrecognition necessary to any liturgical enactment of the sacred. Theater thus has the capacity to theorize all redemptive media and even to make visible the links between ritual, repression, and social contradiction. The strategy of evacuation through the use of a theatrical pedagogy, though carefully focused on specific unauthentic practices, is paradoxically self-condemnatory in the way it foregrounds the element of collective misrecognition on which charismatic and juridical authority depends.

Despite its capacity to theorize ritual practices, theater is not simply the logical 'opposite' of liturgy. There are important isomorphisms between these two symbolic protocols. Ritual and theater are based on formalities, on conventional social etiquette, and on the use of selected artifacts or symbols within a well-defined spatial frame. In addition, theater resembles ritual in that it requires its own particular brand of 'misrecognition' in the form of a temporary and contractual make-believe. However, a fiction does not require the unselfconscious and unreflective misrecognition necessary for ritual (Greenblatt 1988: 106). Fictions may, however, inspire powerful feelings of acute discomfort experienced, for example, at performances of *Othello*. The apparent dilemma between a classic sociology of religion that interprets ritual as a necessary though wholly unselfconscious misrecognition and a classic sociology of theatrical reception that interprets performance in light of the necessarily lucid recognition of make-believe may be resolved in part by an appeal to Mikhail Bakhtin's category of the carnivalesque. Carnival is an ensemble of practices that seems to be both 'full' of positive social content, like a ritual, and 'empty' of any substantive social meaning, like a theatrical performance. This theory can help to make sense of the apparently paradoxical notion of a knowledgeable misrecognition that seems to be the condition of the possibility of a proper response to a theatrical performance. One of the salient features of carnival is its capacity to open up an alternative space for social action (Bakhtin 1968: 145–196). Within the spatio-temporal boundaries of a carnivalesque event, the individual subject is authorized to renegotiate identity and to redefine social position *vis-à-vis* others. In Bakhtin's reading of carnival, the social effervescence and the energy generated by a radical popular will to otherness is not simply recaptured for the purposes of the official culture. In its capacity for excess and derangement, carnival empowers the popular element to voice its opposition to the imperatives of official culture.

The theory of carnival distinguishes between the affirmative character of ritual consciousness as such, and the negative and corrosive force of popular festive form. This distinction corresponds to the distinction between official culture – the legitimated stories and interpretations of social hierarchy reproduced in the ideological

apparatus – and popular culture – the alternative values and interpretations of the social life-world sedimented in the symbolic practices of various excluded or partially excluded groups. Carnival
analyzes and dismantles the official order of things, not in a spirit of
pure negation, but rather as the expression of an alternative understanding of the social world as an ensemble of material practices
(Bristol 1985: 59–111). To be sure, this alternative understanding
may be profoundly conservative in its thematic content and in its
evaluation of various social practices. However, such a conservatism
by no means implies a blanket endorsement of all decisions taken by
individuals and groups with access to mechanisms of political
power, or an indiscriminate willingness to submit to authority.
In fact, the knowledge sedimented in the artifacts and the symbolic
vocabularies of carnival is a reaffirmation of practical consciousness
that may be significantly at odds with the ideologies officially sanctioned by ruling elites. This practical consciousness is best thought
of as the outlook of social agents sufficiently knowledgeable to 'get
on' within the constraints of economic and institutional reality
(Giddens 1984: 3–4). Such knowledgeability is not always equivalent to the self-understanding of a particular social agent but is
instead sedimented within certain institutional practices, including
but not limited to the conventions of theater and theater-going.

Bakhtin's view of carnival is in some sense a development of
what appears to be the contrasting position articulated in
Durkheim's sociology of religion. It is important to realize, however,
that Bakhtin's anthropology preserves the central insight of
Durkheim's sociology of religion and of the view that both official
ritual and its popular cognates, as moments of greatly intensified
social life, tend powerfully towards the reaffirmation of a deeply
felt 'way-of-being-together-in-the-world' (Bristol 1985: 26–59). The
notion of the carnivalesque, however, adds an element to the sociology of religion which helps to account for the possibility of social
change, and for the presence of differentiated interests that have to
participate in the negotiation of that change. The carnivalesque
would thus be a mode of authentic cognition, a kind of para-
scientific and pre-theoretical understanding of social forms that
would disclose whatever is hidden by ritual misrecognition.

The following analysis outlines a hypothesis that would interpret
Othello as a carnivalesque text in the Bakhtinian sense. Carnival is
operative here as something considerably more than a novel decor
for the *mise-en-scène* or an alternative thematics for interpretation.

The play is read here as the carnivalesque derangement of marriage as a social institution and of the contradictory role of heterosexual desire within that institution. As a serio-comic or carnivalesque masquerade, the play makes visible the normative horizons against which sexual partners must be selected, and the latent social violence that marriage attempts to prevent, often unsuccessfully, from becoming manifest. More specifically, I want to draw attention to the play as an adaptation of the social custom, common throughout early modern Europe, of charivari (Underdowne 1985: 99–103; See also LeGoff and Schmitt 1977; Rey-Flaud 1985; Thompson 1972). This was a practice of noisy festive abuse in which a community enacted its objection to inappropriate marriages and more generally exercised a general surveillance of sexuality. As Natalie Davis has pointed out, this 'community' actually consists of young men, typically the unmarried ones, who represent a social principle of male solidarity which is in some respects deeply hostile to precisely that form of institutionally sanctioned sexuality whose standards they are empowered to oversee (Davis 1981).

CHARIVARI

The abusive language, the noisy clamor under Brabantio's window, and the menace of violence of the opening scene of *Othello* link the improvisations of Iago with the codes of a carnivalesque disturbance or charivari organized in protest over the marriage of the play's central characters. Charivari does not figure as an isolated episode here, however, nor has it been completed when the initial on-stage commotion ends (Laroque 1987: 13–16). Despite the sympathy that Othello and Desdemona seem to be intended to arouse in the audience, the play as a whole is organized around the abjection and violent punishment of its central figures. If certain history plays can be read as rites of 'uncrowning' then this play might be read as a rite of 'un-marrying' (Neely 1985). In staging the play as a ceremony of broken nuptials, Iago assumes the function of a popular festive ringleader whose task is the unmaking of a transgressive marriage.

As the action of *Othello* unfolds, the audience is constrained to witness to a protracted and diabolical parody of courtship leading to a final, grotesquely distorted consummation in the marriage bed. To stage this action as the carnivalesque thrashing of the play's central characters is, of course, a risky choice for a director to make, since it can easily transform the complex equilibrium of the play from tragedy to *opera buffo*. Although the play is grouped with the tragedies in the first folio and has always been viewed as properly belonging to this genre, commentators have recognized for a long time the precarious balance of this play at the very boundaries of farce (Snyder 1979: 70–74). *Othello* is a text that evidently lends itself very well to parody, burlesque and caricature (Levine 1988: 14–20; Neill 1989: 391–393). Alteration of the play's formal characteristics, however, would not be the most serious problem encountered in contemplating a carnivalized performance. Since the basis for the charivari is an interracial marriage, many of the strongest effects of this ritual practice would be realized here through use of derisory and stereoptypical images of 'The Moor'.

It is important to remember that Othello does not have to be a black African for this story to work itself out. Racial difference is not absolutely required to motivate any of the play's fundamental plot moves. The feelings expressed by the various characters that prompt each of the turns in the action could just as well be tied to some other difference between the two romantic protagonists and in fact the difference in age seems as important if not more important than the fact of Othello's blackness in the concrete unfolding of the story (Stavropoulos 1987: 125–141). The image of racial otherness is thus tangential to the primary narrative interest here. At the time of the play's earliest performances, the supplementary character of Othello's blackness would be apparent in the white actor's use of black-face makeup to represent the conventionalized form of 'The Moor'. In the initial context of its reception, it seems unlikely that the play's appeal to invidious stereotypes would have troubled the conscience of anyone in the audience. Since what we now call racial prejudice did not fall outside prevailing social norms in Shakespeare's society, no one in the early audience would have felt sympathy for Othello simply on grounds that he was the victim of a racist society (Hunter 1964, 1967; Orkin 1987). It is far more probable that 'The Moor' would have been seen as comically monstrous. Under these conditions the aspects of charivari and of the comical abjection of the protagonists would have been entirely visible to an audience for whom a racist sensibility was entirely normal.

At the end of the sixteenth century racism was not yet organized as a large-scale system of oppressive social and economic arrangements, though it certainly existed as a widely shared set of feelings and attitudes. Racism in this early, prototypical form entails a specific physical repugnance for the skin color and other typical features of black Africans. The physical aversion of the English towards the racial other was rationalized through an elaborate mythology, supported in part by scriptural authority and reinforced by a body of popular narrative (Jordan 1968; Tokson 1982). Within this context, the image of the racial other is immediately available as a way of encoding deformity or the monstrous.

For Shakespeare and for his audience, the sensibilities of racial difference are for all practical purposes abstract and virtually disembodied, since the mythology of African racial inferiority is not yet a fully implemented social practice within the social landscape of early modern Europe. Even at this early stage, however, it had already occurred to some people that the racial other was providentially pre-ordained for the role of the slave, an idea that was fully achieved in the eighteenth- and nineteenth-century institutions of plantation slavery and in such successor institutions as segregation and apartheid. The large-scale forms of institutional racism that continue to be a chronic and intractable problem in modern societies are, of course, already latent within the abstract racial mythologies of the sixteenth century, since these mythologies enter into the construction of the social and sexual imaginary both of the dominant and of the popular culture. In more recent contexts of reception the farcical and carnivalesque potentiality of the play is usually not allowed to manifest itself openly. To foreground the elements of charivari and comic abjection would disclose in threatening and unacceptable ways the text's ominous relationship to the historical formation of racism as a massive social fact in contemporary Europe, and in the successor cultures of North and South America as well as in parts of the African homeland itself. Against this background the text of *Othello* has to be construed as a highly significant document in the historical constitution both of racist sensibility and of racist political ideology.

The relationship of marriage is established through forms of collective representation, ceremonial and public enactments that articulate the private ethos of conjugal existence and which mark out the communal responsibilities of the couple to implement and sustain socially approved relations of reproduction. In the early modern period the ceremonial forms of marriage are accompanied (and opposed) by parodic doubling of the wedding feast in the forms of charivari (Alford 1959: 505–518). This parodic doubling is organized by a carnivalesque wardrobe corresponding to a triad of dramatic agents – the clown (who represents the bridegroom), the transvestite (who represents the bride) and the 'scourge of marriage', often assigned a suit of black (who represents the community of unattached males or 'young men'). Iago of course is neither unattached nor young, but part of his success with his various dupes is his ability to present himself as 'one of the boys'. Iago's misogyny is expressed as the married man's resentment against marriage, against wives in general, and against his own wife in particular. But this resentment is only one form of the more diffuse and pervasive misogyny typically expressed in the charivari. And of course Iago's more sinister function is his ability to encourage a kind of complicity within the audience. In a performance he makes his perspective the perspective of the text and thus solicits from the audience a participatory endorsement of the action.

The three primary characters in charivari each has a normative function in the allocation of marriage partners and in the regulation of sexual behavior. These three figures parody the three characters of the wedding ceremony – bride, groom, and priest. It is the last of these three figures who confers both social and sacred authority on the marriage. The ensemble as a whole, however, is a travesty of the wedding ceremony itself. The counter-festive vocabulary of charivari provides the community with a system of critical resources through which marriage as a social arrangement and as a private form of sexuality may be either negated or reaffirmed.

Charivari features the three primary figures mentioned above; that is, a bride, a groom, and a ringleader who may in some instances assist the partners in outwitting parental opposition, but who may also function as a nemesis of erotic desire itself and attempt to disrupt and to destroy the intended bond. In the actual practice of charivari, the married couple are forced to submit to public ridicule and sometimes to violent punishment. In its milder forms, a charivari allows the husband and wife to be represented by parodic doubles who are then symbolically thrashed by the ringleader and his followers. This triad of social agents is common to many of Shakespeare's tragedies of erotic life and it even appears in the comedies. Hamlet stages 'The Murder of Gonzago' partly as a public rebuke to the unseemly marriage of Claudius and Gertrude (Davis 1981: 75). This is later escalated to a fantasy of the general abolition of the institution of monogamy, 'I say we will have no more marriages'. Hamlet's situation here expresses the powerful ambivalence of the unattached male towards marriage as the institutional format in which heterosexual desire and its satisfaction are legitimated. His objection to the aberrant and offensive union of mother and uncle is predicated on the idealization of marriage and in this case on the specific marriage of mother and father. This idealization is, however, accompanied by the fantasy of a general dissolution of the institution of monogamy back into a dispensation of erotic promiscuity and the free circulation of sexual partners. A similar agenda, motivated by a similar ambivalence, is pursued by Don John in *Much Ado About Nothing*, and by Iachimo in *Cymbeline*.

The argument I hope to outline out here requires that readers or viewers of *Othello* efface their response to the existence of Othello, Desdemona, and Iago as individual subjects endowed with personalities and with some mode of autonomous interiorized life. The reason for such selective or wilful ignorance of some of the most compelling features of this text is to make the determinate theatrical surfaces visible. To the extent that the surface coding of this play is openly manifested, the analysis presented here will do violence to the existence of the characters in depth. Instead of striving to understand the grandeur and the sublime dignity of the play's hero and heroine, this argument seeks to stop at the surface in order to focus attention on the carnivalesque scenario or charivari that governs the dramatic action.

In order to grasp the primary characters of *Othello* at this level of representation, it is necessary to withdraw from the position of empathy for the characters as subjects constituted in the way we are constituted and to seek out an appropriate mode of counter-identification. I believe that the withdrawal of empathy and identification from the play's main characters is difficult, not least because the experience of individual subjectivity as we have come to know it *is* objectively operative in the text. The constellation of interests and goal values most characteristic of the institutional processing of literary texts has given rise to an extremely rich critical discourse on the question of the subject; it is precisely the power and the vitality of this discourse that makes the withdrawal of empathy from the characters so difficult. I have already discussed the claim that the pathos of individual subjectivity was actually invented by Shakespeare, and that this experience appears for the first time in the history of Western representation in his plays. Whether or not arguments of this kind are historically accurate, however, there is the more immediate difficulty that modern readers and viewers naturally desire to reflect on and identify with the complex pathos of individual subjectivity as it is represented in Shakespeare's *oeuvre*. This is especially so, perhaps, for professional readers and viewers, who are likely to have strong interests in the experience of the speaking/writing subject and in the problematic of autonomy and expressive unity. Nevertheless, for Shakespeare's characters to exist as Othello, Desdemona, and Iago, they have to use the carnival-esque 'wardrobe' inscribed within this text, and this wardrobe assigns them the roles of clown, transvestite, and 'scourge of marriage' in a charivari.

The clown is a type of public figure who embodies the 'right to be other', as Bakhtin would have it, since the clown rejects the categories available in routine institutional life (Bakhtin 1981: 158–167). The clown is therefore both criminal and monster, although such alien and malevolent aspects are more often than not disguised. Etymologically, clown is related to *colonus* – a farmer or settler, someone not from Rome but from the agricultural hinter-land. As a rustic or hayseed the clown's relationship to social reality is best expressed through such contemporary idioms as 'He's out of it!' 'He doesn't know where it's at!' or simply 'Mars!' In the drama of the early modern period a clown is often by convention a kind of country bumpkin, but he is also a 'professional outsider' of extremely flexible social provenance. Bakhtin has stressed the emancipatory capacity of the clown function, arguing that the clown mask embodies the 'right to be other' or *refus d'identité*. However, there is a pathos of clowning as well, and the clown mask may represent everything that is social and sexually maladroit, credulous, easily victimized. And just as there is a certain satisfac-tion in observing an assertive clown get the better of his superiors, so there is also satisfaction in seeing an inept clown abused and stripped of his dignity. This abuse or 'thrashing' of the doltish out-sider provides the audience with a comedy of abjection, a social genre in which the experience of exclusion and impotence can be displaced on to an even more helpless caste within society.

To think of Othello as a kind of black-faced clown is perhaps dis-tasteful, although the role must have been written not for a black actor, but with the idea of black makeup or a false face of some kind. Othello is a Moor, but only in quotation marks, and his blackness is not even skin-deep but rather a transitory and superficial theatrical integument. Othello's Moorish origins are the mark of his exclusion; as a cultural stranger he is, of course, 'out of it' in the most compel-ling and literal sense. As a foreigner he is unable to grasp and make effective use of other Venetian codes of social and sexual conduct. He is thus a grotesque embodiment of the bridegroom – an exotic, monstrous, and funny substitute who transgresses the norms associated with the idea of a husband.

To link Othello to the theatrical function of a clown is not necessarily to be committed to an interpretation of his character as a fool. Othello's folly, like his nobility and personal grandeur, are specific interpretations of the character's motivation and of his competence to actualize those motives. The argument here, however, is that the role of Othello is already formatted in terms of the abject clown function and that any interpretation of the character's 'nature' therefore has to be achieved within that format. The eloquence of Othello's language and the magnanimity of his character may in fact intensify the grotesque element here. His poetic self-articulation is not so much the *expression* of a self-possessed subject but is instead a form of discursive indecorum that strains against the social meanings objectified in Othello's counter-festive *persona*. Stephen Greenblatt identifies the joke here as one of the 'master plots of comedy', in which a beautiful young woman outwits an 'old and outlandish' husband (1980: 234). Greenblatt reminds us here that Othello is functionally equivalent to the gull or butt of an abusive comic action, but he passes over the most salient feature of Othello's outlandishness, which is actualized in the black face makeup essential to the depiction of this character. This discretion is no doubt a political judgement rather than an expression of a delicacy of taste. To present Othello with a black face, as opposed to presenting him as a black man, would confront the audience with a comic spectacle of abjection rather than with the grand opera of misdirected passion. Such a comedy of abjection has not found much welcome in the history of the play's reception.

The original audience of this play in Jacobean England may have had relatively little inhibition in its expression of invidious racial sentiments, and so might have seen the derisory implications of the situation more easily. During the nineteenth century, when institutional racism was naturalized by recourse to a 'scientific' discourse on racial difference, the problem of Othello's outlandishness and the unsympathetic laughter it might evoke is 'solved' by making him a Caucasoid Moor, instead of a 'Veritable Negro' (Newman 1987: 144). Without such a fine discrimination, a performance of *Othello* would have been not so much tragic as simply unbearable, part farce and part lynch mob. In the present social climate, when

racism, though still very widespread, has been officially anathema-
tized, the possibility of a black-faced Othello would still be an
embarrassment and a scandal, though presumably for a different set
of reasons. Either way, the element of burlesque inscribed in this
text is clearly too de-stabilizing to escape repression.

If Othello can be recognized as an abject clown in a charivari,
then the scenario of a such a charivari would require a transvestite
to play the part of the wife. In the context of popular culture in the
early modern period, female disguise and female impersonation
were common to charivari and to a variety of other festive observances (Davis 1974: 147ff.). This practice was, among other things,
the expression of a widespread 'fear' of women as both the embodiment of and the provocation to social transgression. Within the
pervasive misogyny of the early modern period, women and their
desires seemed to project the threat of a radical social undifferentiation (Woodbridge 1984). The young men and boys who appeared in
female dress at the time of carnival seem to have been engaged in
'putting women in their place' through an exaggerated pantomime
of everything feminine. And yet this very practice required the
emphatic foregrounding of the artifice required for any stable
coding of gender difference. Was this festive transvestism legitimated by means of a general misrecognition of the social constitution of gender? Or did the participants understand at some level
that the association of social badness with women was nothing more
than a patriarchal social fiction that could only be sustained in and
through continuous ritual affirmation?

Female impersonation is, of course, one of the distinctive and
extremely salient features of Elizabethan and Jacobean dramaturgy
and yet surprisingly little is known of how this mode of representation actually worked (Rackin 1987: 29–42). The practice of using
boy actors to play the parts of women is derivative of the more
diffuse social practice of female impersonation in the popular festive
milieu. Were the boy actors in Shakespeare's company engaging in
a conventional form of ridicule of the feminine? Or were they
engaged in a general parody of the artifice of gender coding itself?
A transvestite presents the category of woman in quotation marks,
and reveals that both 'man' and 'woman' are socially produced
categories. In the drama of Shakespeare and his contemporaries,
gender is at times an extremely mobile and shifting phenomenon
without any solid anchor in sexual identity. To a considerable
degree gender is a 'flag of convenience' prompted by contingent

social circumstances, and at times gender identity is negotiated with considerable grace and dexterity. The convention of the actor 'boying' the woman's part is thus doubly parodic, a camp put-down of femininity and, at another level, a way to theorize the social misrecognition on which all gender allocations depend.

Desdemona's 'femininity' is bracketed by the theatrical 'boying' of her or his part. This renders her or his sexuality as a kind of sustained gestural equivocation and this corresponds to the exaggerated and equivocal rhetorical aspect of Desdemona's selfpresentation. As Desdemona puts it, 'I saw Othello's visage in his mind'; in other words, her initial attraction to him was not provoked by his physical appearance. The play thus stipulates that Desdemona herself accepts the social prohibition against miscegenation as the normative horizon within which she must act. On the face of it she cannot be physically attracted to Othello, and critics have usually celebrated this as the sign of her ability to transcend the limited horizons of her acculturation. These interpretations thus accept the premise of Othello as physically undesirable and thus insinuate that Desdemona's faith is predicated on her blindness to the highly visible 'monstrosity' of her 'husband'. In other words, her love is a misrecognition of her husband's manifestly undesirable qualities. Or is it a misrecognition of her own socially prohibited desire? Stanley Cavell interprets her lines as meaning that she saw his appearance in the way that he saw it: that she is able to enter into and to share Othello's self-acceptance and self-possession (Cavell 1987: 129). According to this view Desdemona is a kind of idealization of the social category of 'wife', who can adopt the husband's own narrative fiction of self as her own imaginary object. Desdemona is thus both a fantasy of a sexually desirable woman and a fantasy of absolute sexual compliance. This figure of unconditional erotic submission is the obverse of the rebellious woman or shrew, but, as the play shows us, this is also a socially prohibited *métier* for a woman. In fact, as Stephen Greenblatt has shown in his very influential essay, the idea that Desdemona might feel an ardent sexual desire for him makes Othello perceive Iago's insinuations of infidelity as plausible and even probable (Greenblatt 1980: 237–252). The masculine fantasy projected in the figure of Desdemona cannot recognize itself as the object of another's desire.

Like all of Shakespeare's woman characters, Desdemona is an impossible sexual object, a female artifact created by a male imagination and objectified in a boy actor's body. This is, in its own way, just as artificial and grotesque a theatrical manifestation as the black-faced Othello who stands in for the category of the husband. What is distinctive about Desdemona is the way she embodies the category of an 'ideal wife' in its full contradictoriness. She has been described as chaste or even as still a virgin and also as sexually aggressive, even though very little unambiguous textual support for either of these readings actually exists (Nelson and Haines 1981: 1–18; Booth 1989: 332–336). Her elopement, with a Moor no less, signals more unequivocally than a properly arranged marriage ever could that the biblical injunction to leave mother and father has been fulfilled. It is probably even harder to accept the idea of Desdemona as part of a comedy of abjection than it is to accept Othello in such a context. It is, however, only in such a theatrical context that the hyperbolic and exacerbated misrecognition on which marriage is founded can be theorized.

At the level of surface representation then, the play enacts a marriage between two complementary symbols of the erotic grotesque. This is a marriage between what is *ipso facto* hideous and repellent with what is most beautiful and desirable. The incongruity of this match is objectified in the theatrical hyper-embodiment of the primary categories of man and woman or husband and wife. It is not known to what extent Elizabethan and Jacobean theater practice deliberately foregrounded its own artifice. However, the symbolic practice of grotesque hyper-embodiment was well known in popular festive forms such as charivari. The theatrical coding of gender in the early modern period is thus still contaminated by the residue of these forms of social representation.

The marriage of grotesque opposites is no more a private affair or erotic dyad than a real marriage. Marriage in the early modern period, among many important social classes, is primarily a dynastic or economic alliance negotiated by a third party who represents the complex of social sanctions in which the heterosexual couple is inscribed. The elopement of Desdemona and Othello as well as their reliance on Cassio as a broker or clandestine go-between already signals their intention deliberately to evade and thwart the will of family interests. To the extent that readers or viewers are conditioned by the normative horizons that interpret heterosexual love as mutual sexual initiative and the transcendence of all social obstacles, this elopement will be read as a romantic confirmation of the spiritual and disinterested character of their love. However, it can also be construed as a flagrant sexual and social blunder.

Private heterosexual felicity of the kind sought by Othello and Desdemona attracts the evil eye of erotic nemesis.

The figure of erotic nemesis and the necessary third party to this union is Othello's faithful lieutenant, Iago. It is Iago's task to show both his captain and his audience just how defenseless the heterosexual couple is against the resources of sexual surveillance. The romantic lovers, represented here through a series of grotesque distortions, do not enjoy an erotic autonomy, though such autonomy is a misrecognition of the socially inscribed character of 'private' sexuality. His abusive and derisory characterizations of the couple, together with his debasement of their sexuality, are a type of social commentary on the nature of erotic romance. The notion of mutual and autonomous self-selection of partners is impugned as a kind of mutual delusion that can only appear under the sign of monstrosity. In other words, the romantic couple can only 'know' that their union is based on mutual love *and on nothing else* when they have 'transcended' or violated the social codes and prohibitions that determine the allocation of sexual partners.

Iago is a Bakhtinian 'agelast'; that is, one who does not laugh. He is, of course, very witty, but his aim is always to provoke a degrading laughter at the follies of others rather than to enjoy the social experience of laughter *with* others. He is a demythologizer whose function is to reduce all expressivity to the minimalism of the *quid pro quo*. The process represented here is the reduction of quality to quantity, a radical undifferentiation of persons predicated on a strictly mechanistic, universalized calculus of desire. Characters identified with this persona appear throughout Shakespeare's *oeuvre*, usually in the guise of a nemesis of hypocrisy and dissimulation. Hamlet's 'I know not seems' and Don John's 'it cannot be denied I am a plain dealing villain' are important variants of a social/cognitive process that proclaims itself to be a critique of equivocation and the will to deception. It is ironic, of course, that these claims of honesty and plain dealing are so often made in the interests of malicious dissimulation. What appears to be consistent, however, in all the variants of this character type is the disavowal of erotic attachment and the contemptuous manipulation of the erotic imagination.

The supposedly 'unmotivated' malice enacted by this figure is puzzling, I believe, only when read individualistically. Is Iago envious of the pleasure Othello enjoys with Desdemona, or is he jealous of Othello's sexual enjoyment of Emilia? Of course, both these ideas are purely conjectural hypotheses that have no apparent

bearing on Iago's actions. In any case there is no sustained commitment to either of these ideas, as numerous commentators have
pointed out. Nevertheless, there is an important clue to understanding Iago as a social agent in these transitory ruminations. Iago
seems to understand that the complex of envy and jealousy is not an
aberration within the socially distributed erotic economy, but
rather the fundamental pre-condition of desire itself. Erotic desire is
not founded in a qualitative economy or in a rational market, but
rather in a mimetic and histrionic dispensation that Iago projects as
the envy–jealousy system. In this system men are the social agents
and women the objects of exchange. Iago's actions are thus socially
motivated by a diffuse and pervasive misogyny that slides between
fantasies of the complete abjection of all women and fantasies of an
exclusively masculine world.

Iago's success in achieving these fantasies is made manifest in the
unbearably hideous tableau of the play's final scene. If the play as a
whole is to be read as a ritual of unmarrying, then this ending is the
monstrous equivalent of a sexual consummation. What makes the
play unendurable is the suspicion that this climax expresses all too
accurately an element present in the structure of every marriage.
This is an exemplary action in which the ideal of companionate
marriage as a socially sanctioned erotic union is dissolved back
into the chronic violence of the envy–jealousy system. Iago
theorizes erotic desire and thus marriage, primarily by a technique
of emptying out Othello's character, so that nothing is left at the
end except the pathetic theatrical integument, the madly deluded
and murderous black-faced clown. Desdemona, the perfect wife,
remains submissive to the end. And Iago, with his theoretical or
pedagogical tasks completed, accepts in silence his allocation to the
function of sacrificial victim and is sent off to face unnamed 'brave
punishments'.

The cultural text of charivari has had a durable life of its own,
especially in rural settings where it has from time to time been used
to police interracial marriages. Such events can have grim consequences. In *Roughing it in the Bush*, a journal of her life in upper
Canada in the 1830s, Susanna Moodie has devoted an entire
chapter to the custom of charivari, which was evidently common
throughout the region during this period. Moodie herself is unfamiliar with the practices of charivari, but her neighbor explains that
the Canadians 'got it from the French' in the Lower Province
(Moodie 1989: 208). After explaining the purposes of charivari and

the various functions of disguise, the neighbor recounts the following
example.

> There was a runaway nigger from the States came to the village,
> and set up a barber's poll, and settled among us. I am no friend
> to the blacks; but really Tom Smith was such a quiet, good-
> natured fellow, and so civil and obliging that he soon got a good
> business. . . . Well, after a time he persuaded a white girl to
> marry him. She was not a bad-looking Irishwoman, and I can't
> think what bewitched the creature to take him. The girl's
> marriage to the black man created a great sensation in the town.
> All the young fellows were indignant at his presumption and her
> folly, and they determined to give them the charivari in fine
> style, and punish them both for the insult they had put upon the
> place. Some of the young gentlemen in the town joined in the
> frolic. They went so far as to enter the house, drag the poor
> nigger from his bed, and in spite of his shrieks for mercy, they
> hurried him out into the cold air – for it was winter – and almost
> naked as he was, rode him upon a rail, and so ill-treated him
> that he died under their hands.
>
> (Moodie 1989: 210)

I am not suggesting here that the murder of 'Tom Smith' was in any
sense scripted from the text of *Othello*, though the insinuation that
the young Irishwoman must have been 'bewitched' is a suggestive
detail. What I do insist upon, however, is that both Moodie's
anecdote and any given performance of *Othello* necessarily express
the historical exigencies of race within the successor cultures of
Western modernity. The fate of Tom Smith's Irish wife is unknown.
It is nevertheless clear that the aim of the ringleaders was not only
to punish her, but also in a sense to rescue her from the consequences
of her own folly. The fantasy of rescue has also figured prominently
throughout the reception history of *Othello*.

RESCUING DESDEMONA

Othello is a text which severely tests the willingness of an audience to
suspend its disbelief, although the problem is not necessarily that the
situation can degenerate into farce. For many commentators it is
not the potentially ludicrous character of the action, but the exacerbated pathos of the ending that have provoked discomfort amounting to revulsion with this play. Horace Howard Furness found the

play horribly painful, and wished that Shakespeare had never written it (Furness 1922: 2,149). The problem was not simply that an innocent woman is murdered by her husband, though Furness was clearly very sensitive to the play's candid suggestions of erotic intimacy. His discomfiture is aggravated by the even more candid spectacle of miscegenation. Furness' *Variorum* edition of *Othello* was published in 1885, just twenty years after the end of the American Civil War. Although plantation slavery had been officially ended by the defeat of the South, race relations scarcely improved. This is the period of the rise of the Ku Klux Klan, and of other institutions that aimed to enforce racial separateness. In this context it is not altogether surprising that Furness would find the play unbearably difficult, or that he would yearn for some way to rescue Desdemona from her intolerable predicament.

One way to rescue Desdemona of course is simply to rewrite the story, so that Othello's stark blackness is modulated to a more acceptable and less threatening skin color. Edmund Kean was evidently the crucial innovator in this respect, repudiating the venerable tradition maintained by Betterton, Garrick, and Kemble, all of whom played Othello with black faces, in favor of a light brown that preserves a desirable exoticism without troubling the racial sensibilities of a white audience. By changing the makeup used to portray Othello's Moorishness, Kean solved the problem first hinted at in Rymer's critique and later articulated more emphatically by Charles Lamb.

> [Desdemona] sees Othello's colour in his mind. But . . . I appeal to every one that has seen *Othello* played, whether he did not . . . sink Othello's mind in his colour; whether he did not find something extremely revolting in the courtship and wedded caresses of Othello and Desdemona.
>
> (Lamb 1893: 191)

Lamb's solution to this insuperable difficulty is simply not to attend theatrical productions, which can only coarsen the response of the imagination to Shakespeare's works. It is much better to read the texts, and to permit the mind to 'overpower and reconcile the first and obvious prejudice' (Lamb 1893: 191).

For Lamb, 'the Moors are now well enough known to be by many shades the less unworthy of white woman's fancy' (1893: 191). Changing Othello's skin color and his racial identity does nothing, of course, to save Desdemona's life. It does, however, permit her to suffer death with her dignity intact, a thought that many readers have found consoling. Coleridge's assessment of Shakespeare's achievement in conceiving *Othello* depends on maintaining a sharp distinction between 'negro' and 'Moor'. 'It would be something monstrous to conceive this beautiful Venetian girl falling in love with a veritable negro' (Coleridge 1849: I, 42). As a 'negro', Othello must be read as a savage and a slave, and his murder of Desdemona is thus the expression of brutal passion. As a 'Moor', Othello is a warrior, and the murder, though tragically misguided, is nevertheless transmuted into a sacrifice made in the name of honor.

The amendment of Othello's color from black, to light brown, and finally to 'tawny' becomes the orthodox solution to the play's racial difficulties throughout the nineteenth and well into the twentieth century. The compromise settlement allows the play to be accommodated to the sensibilities of a white audience. It even makes possible a way to teach the play to young, southern women. In the volume of *Shakespeariana* for 1884, Professor William Taylor Thom arranges to publish the 'prize examination on the play of *Othello*' written by Miss Fanny E. Ragland, his pupil at Hollins Institute in Roanoke, Virginia. Among the many questions posed, Thom asks his students the following question: 'Do you agree with Schlegel's view, that Othello is of the African type?' Miss Ragland's response to this question is admirable for its clarity and directness.

> Othello is not of the African type, I think, either mentally and morally or physically. He is distinctly spoken of all through the play as a 'Moor,' and the Moors differed widely from the mere negroes in both intellect and color. Roderigo calls Othello '*Thick lips,*' but we must remember that he speaks as an unsuccessful rival. Othello is several times spoken of as 'black,' but then, as now, 'black' was often used of a dark complexion in contradistinction to a fair one. . . . Besides, there is something repulsive to my mind in the idea of a beautiful Venetian girl falling in love with an African prince, and Shakespeare would hardly have made Othello a prince if he had intended him for a negro.
>
> (Ragland 1884: 252)

Miss Ragland, closely following Coleridge, rescues Desdemona's honor by carefully distinguishing Moors from 'mere negroes'. Her use of this precise 'physical anthropology' opens up the possibility for much fuller interpretive response. Othello is 'a type of moral grandeur'; the killing of Desdemona is prompted not by jealousy, but by honor (p. 252). The 'final scene of agony' is the consequence of injured moral laws (p. 254). Ragland was well acquainted with the important critical literature on the play; she refers not only to Schlegel and to Coleridge, but to Johnson, Macauley, Wordsworth, and several times to Hudson. It's clear however, that the examination is something more than a purely academic exercise. Behind the always tactful and confident language of the examination it is easy to sense a deeper uneasiness occasioned by the politics of racial difference in the American South.

The critical revisions of Lamb and Coleridge, along with the theatrical innovations introduced by Kean, rescue Desdemona from the crude spectacle of miscegenation and vulgar domestic violence. At the same time they eradicate the comedy of abjection from the play, and thus absolve audiences of any need to confront their own racial attitudes. The motives that prompt this revisionary strategy are very complex. On one level it simply expresses commonly held racist beliefs in the naturally abject and servile nature of black Africans. At the same time, however, the bleaching of Othello's skin is a powerfully effective way to hide the truth of white racism. The slave trade was abolished in England and her colonies in 1807, though slavery persisted in the United States until Emancipation in 1865. In this context an honest production of *Othello* would be just as intolerable as an honest production of *The Merchant of Venice* in the post-Holocaust context. The rescue of Desdemona through the resources of nineteenth-century physical anthropology is a kind of misrecognition for a collective guilty conscience.

The transformation of Othello from a 'mere negro' into a caucasoid Moor saves Desdemona by suppressing the play's comedy of abjection and thus permitting a less difficult imaginative compromise. A more direct and violent form of rescue is described in the following anecdote recounted by Stendhal (1925).

> *L'année dernière (août 1822), le soldat qui était en faction dans l'intérieur du théâtre de Baltimore, voyant Othello qui, au cinquième acte de la tragédie de ce nom, allait tuer Desdemona, s'écria: 'Il ne sera jamais dit qu'en ma présence un maudit nègre aura tué une femme blanche.' Au même moment le soldat tire son coup de fusil, et casse un bras à l'acteur qui faisait Othello. Il ne se passe pas d'années sans que les journaux ne rapportent des faits semblables.*

[Last year (August of 1822), the soldier standing guard at the interior of the theater in Baltimore, seeing Othello who, in the fifth act of the tragedy of that name, was going to kill Desdemona, cried out 'It will never be said that in my presence a damned black would kill a white woman.' At that moment the soldier fired his gun, and broke the arm of the actor who played Othello. Not a year goes by withou newspapers reporting similar facts.]

(My translation)

The moral that Stendhal wants to draw from the story of the soldier in Baltimore is that only someone who is extremely ignorant or stupid – i.e. an American – fails to distinguish an actual murder from a dramatic representation of one. In the perhaps more definitive variant of the anecdote the performance takes place in a barn, and the unlucky actor playing Othello is not merely wounded but killed outright. In this version the soldier's behavior is less a matter of the 'perfect illusion' described by Stendhal than a militant defense of white women notwithstanding the fictional status of Desdemona's 'murder'.

It is difficult to confirm whether the Baltimore incident described by Stendahl in such circumstantial detail actually took place. There was, however, a theatrical riot in Paris at about the same time. A group of young French liberals hounded a troop of English performers off the stage with the cry *A bas Shakespeare, c'est un aide-de-camp du duc de Wellington!* The play scheduled for the night in question was almost certainly *Othello*. Conservatives at the time were appalled by the rioters' lack of civility, but the liberal press defended the protesters for their spirited defense of the national honor of France. Stendahl, who was otherwise sympathetic to the liberal position, none the less defended Shakespeare as the author of *chef-d'oeuvres de l'esprit humain* that transcend the lively but ephemeral conflicts inspired by nationalist feeling. Still, the nativist and chauvinistic strain of the protests should not be allowed to obscure the real sense of threatened group consciousness that inspired the protesters.

Stendahl's editor claims that the story of Othello's wounding by an outraged security guard in Baltimore is repeated in *l'Almanach des spectacles* for 1823, but there is no local corroboration for the story in any Maryland newspapers of this period. There is, however, an item in the *Maryland Republican and Political and Agricultural Museum* for 27 August 1822, concerning a violent attack on the 'African theater'.

Unmanly Outrage. – Saturday night a gang of fifteen or twenty ruffians, among whom was arrested and recognized one or more of the Circus riders, made an attack upon the *African Theater*, in Mercer-street, with full intent, as is understood, to break it up root and branch . . . entering the house by regular tickets, they proceeded, at quick time, to extinguish all the light in the house, and then to destroy every thing in the shape of furniture, scenery &c. . . . The actors and actresses, it is said, were fairly striped like so many squirrels, and their glittering apparel torn in pieces over their heads.

The reasons for the attack remain obscure, except for the tantalizing reference to 'Circus riders'. Was the incident prompted only by commercial rivalry and carried out by a group of itinerant performers? Or was it the expression of local sentiment, enforced by the actions of local thugs? The item reports only that several of the perpetrators were arrested, and that the public prosecutor would attempt to seek a compromise.

Stendahl may have conflated information about these two actual incidents to create the philosophically more interesting story about shooting Othello. The ideas of summary popular censorship and violent racial antagonism are related as crucial elements in the level of public tolerance of fictional provocations. Although the actual tale about the misguided soldier and the luckless actor in Baltimore may in all likelihood be itself a fiction, the *fantasy* of rescuing the beautiful Venetian girl from the clutches of a murderous black man has probably occurred more than once to various spectators in the history of the play's many performances. Such a fantasy has also been realized in a range of derivative forms.

Perhaps the most stirring and influential re-enactment of Desdemona's rescue is the ride of the Ku Klux Klan to save young Elsie Stoneman from a menacing black rapist in D. W. Griffith's *Birth of a Nation*. Here the story is re-told, as if from the point of view of Brabantio, as a forcible abduction rather than an elopement. Unless she were a completely abandoned whore, Desdemona/Elsie has no business 'seeing Othello's visage in his mind'. There is in principle no possibility for mutual attraction of any kind between racial opposites. And there is no question here of wishy-washy compromises with Othello's blackness. This is a much more severe rewrite of the play than the traditional nineteenth-century compromise that preserves the dignity of the characters by making Othello a 'tawny Moor'. Instead the film heightens and intensifies the radically antipathetic valences of black man and white woman in a sexual context. Elsie is virginal and completely defenceless. Her abductor represents the menace of black sexual aggression in the most crudely stereotypical way, without the extenuation of exotic origins and certainly without any trace of heroic dignity (Rogin 1985: 161ff.). Her rescue must therefore take the form of virile and direct action, as Elsie's captor is summarily punished by the outraged Klansmen.

Later films return more directly to *Othello* and to the way in which the story tends to breach the fragile boundary between actuality and make-believe. In George Cukor's *A Double Life* (1947), Ronald Coleman plays an actor who becomes obsessively preoccupied with his wife's infidelity as he rehearses the role of Othello. Here the iterative recitation of the dramatic text becomes internalized as the character becomes more fully identified with his theatrical role. The actor is literally possessed by Othello. André Forcier's *Une Histoire Inventée* (1990) develops the more farcical possibilities of the situation. In this film the roles of Othello and Desdemona are played by a young couple who are initially lovers in their off-stage existence. When she discovers her boy-friend with another woman she immediately ends the relationship, though they continue to work together in their theatrical capacity. In the meantime the play's chief financial backer becomes increasingly anguished over the suffering and death of 'beautiful Desdemona'. Each rehearsal is more painful than the last, until finally on opening night, during the final scene, he takes out a pistol and kills not only the murderous 'Othello', but 'Desdemona's's new lover as well. The recurring wish to prevent the catastrophe, to rewrite the play by disrupting its performance, has its partial basis in the equivocal ontological and social status of theater as a form of representation. The tension and uneasiness provoked by the ambiguous 'reality' of every theatrical performance is, however, greatly heightened in the case of *Othello*.

In his discussion of the ontological status of the theatrical representations, Stanley Cavell identifies *Othello* as the exemplary instance where acute theatrical discomfort may provoke an outright refusal of the *mise-en-scène*.

What is the state of mind in which we find the events in a theater neither credible nor incredible? The usual joke is about the

Southern yokel who rushes to the stage to save Desdemona from
the black man. What is the joke?

(Cavell 1987: 98ff.)

Cavell's willingness to take this joke seriously suggests that the
impulse to rescue Desdemona is not some sort of fantastical aberration, but is in fact a response common to a great many (male?)
viewers. Something real is at stake for the audience of *Othello*, even
though the actual performance of the play depends on recognition
of its status as a fiction.

At the opening of the play it is fully true that I neither believe nor
disbelieve. But I am something, perplexed, anxious . . . . Much
later, the warrior asks his wife if she has said her prayers. Do I
believe he will go through with it? I know he will; it is a certainty
fixed forever; but I hope against hope he will come to his senses;
I appeal to him, in silent shouts. Then he puts his hands on her
throat. The question is: What, if anything, do I do? I do nothing;
that is a certainty fixed forever. And it has its consequences. *Why*
do I do nothing? Because they are only pretending? . . . Othello is
not pretending.

(Cavell 1987: 100)

Does Cavell want to suggest that the Southern yokel is somehow
doing the right thing, and that performances of *Othello* should hence-
forth be disrupted? Such disruption is not actually recommended
here, but Cavell is willing to take such a possibility seriously in order
to point out that such a violation of theatrical etiquette has substantive moral content. But if this is true, then behaving properly in
a theater also has a moral content *vis-à-vis* the action represented.

Cavell does not push the argument to the point of suggesting that
knowing how to make-believe and agreeing to acquiesce in the
social conventions of performance here is the moral equivalent of
complicity in a murder. On the contrary, the disruption of the
mise-en-scène would really be a trivial gesture, since the murder will
take place no matter what anyone does at any given theatrical performance. For, as Cavell puts it, 'Quiet the house, pick up the
thread again, and Othello will reappear, as near and as deaf to us as
ever. – The transcendental and the empirical crossing; possibilities
shudder from it' (p. 101). Cavell does want to make himself and his
readers accountable for their response as moral agents to what the
play discloses, and therefore he must insist on the element of consent

and affirmation that theater demands from the members of an audience.

Given the painful nature of the story, the history of both the interpretation and the performance of *Othello* has been characterized by a search for explanations that allow the show to go on. These consoling interpretations usually work to prevent disruptions of the play in performance. Nevertheless, the history of anguished responses to this play signals a chronic unwillingness amounting at times to outright refusal to participate in the performance of a play as the ritual or quasi-ritual affirmation of certain social practices. *Othello* occupies a problematic situation at the boundary between ritually sanctioned reality and theatrically consensual fiction. Does the play simply depict an inverted ritual of courtship and marriage, or does its performance before an audience that accepts it status as a fiction also invite complicity in a social ritual of comic abjection, humiliation, and victimization? At a time when large-scale social consequences of racist sensibilities had not yet become visible, it may well have been easy to accept the formal codes of charivari as the expression of legitimate social norms. In later contexts of reception it is not so easy to accept *Othello* in the form of a derisory ritual of racial persecution, because the social experience of racial difference has become such a massive scandal.

Finita la commedia. What does it mean to accept the *mise-en-scène* of this play? And what does it mean to *know* that we wish it could be otherwise? To the extent that we want to see a man and a woman defying social conventions in order to fulfill mutual erotic initiatives, the play will appear as a thwarted comedy and our response will be dominated by its pathos. But the play also shows us what such mutual erotic initiatives look like from the outside, as a comedy of abjection or charivari. The best commentators on this play have recognized the degree to which it prompts a desire to prevent the impending débâcle and the sense in which it is itself a kind of theatrical punishment for the observers (Burke 1951; Neely 1980; Parker 1985; Stallybrass 1986). This helpless and agonized refusal of the *mise-en-scène* should suggest something about the corrosive effect on socially inscribed rituals of a radical or 'cruel' theatricality.

The idea of theatrical cruelty is linked to the radical aesthetics of Antonin Artaud. However, the English term 'cruelty' fails to capture an important inflection that runs through all of Artaud's discussion of theater. The concept is derived from words that mean 'raw' or 'unprocessed'. In French, *'cruauté'* expresses with even greater candour this relationship with 'le cru' and its opposition to 'le cuit'. Cruelty here has the sense of something uncooked, or something prior to the process of a conventional social transformation or adoption into the category of the meaningful (Artaud 1958: 42 *et passim*). *Othello*, perhaps more than any other Shakespeare play, raises fundamental questions about the institutional position and aesthetic character of Shakespearean dramaturgy. Is Shakespeare raw – or is he cooked? Is it possible that our present institutional protocol for interpreting his work is a way of 'cooking' the 'raw' material to make it more palatable, more fit for consumption?

The history of the reception of *Othello* is the history of attempts to articulate ideologically correct, that is, palatable interpretations. By screening off the comedy of abjection it is possible to engage more affirmatively with the play's romantic *Liebestod*. Within these strategies, critics may find an abundance of meanings for the tragic dimension of the play. In this orientation the semantic fullness of the text is suggested as a kind of aesthetic compensation for the cruelty of it final scenes. Rosalie Colie, for example, summarizes her interpretation with an account of the play's edifying power.

> In criticizing the artificiality he at the same time exploits in his play, Shakespeare manages in *Othello* to reassess and to reanimate the moral system and the psychological truths at the core of the literary love-tradition, to reveal its problematics and to reaffirm in a fresh and momentous context the beauty of its impossible ideals.
>
> (Colie 1974: 167)

This is recognizably the language of the ritual misrecognition of what the play as a comedy of abjection is capable of theorizing. The fullness of the play, of course, is what makes it possible for viewers and readers to participate, however unwillingly, in the charivari or ritual victimization of the imaginary heterosexual couple represented here. Such consensual participation is morally disquieting in the way it appears to solicit at least passive consent to violence against women and against outsiders, but at least we are not howling with unsympathetic laughter at their suffering and humiliation.

Colie's description of the play's semantic fullness is based in part on her concept of 'un-metaphoring' – that is, the literalization of a metaphorical relationship or conventional figuration. This is a moderate version of the notion of theatrical cruelty or the unmaking

Chapter 8

Calvin and Hobbes, or what was democracy

I don't take no stock in dead people.

(Huckleberry Finn)

In *Characters of Shakespear's Plays*, William Hazlitt proclaims 'It is *we* who are Hamlet', though without specifying very clearly just who is to be included by the emphatic first person plural (Hazlitt 1817: 105). Emerson urges even more forcefully that Hamlet represents the 'speculative genius' of a rapidly developing modernity (Emerson 1968: 127). These vague but in many ways crucial intuitions receive more detailed and explicit articulation in the writings of François Guizot.

> Hamlet alone presents the confused spectacle of a mind formed by the enlightenment of society, in conflict with a position contrary to its laws; and he needs a supernatural apparition to determine to act, and a fortuitous event to accomplish his project . . . the world now presents to the poet minds like Hamlet's, deep in the observation of those inward conflicts which our classical system has derived from a state of society more advanced than that of the time in which Shakespeare lived. So many feelings, interests, and ideas, the necessary consequences of modern civilization, might become, even in their simplest form of expression, a troublesome burden.

> (Guizot 1821/1852: 178–179)

Guizot came to Shakespeare in the course of an active political career in various ministries of the French government. His career was devoted to efforts to establish a constitutional basis for democracy, during the prolonged and complicated aftermath of the French Revolution. He was convinced that seventeenth-century

England offered an exemplary model for the growth of democratic institutions, and he spent the latter part of his life in political retirement writing a series of historical studies about these developments. His earlier work on Shakespeare was an important element in the formation of his larger political projects, partly because Guizot saw in theater a fundamental resource for mobilization and articulation of the popular collective will. As the quotation suggests, Hamlet has a vividly distinctive role to play in Guizot's own larger drama, namely the struggle to bring into existence the institutions of modern, Western liberal democracy.

In many ways Hamlet really does represent with extraordinary clarity the unencumbered, deeply reflective subjectivity that figures so prominently in nineteenth-century political theory. The agonizing pathos of that subjectivity is acknowledged in Bertolt Brecht's *A Short Organum for the Theatre*, written in Zurich in 1948 towards the end of Brecht's lengthy career after the catastrophic upheavals of the Second World War.

> Given the dark and bloody period in which I am writing – the criminal ruling classes, the widespread doubt in the power of reason, continually being misused – I think that I can read the story thus: It is an age of warriors . . . the young Hamlet is summoned by his warrior father's ghost to avenge the crime committed against him. After at first being reluctant to answer one bloody deed by another, and even preparing to go into exile, he meets young Fortinbras at the coast. . . . Overcome by this warrior like example, he turns back and in a piece of barbaric butchery he slaughters his uncle, his mother and himself. . . . These events show the young man . . . making the most ineffective use of the new approach to reason which he has picked up at the University of Wittenberg. In the feudal business to which he returns it simply hampers him.
>
> (Brecht 1964: 201)

Brecht's reading of *Hamlet*, as with his reading of Shakespeare generally, has been controversial. The interpretation proposed here is linked to his larger program of *Verfremdung* or 'alienation', a program with frankly political and strongly partisan aims.

Brecht understood theater as not only and not even principally an art form, especially in the sense given to notions of art and the aesthetic within the actually existing conditions of his own time. He construed theater in a radically non-aesthetic way as an element in the ensemble of productive forces. This entails a rejection of notions of the autonomy of art. Brecht's argument takes up a frankly pragmatic view of dramatic art as a strategically oriented social practice. The heuristic value of 'the old works' is, however, based on a carefully delimited belief in historical continuity. There is never, for Brecht, a complete and utter break with the past; we are the children of earlier cultural formations, and in fact share some of the feelings expressed in these earlier works (Brecht 1965: 16). On this view the work of art may appear difficult, inaccessible, or even unintelligible, but it is not in the end fundamentally alien. With the right sort of critical alacrity and discernment even the most archaic works can be made to serve contemporary interests. For Brecht, however, the contemporary value of the past can only be realized by means of active and disciplined political commitment.

The 'alienation effect' is a heuristic protocol rather than a set of stylistic devices. The crucial element here is what Brecht calls 'the exposition'; other features of Brechtian theater, such as the suppression of empathy or baring the device, are clearly secondary to this fundamental principle.

> What needs to be alienated, and how this is to be done, depends on the exposition demanded by the entire episode; and this is where the theater has to speak up decisively for the interests of its own time.
>
> (Brecht 1964: 201)

The small-time element of transitoriness or topical currency has a positive value in Brecht's view of dramatic art. Knowing what needs to be alienated implies that an old play text can have a precise historical moment of truth, and that the epic theater is above all a kind of alertness towards that moment. This is what is meant by the theater 'speaking up for the interests of its own time'.

A work of Shakespeare's, like 'the old play *Hamlet*', continues to have a socially significant afterlife in the prolonged and complicated aftermath of the Second World War. Brecht's own precise sense of the interests of his own time have in many ways been fatally compromised by more recent historical developments. Ironically, the actual terms of his reading of *Hamlet* may prove far more durable than any of his larger projects. Brecht's *Hamlet* is, of course, not fundamentally different from the *Hamlet* of the nineteenth century. The character of Hamlet and his extraordinary predicament continue to reflect a distinctively modern experience of subjectivity.

This is apparent not only in the recent theatrical history of the play, but also and even more emphatically in powerfully derivative forms such as Müller's *Hamletmaschine* or in the endless proliferation of parodies in episodes of *Gilligan's Island*, *Happy Days*, or *The L.A. Story*. Hamlet's resources are those of an unencumbered, sovereign subject with exceptional powers of intellect and imagination. In the event, however, these resources are precisely the liabilities of a deracinated and fatally disoriented modern agency, unable to confront the massive encumbrances of its own historical past. The irresistibly seductive melancholy of Hamlet continues to resonate through contemporary popular culture, because Hamlet continues to explain who and what we are. Or, as Walt Kelly's Pogo puts it, 'we have met the enemy, and he is us'.

THE FIRST TIME AS HISTORY

As Stanley Cavell and other critics have pointed out, the theme of succession within the family and the nation is of paramount importance in many of Shakespeare's plays. In *Hamlet*, succession is enacted in relation to the complexity of social time and collective memory. As Horatio points out in his explanation to the sentries, a problematic and contested succession accounts for the elaborate military preparations that they have witnessed, and in all likelihood for the appearance of the ghost as well.

> HORATIO: our last king,
> Whose image even now appeared to us,
> Was, as you know, by Fortinbras of Norway,
> Thereto pricked on by a most emulate pride,
> Dared to the combat; in which our valiant Hamlet
> (For so this side of our known world esteemed him)
> Did slay this Fortinbras, who by a sealed compact
> Well ratified by law and heraldry,
> Did forfeit (with his life) all [those] his lands
> Which he stood seized of, to the conqueror;
> Against the which a moiety competent
> Was gaged by our king, which had [returned]
> To the inheritance of Fortinbras,
> Had he been vanquisher; as by the same comart
> And carriage of the article [designed]

His fell to Hamlet. Now, sir, young Fortinbras,
Of unimproved mettle hot and full,
Hath in the skirts of Norway here and there
Sharked up a list of lawless resolutes
For food and diet to some enterprise
That hath a stomach in't, which is no other,
As it doth well appear unto our state,
But to recover of us, by strong hand
And terms compulsatory, those foresaid lands
So by his father lost.

(1.1.80–104)

The notion of 'emulate pride' that motivates this conflict is
elaborated in the vocabulary of a 'sealed compact' that spells out
the terms under which the estate of the two kings can be altered
according to the outcome of the battle. Horatio interprets these
arrangements in the framework of contractual obligation. On
Horatio's understanding the relationship between the two kings is
based on a formal agreement that stipulates the terms of a final
settlement or audit of their differences. Once the deal goes down,
title to property is to change hands once and for all, as in the case of
an outright sale.

According to Horatio, young Fortinbras proceeds in lawless dis-
regard of prior binding agreements. Fortinbras himself, on the other
hand, evidently bases his actions on the more complex and open-
ended law of reciprocity characteristic of a gift economy. The
imperatives of gift exchange demand that all gifts must in time be
repaid, though this repayment will usually require a significant
interval of time to pass before it can be accomplished. It is important to realize here that the dynamic of the gift includes *both* the
obligation of repayment for benefits received *and* the redress of
injuries or grievances. Horatio prefers to read past events according
to an official history that considers the conflict between Norway and
Denmark in terms of a fixed and permanent settlement of national
boundaries. Young Fortinbras remembers these same events within
the more personal ethical dispensation of a warrior society, where
the gift of his father's violent death must be returned in some
manner to the giver.

The position of the sentries in this context is interesting. Although
they are soldiers on active duty for the Danish King, they nevertheless have to ask Horatio to inform them about the obvious national

crisis evident in what he describes as 'post-haste and romage in the land' (1.1.107). Even Marcellus, an officer in the palace guard, has evidently not been officially briefed, though he is clearly shrewd and experienced enough to realize that something out of the ordinary is going on. The founding of artillery, the construction of ships, and the heightened military alerts all point unmistakably to impending military conflict on a large scale. Ordinary soldiers like Francisco, Bernardo, and Marcellus have no access to fuller knowledge about these military preparations because there simply is nothing like a public sphere, no institutional forms of publicity, which would supply them with appropriate information. News circulates only in a haphazard and fortuitous manner, through hearsay, rumor, and insider accounts. Horatio interprets the news by looking at the recent history of Denmark and Norway. The ghost of 'the king that's dead' suggests that current events are not so easily or so rationally explicable.

The ghost has a message to impart, exactly as the sentries suspect, though that message is not a matter for the public record. The ghost returns not as a king with an interest in matters of national policy, but as a father with a very particular burden to impose on a son. Prince Hamlet's deeply troubled sense that he is under an obligation to the past is, of course, elaborately developed and ostentatiously foregrounded throughout the play. The full moral implications of this obligation never become exactly clear to him. What precisely is owed to the past, and why are its injunctions binding on present actions? Lawrence Becker interprets this larger philosophical question in terms of reciprocity and the obligation to make appropriate return for gifts received. But what are the gifts Hamlet has received from the past? He says he loved his father, but, as Harold Bloom has pointed out, we are never given any indication that his father loved him (Bloom 1990a: 3). Hamlet's sense of filial obligation does not have its source in memories of fatherly affection and companionship. That feeling arises instead from Hamlet's deeply held conviction that his father was an exemplary figure of courage and probity; these are the goods that demand reciprocity.

Hamlet's actual memories of affection and personal warmth appear to come from another, quite incongruous source.

> HAMLET: Alas, poor Yorick! I knew him, Horatio, a fellow of in-
> finite jest, of most excellent fancy. He hath borne me on his back
> a thousand times, and now how abhorred in my imagination it is!

my gorge rises at it. Here hung those lips that I have kissed I
know not how oft. Where be your gibes now? Your gambols, your
songs, your flashes of merriment that were wont to set the table
on a roar?

(5.1.185–193)

In an important sense Yorick is Hamlet's real father, and under the
law of reciprocity he is obligated to make return for the 'flashes of
merriment' he remembers. It could be argued that Hamlet does
exactly this throughout the play. Hamlet's 'antic disposition' is a
continuation of the past as he takes up the role of court jester. As
Yorick's 'son', Hamlet embodies the radical and grotesque tradition
of the carnivalesque not only in speech and behavior, but also in his
fundamental way of understanding the social world (Bristol 1994:
359–363). Carnival is based on a principle of distributive justice in
which social goods are to achieve the widest possible circulation in
the long run. But carnival is also a process of violent expulsion of
everything that is moribund or resented in social life. Hamlet's
clowning masks a sinister and murderous intent.

There is, then, a darker side to the law of reciprocity, and Hamlet
evokes this in his encounter with the players, who supply him with
another point of contact with early modern popular culture.
Hamlet has a particularly vivid memory of a speech he heard the
first player make, about Priam's slaughter. He recites the first few
lines to cue his friends' performance:

HAMLET: The rugged Pyrrhus, like th' Hyrcanian beast –
'Tis not so, it begins with Pyrrhus:
The rugged Pyrrhus, he whose sable arms,
Black as his purpose, did the night resemble
When he lay couched in th' ominous horse,
Hath now this dread and black complexion smeared
With heraldry more dismal: head to foot
Now is he total gules, horridly tricked
With blood of fathers, mothers, daughters, sons,
Baked and impasted with the parching streets,
That lend a tyrannous and a damned light
To their lord's murther.

(2.2.450–461)

It is significant that Hamlet must struggle to remember these lines,
because in this evidently literary recollection lies an important

element of self-recognition. Hamlet is himself a sable-armed father-revenger destined to be 'horridly tricked/With blood of fathers, mothers, daughters, sons', though the point of this connection seems to escape him at just this moment. The image of 'rugged Pyrrhus' links up with Horatio's account of 'emulate pride', and with the ethos of honor and retribution that governs international conflict. It also mandates the more strictly personal tasks of retaliation assumed by sons against the murderers of their fathers. As we see again when the players perform 'The Murder of Gonzago', Hamlet is himself an iterative figure in an interminable fugue of revenge and retribution.

The ending of *Hamlet* is interesting in this respect because the total carnage on stage leaves no one to carry out the obligations of reciprocity that would eventually make this new Fortinbras the object of further retaliation. The final settling of accounts, if that is what this is, has been made possible by an earlier, unforeseen consequence of some of Hamlet's own actions.

> QUEEN: Sweets to the sweet, farewell!
> I hoped thou shouldst have been my Hamlet's wife.
> I thought thy bride-bed to have decked, sweet maid,
> And not have strewed thy grave.
>
> (5.1.242–245)

This moment is connected with an earlier linking of wedding and funeral rites in Claudius' official proclamation of his marriage with Gertrude, and with the frankly carnivalesque linkage of life with death so disturbing to Hamlet in his odd and troubling image of 'funeral baked meats' that 'did coldly furnish forth the marriage table' (Bristol 1994: 356).

The law of reciprocity, it would appear, entails two binding obligations, namely retaliation or the redress of injuries and reproduction or social continuity. More specifically, the idea of an obligation to the past seems to carry with it some sort of orientation to the future. Hamlet, of course, has decreed that there will be no more marriages, hoping by this means to prevent any future betrayal of the past. In a sense he is successful, though exactly what the future holds for Denmark is unclear. Hamlet's death clears the way for young Fortinbras to secure his claim to the Danish throne. Since the Danish lineage is now extinct, the chain of serial reciprocity and revenge may come to its end.

FORTINBRAS: For me, with sorrow I embrace my fortune.
I have some rights, of memory in this kingdom,
Which now to claim my vantage doth invite me.

(5.2.388–390)

Fortinbras has his rights. Memory here serves to buttress his sense of political entitlement rather than any compelling feelings of ethical obligation. What matters to Fortinbras are strategic alertness and *force majeure* that make it possible for him to cash in on an opportunity. Hamlet dies with the more modest but tenuous hope that someone will get his story straight.

Hamlet's sense of obligation to the past is cobbled together from the ghostly injunction of a dead father, from memories of a dead jester, and from literary recollections of classical antiquity. As most commentators have seen, these complex obligations are in fundamental conflict with Hamlet's extraordinary capacity for critical reflection. Despite the 'ineffective use' he makes of 'the new approach to reason', the seductive promise of the fully sovereign, self-determining subjectivity Hamlet represents is what accounts for this character's hold on the modern imagination. The accession of Fortinbras seems a trifling compensation for the loss of Hamlet, whatever it may do by way of setting things right in the troubled state of Denmark. Fortinbras may be what is politically necessary or expedient, but he is simply not interesting in narrative terms. Hamlet, on the other hand, continues to be the source and provocation for an abundant derivative creativity.

When Emerson maintained that Shakespeare drew 'the father of the man in America' he may well have intended his readers to think specifically of Hamlet as a son unable to come to terms with binding imperatives insisted upon by a ghostly father. In political terms Hamlet occupies the subject position of the colonist who can neither fully reject nor fully embrace the traditions of the mother country. For Emerson, Hamlet's 'speculative genius' is nothing less than the prototype for the achievements of nineteenth-century science and for the creativity of its social innovations, especially in the United States. In this recognition of Hamlet as his own precursor, however, Emerson selectively ignores the disaster towards which 'speculative genius' is ultimately drawn, evidently believing that the social formations of modernity emerging in America would be successful in disburdening themselves of traditional obligations to the past by means of critical intelligence and radical originality. The burdens imposed by past history are not, however, so easily discharged, particularly in the deracinated and hyperactive variant of modernity characteristic of America.

Leslie Fiedler, no doubt following the suggestions of Emerson, has argued that the two Shakespearean characters who figure most prominently in America's 'deep imagination' are Hamlet and Caliban (Fiedler 1966: 23). Fiedler argues that for Europeans, secure in their social and cultural traditions, Americans can only appear as rebellious slaves; that is, as Caliban. Americans themselves, and most especially American writers, view themselves instead as wronged or dispossessed sons. Hamlet's melancholy, his sense of grievance, is internalized as 'an unanswerable revolt against inherited obligations' (p. 26). These two characters articulate forms of consciousness that take shape within the dialectic of an archaic European past alternately embraced and resisted by an emerging American cultural dispensation. Hamlet as the son unable to come to terms with the injunction of a ghostly father occupies the position of a newly settled immigrant who can neither wholly reject nor wholly carry on the traditions of the 'old country'. Caliban, on the other hand, as many scholars have come to realize in recent years, is the non-white, non-European man whom Fiedler sees most emphatically in the '[American] Negro . . . the living embodiment of that absolute Other dreamed by Europeans – sometimes sympathetically, more often in fascinated horror' (p. 25). In the interactive relationship between these two figures Fiedler sees a durable pattern of motives operative throughout American culture.

> [Caliban symbolizes] a desire to re-establish culture on a denial of that Western cosmopolitanism whose political face is White Imperialism. . . . While Europeans tend to think of us mythologically as rebellious slaves [i.e. Caliban] which is to say, politically and in the context of society, we need to regard ourselves as wronged sons, [i.e. Hamlet] which is to say, psychologically and in the context of the family.
>
> (p. 26)

Fiedler views this rather schematic mythology as a kind of dark prophecy. Neither Hamlet nor Caliban can escape the narrative logics in which they are inscribed. Hamlet always postpones revenge, always bungles its execution, and then achieves it but only suicidally. Caliban's plan to overthrow his master is always defeated.

In Fiedler's sketch of American literary history, the figure of Hamlet reappears most vividly in Melville's Pierre but also in Poe's Roderick Ussher, Hawthorne's Dimmesdale, Faulkner's Quentin Compson, and Bellows' Herzog (pp. 25–26). Hamlet is even suggested as the archetype for Lee Harvey Oswald. Caliban, by contrast, anticipates the rebellious energy and resentment not only of African-American writers, but also of figures like Whitman or Alan Ginsburg. The 'Hamlet–Caliban paradox' endures in the American imagination because Europe's first gift to the new society taking shape in America was plantation slavery (p. 27). These tensions are nowhere more powerfully imagined than in that most popular of nineteenth-century derivative *Hamlets*, Mark Twain's *The Adventures of Huckleberry Finn*. Fiedler never mentions this text, though it is precisely here that Hamlet-Huck and Caliban-Jim join forces for a time and attempt to escape from 'sivilization'.

Twain's highly idiosyncratic relationship with Shakespeare as an origin is suggested in his deeply equivocal handling of the authorship question. His view of this problem is given full elaboration in a text with the provocative title *Is Shakespeare Dead?* Originally a long section of Twain's *Autobiography*, this extended essay appeared in volume form in 1909 and was republished again in 1917 as part of a collection with the equally suggestive title *What Is Man?* Twain's strategy is to use the relative paucity of documentation and biographical detail as evidence that Shakespeare, the player manager who spent half of his life in Stratford, was not the real author of the plays circulated under his name.

> When Shakespeare died in 1616, great literary productions attributed to him as author had been before the London world and in high favor for twenty-four years. Yet his death was not an event. It made no stir, it attracted no attention. Apparently his eminent literary contemporaries did not realize that a celebrated poet had passed from their midst. Perhaps they knew a play-actor of minor rank had disappeared, but did not regard him as the author of his Works.
>
> (Twain 1909: 27)

It is extremely difficult to know what to make of Twain's position in the Shakespeare–Bacon authorship controversy, since the text of *Is Shakespeare Dead?* is an exceptionally vertiginous piece of serio-comic writing. At various points Twain indicates that his motives are just a perverse desire to take the 'opposing side' or to challenge dogmatic authority that supports itself by combining scant pieces of evidence with abundant conjecture and inference. At another point, in a discussion of 'irreverence', he ends up claiming for himself the exclusive privilege of determining what will be recognized as sacred and canonical. Authority is dogmatic, evidently, when it is someone else's.

As a self-appointed authority, Twain (pseudonym 'Samuel Clemens') devotes certain chapters to 'claimants historically notorious'. These 'claimants' include, among others, Satan, Mary Baker Eddy, and William Shakespeare, all founders of spurious cults, unlike Samuel Clemens himself, the honest debunker of false claimants. At the beginning of the penultimate chapter of this very odd book he asks, 'Am I trying to convince anybody that Shakespeare did not write Shakespeare's *Works*? Ah, now what do you take me for?' (Twain 1909: 56). What would be the use of such a project, he suggests, in light of the irrational character of traditional 'knowledge' and the credulity of the human race?

The point of this discussion of Shakespeare's authorship is that it really makes no difference whether Mark Twain believes that Shakespeare wrote the plays or whether he believes that Bacon wrote them, since beliefs are in any case beyond the reach of rational argument. The real question raised by asking 'Is Shakespeare Dead?' has to do with the search for and the confirmation of origins. Shakespeare is disqualified as an origin on the grounds that he is a mere copy-cat in his efforts to reproduce a diversity of speech types; in other words, that his 'shop-talk' is mostly unconvincing and second-hand. By the same token his grasp of legal vocabularies and courtroom idiom are *too* convincing and lifelike to have been written by anyone without extensive legal experience. Therefore Bacon wrote the plays. The argument is transparently nonsensical but what makes it almost compelling is its maniacal insistence on discovering the 'real' or 'hidden' origins: the origin of the origin so to speak. In this sense it reproduces, probably unintentionally, a distinctively American fundamentalist paranoia, a paranoia of absolute beginnings. The real point of the argument is the displacement of the spurious claimant – Shakespeare – by the authentic origin – Bacon. The story doesn't have to be true; it works just as well if it is only make-believe. What Twain wants to do is assert his own priority. William Shakespeare the false claimant was not much thought of by his neighbors. The genuine claimant (Clemens) left

Hannibal, Missouri when he was only 15 years old, but he is still fondly remembered by his schoolfellows.

Twain's effrontery – 'I am a bigger celebrity than Shakespeare ever was' – is one answer to 'Is Shakespeare Dead?' The other, equally important answer is provided in Twain's account of George Ealer, his commanding officer on the steamboat *Pennsylvania* and an ardent amateur and scholar of Shakespeare. Ealer's gift was his ability to recite Shakespeare from memory and to simultaneously give commands, so that his own discursive mastery over the idiom of river boat piloting blended into the poetry in one common Shakespeare effect. George Ealer was a true amateur of Shakespeare, and Twain speaks with respect and admiration of his ability to recite passages from the plays while engaged in the intricacies of river boat navigation. A different, much darker view of Shakespeare appears in *Huckleberry Finn*.

In his essay on 'politics', published in 1844, Emerson quotes Fisher Ames' comparison of a monarchy and a republic: 'a monarchy is a merchantman, which sails well, but will sometimes strike a rock and go to the bottom; whilst a republic is a raft, which would never sink, but then your feet are always in the water' (Emerson 1987: 341). The raft as the symbol of a republic, inconvenient, inefficient, but unsinkable, a durable form precisely because of its ramshackle construction and unstable behavior, receives its full imaginative elaboration in Mark Twain's *Huckleberry Finn*. The raft is, of course, invaded by monarchy in the persons of the Duke and the Dauphin, and, along with other cultural baggage, these two representative men bring with them a version of Shakespeare quite different from the one admired and idealized by Emerson. Mark Twain's carnivalized reconstruction of Shakespeare is very carefully positioned within his equally carnivalized reconstruction of America. These reconstructions represent a critical refusal of Emersonian optimism.

In the discussion that follows, *Huckleberry Finn* will not be analyzed as an affirmative text of nineteenth-century American culture or of freedom and individuality as the ideological legitimation of that culture. The journey down the Mississippi River is not a liberating and ultimately hopeful rite of passage for Huck, but rather the utter defeat of his hopes, nebulous and inarticulate as these may be. The raft drifts, mainly in the wrong direction, ever deeper into an America bound over to residual forms of feudal violence and racial oppression, until in the end Huck is recaptured for 'sivilization' by

Tom Sawyer, the ideologue and legitimator of American 'piracy'. Huck, who is endlessly resourceful on the raft, is maladroit and uncomprehending in most situations on land, and his final escapade amounts to a pointless and sadistic parody of the emancipatory impulse that begins his adventure.

Huck's adventures begin when he determines to escape from 'Pap', whose authority has become increasingly violent and threatening. Pap objectifies the resentment of the economically and culturally excluded, a resentment expressed in his hatred of upper-class white society and of the 'free nigger from Ohio'. That resentment takes on quasi-mythical proportions, however, once Pap and Huck are isolated in their remote and lonely shack. In his drunken rage, Pap forces Huck to participate in a manic and deplorable re-enactment of the sacrifice of Isaac. Pap, a demented and farcical Abraham, pursues an unwilling and terrified Huck/Isaac with a knife until he drops unconscious, exhausted by his efforts. Huck, as the son who is to be sacrificed, places no trust either in his father or his father's god, and so he must see to the provision of a substitute sacrificial victim on his own. The substitute victim is not a ram, but a wild pig, obtained not through divine intervention but by laborious effort. Huck's improvisatory revision of the Abraham-Isaac story allows him to escape from a baleful and violent covenant, to renounce entirely all patriarchal authority, and to make 'a complete exit from the present order of life'.

The patriarchal order that Huck flees entails both the hier-archization of social life, and a fear of the malevolent dead, whom, Pap asserts, are 'coming after me'. Huck knows he must flee from this dispensation but his sense of where he is going is much less sure. Solidarity and harmonious communal life are achieved by Huck and Jim on the raft, though the raft can hardly be thought of as a destination. But although the comradeship of the fugitives does suggest utopian harmony, the text makes clear the utter impossibility of achieving those possibilities.

The citizens of this fragile and ephemeral republic are not heroes either of an affirmative or a counter-cultural success story. In *Huckleberry Finn*, a fugitive Hamlet and a fugitive Caliban jointly engineer an escape from their oppressive master narratives. The two characters represent contrasting cognitive styles that comple-ment each other in their mutual emancipatory project. Huck's self-reflecting, speculative consciousness is most frequently divided against itself as he adjudicates between the demands of a social orthodoxy that requires him to betray Jim to his 'owners' and the affective loyalties he feels towards his companion. Huck's attempt to 'educate' Jim by transmitting the knowledge he has of history and world culture are met by Jim's characteristic 'refusal to understand', an intellectual strategy with its own incisive force. When Huck tries to explain kingship, for example, Jim replies with his exegesis of the 'wisdom of Solomon'.

> I's Sollermun: en dish-yer dollar bill's de chile. Bofe un you claims it. What does I do? Does I shin aroun' mongs' de neighbors en fine out which un you de bill do b'long to, en han' it over to de right one, all safe en soun', de way dat anybody dat had any gumption would? No – I take en whack de bill in two . . . I reckon I knows sense when I sees it; en dey ain't no sense in sich doin's as dat. De 'spute warn't 'bout half a chile, de 'spute was 'bout a whole chile; end de man dat think he kin settle a 'spute 'bout a whole chile wid a half a chile, doan know enough to com in out'n de rain.
>
> (Twain 1986: 83)

This is the uncrowning of traditional scriptural authority by everyday practical consciousness; Jim firmly rejects Huck's inference that he has missed the point, arguing that he isn't interested in points, but only in sense. Despite this canny refusal to be taken in by allegorical narrative, however, Jim is not immunized against fraud and humbug when they appear on the raft in the persons of the Duke and the Dolphin.

Huck and Jim trust the raft as a haven from the violence and oppression prevalent on shore. The dangers of land-based culture invade the raft in the persons of the Duke and the Dolphin. Two aspects of these characters are central to understanding their critical function within the novel. First, they claim to represent the traditional ruling classes of Europe. As a corollary to this they also claim to represent the traditional culture of Europe, embodied most significantly in their knowledge of Shakespeare. Second, they represent the dissimulation at the heart of the dispensation of accumulation form in its most fraudulent, meretricious, and piratical manifestations. There's no business except show business. Shakespeare means something very different here from what is imagined in the philosophy of Emerson. In the discourse of the Duke and the Dolphin Shakespeare has been transmuted from a transcendent cultural authority to a repertoire of profitable speeches and gestures.

That repertoire is organized by the device paradigm to generate immediate profit rather than to reproduce the complexity of Shakespeare's originality, whether in Emerson's or in some other sense.

The Duke and the Dolphin illustrate the importance of the device paradigm as they begin to train Huck as a boy actor.

> THE KING: Hamlet's soliloquy. you know; the most celebrated thing in Shakespeare. Ah, it's sublime, sublime! Always fetches the house.
>
> HUCK: So he went to marching up and down, thinking, and frowning horrible every now and then; then he would hoist up his eyebrows; next he would squeeze his hand on his forehead and stagger back and kind of moan; next he would sigh, and next he'd let drop a tear. It was beautiful to see him.
>
> (Twain 1986: 150)

The King's version of 'Hamlet's soliloquy' is an obvious satire on pretentious actors who have no idea what they are saying, and are only concerned with producing impressive histrionic effects. It is, incidentally, a satire on the credulity of audiences. Mark Twain's own views of Shakespeare in performance were quite complicated. In an early theater review he expressed concern over a visit to San Francisco by Edwin Forrest.

> In God's name let him stay where he is . . . . I have looked upon him as the bulwark which enables us to defy the waves of European criticism . . . and now, after all this, they would bring the illustrious tragedian out here and turn the inspired critics of the San Francisco press loose upon him . . . I do hope they will never get a chance to expose to the world what a poor, shabby, stuck-up imposter Mr Forrest is.
>
> (Krause 1967: 63)

The King, of course, is the ultimate in shabby impostors, but Twain is concerned more with the depiction of this character than meretricious acting styles. Shakespeare, as 'done' by the King, is part of a repertoire of deception and fraud that also includes the obscene spectacle of the camel-leopard, the exploitation of vulgar religiosity by fake evangelists, and the risky impersonation of William and Harvey Wilks to cheat a young girl of her inheritance.

As for the King's version of Hamlet's soliloquy, it is perhaps something more than a nonsensical parody.

To be or not to be; that is the bare bodkin
That makes calamity of so long life;
For who would fardels bear, till Birnam Wood do come to
    Dunsinane,
But that the fear of something after death
Murders the innocent sleep,
Great nature's second course,
And makes us rather sling the arrows of outrageous fortune
Than fly to others that we know not of.
There's the respect must give us pause:
Wake Duncan with thy knocking! I would thou couldst;
For who would bear the whips and scorns of time,
The oppressor's wrong, the proud man's contumely,
The law's delay, and the quietus which his pangs might take,
In the dead waste and middle of the night, when churchyards
    yawn
In customary suits of solemn black,
But that the undiscovered country from whose bourne no traveler
    returns,
Breathes forth contagion on the world,
And thus the native hue of resolution, like the poor cat in the
    adage,
Is sicklied o'er with care,
And all the clouds that lowered o'er our housetops,
With this regard their currents turn awry,
And lose the name of action.
'Tis a consummation devoutly to be wished. But soft you, the fair
    Ophelia:
Ope not thy ponderous and marble jaws,
But get thee to a nunnery – go!

(Twain 1986: 137–138)

The King's speech recalls Hamlet's anticipatory dread over the
intended murder of Claudius, but this is interrupted by a reminder
of Macbeth's retrospective horror over the already accomplished
murder of Duncan. Together the two characters represent a complex stasis and historical paralysis. Hamlet is constrained to act by a
dead father who has returned from the grave; Macbeth, on the
other hand, cannot ever hope to wake his own 'dead father'. In combining these two moments Twain creates a kind of carnivalized
allegory of a deracinated American consciousness trapped by a

European past it can neither forget nor ever hope to renew. The bare bodkin is the threat of interminable social violence which is a pervasive fact throughout the American landscape of *Huckleberry Finn*. The dead past of Europe's interminable civil war reasserts itself in episodes such as the blood-feud between the Grangerfords and the Shepherdsons. The heritage of violence persists throughout every attempt to find a second social nature free of invidious distinction and the need for domination.

The King's speech is Shakespeare utterly degraded, yet it nevertheless possesses a kind of objective cogency. The confusion of Hamlet with Macbeth is a way of representing a violent assault on political authority. In the anticipatory perspective of Hamlet the usurping king is without legitimate sanction, so that Hamlet's failure of political alacrity results in social calamity. In the retrospective of Macbeth, however, the King's authority is unquestionably legitimate and it is precisely Macbeth's aggressive initiative that leads to calamity. To be or not to be indeed. 'Doing Shakespeare' on Huck's raft suggests that the attempted escape from archaic repression is not really possible. Neither Hamlet (Huck) nor Caliban (Jim) can break free of the master narrative in which they are inscribed.

In 'Jewish Oedipus', Jean François Lyotard makes the following comparison:

> Oedipus fulfils his fate of desire; the fate of Hamlet is the non-fulfilment of desire: this chiasmas is the one that extends between what is Greek and what is Jewish, between the tragic and the ethical.

> (Lyotard 1977: 401)

Hamlet's non-fulfillment of the patriarchal word marks the difference between modernity and classical antiquity. If the movement from Oedipus to Hamlet marks the shift from the tragic to the ethical, what can we say of the movement from Hamlet to Huck Finn, who has never had a feeling of obligation to the past?

> After supper she got out her book and learned me about Moses and the Bulrushers, and I was in a sweat to find out all about him; but by and by she let it out that Moses had been dead a considerable long time; so then I didn't care no more about him, because I don't take no stock in dead people.

> (Twain 1986: 12)

Let the Dead Bury their dead.

To be free for ever of the revenant dead is Huck's most powerful desire. Jim's gift is the emancipatory confirmation of Pap's death. Jim, on the other hand, is denied access to knowledge of his own emancipation, and to the benefits of that emancipation in order to provide a kind of literary entertainment for Tom Sawyer. In any case, it is hard to see how to distinguish between Huck's drive towards absolute freedom, his determination to abscond from 'sivilization', and Huck's militant and conscientious ignorance. Huck's solution to the problem of our obligation to the past seems an equivocal achievement at best. The non-fulfillment of tragic destiny or even of ethical obligation leads to complete but ultimately to completely vacuous freedom.

THE SECOND TIME AS FARCE

Many people have been generous in sending me newspaper clippings about Shakespeare. Among the most important is the Sunday comic strip from Bill Watterson's *Calvin and Hobbes* for 5 March 1994 (Figure 1). Blecchhh! In the first panel of the strip Calvin is confronted with a plate of slimy, lumpy green food, the sort of stuff every little boy's mother expects him to eat. Calvin stares at the food and pokes it with a fork. And then suddenly . . . the lumpy green food rises up off the plate, extends its little green arms, opens its little green mouth and recites:

> To be?? . . . or . . . not to be? [sighhh] that is the question.
> Whether 'tis nobler in the mind to *suffer*
> The *slings* and *arrows* of outrageous fortune . . .
> . . . Or to take *arms* against a sea of troubles . . .
> And by opposing, *end* them? [Thwupp] To die: to sleep; . . .
> No more! and by a sleep to say we *end*
> The *heartache* and the *thousand* natural shocks
> That flesh is heir to . . . [sniff] 'Tis a consummation
> Devoutly to be wished! To die, To sleep!
> To sleep, perchance to *dream*: Ay, *there's* the rub!
> . . . For in that sleep of *death*, what dreams may come
> When we have shuffled off this mortal coil
> Must give us pause.

And then, after a brief pause . . . 'Feeheelinggs . . . . wo wo wo feelings'. And then the green food recedes. When his mother returns,

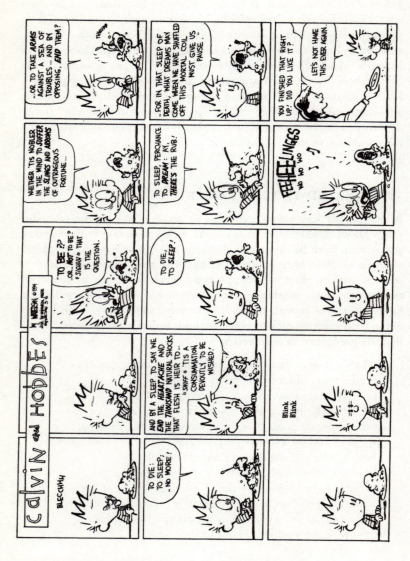

Calvin's plate is empty. She says, 'You finished that right up! Did you like it?' He replies, 'Let's not have this ever again.'

Calvin inhabits the familiar environment of ordinary suburban family life. But his relationship with this everyday social reality is distant and cool. He is fundamentally disengaged from his parents, who rarely appear in his life, and even more radically estranged from the dreaded Miss Wormwood, his teacher. Calvin expresses his protest against all social authority, especially as this is embodied in baby-sitters, when he becomes Stupendous Man. But he truly enters into his real existence as Spiff the Spaceman, whose adventures are rendered with extraordinary comic-book verisimilitude by the artist Bill Watterson. In this post-humanist world Calvin is truly and excitingly on his own, alive only to his own heroic individuality faced with the constant threat of disgusting, drooling monsters.

The radical individuality depicted in *Calvin and Hobbes* marks a kind of end point of a complex trajectory that we know historically as democracy. But what does it portend when Calvin is visited by this apparition of Shakespeare in the guise of an incomprehensibly sickening meal presented to him by his mother? I'm going to begin with the suggestion that Calvin is the post-modern Hamlet, inter-pellated, like Hamlet, by the ghost of his predecessor. Calvin's alac-rity in responding to the ominous transformation of his food, however, stands as an instructive contrast with that earlier Hamlet's protracted deliberation about the demands of a predecessor culture. The strip represents Calvin's heroic and slightly nauseated intro-jection not just of an earlier Hamlet, but of the entire sweep of Western modernity from Shakespeare to Barry Manilow, from philosophical reflection on being to the ethics of inarticulacy. In order to see just what such an introjection of the past entails it will be useful to return to the Hamlet whose pitiful remains have just been ingested – we can't really say digested – in this contemporary comic strip.

Harold Bloom has argued that 'we know the ethos of dis-interestedness only because we know Hamlet . . . a representation so original that conceptually *he contains us*, and has fashioned our psychology of motives ever since'. I have followed Bloom's sugges-tion throughout this discussion in arguing that Hamlet does repre-sent a specifically modern experience of agency and subjectivity, but I want to propose as an alternative to Bloom's largely psycho-analytic account the suggestion that his character can be understood in a more public or, if you will, political way. Hamlet is not, by any stretch of the imagination, democratic in his sympathies or in what we can infer about any of his specific political beliefs. Nevertheless, Hamlet struggles towards an important historical revision of the experience of self in terms of critical self-reflection, deliberative competence, and a strong sense of political vocation that will be fundamental for the possibility of modern liberal democracy. This experience of self entails a complex attitude to the past which combines sentimental longing for lost social cohesion with a critical detachment from the imperatives of tradition. In pursuing this argument I prefer to think of Hamlet's long monologues not as inward, private rumination, but rather as public orations or sermons. I visualize the earliest performances of this play with the figure of Hamlet occupying a heightened zone of public visibility near center stage, sharing a space of open and mutual acknowledgement with members of his audience. In other words I want to situate Hamlet in the early modern equivalent of the public sphere.

The local action of *Hamlet* is intensely focused within the intimate sphere of family politics, characterized by deep emotional investment in issues of succession, reciprocity, and compensation for injuries. But the family drama is played out against a geographical and temporal context organized on the grand scale of international politics, contending nations, diplomatic missions, mobilization, and war. The map of this dynamic and cosmopolitan world corresponds precisely and uncannily to the grand theater of operations which we now know as the Thirty Years' War. The startling and frightful interpellation of Hamlet by his paternal ghost links the action to a temporal depth that recedes far back into the ancient world and the bloody pillage of Troy by 'the rugged Pyrrhus'. Hamlet wants to know what is to be done. For the ghost, however, emanating from an archaic political world of personal loyalty and heroic virtue, there is no real distinction between redress of private grievances and the enactment of public policy, and therefore no real question as to what is to be done. Maynard Mack has described the 'world of Hamlet' as one of radical epistemic uncertainties (Mack 1950). I think Mack's description of the ambient circumstances in which Hamlet has to act is in many ways very apt, but I also think it's important to note why this condition of uncertainty is significant. In the archaic world of heroic virtues from which the ghost speaks, action is mandated by a principle of serial reciprocity. In this kind of regime, benefits, or gifts, are received and held temporarily by beneficiaries, but they are always entailed to a successor generation.

This is even more emphatically felt with respect to what we might call 'negative benefits' or, more simply, injuries and harm. The familiar claim that Hamlet's world is characterized by uncertainty is pertinent only if there is some sense in which it matters whether or not Claudius actually committed the murder. Hamlet, who has presumably been trained in habits of critical reflection at Wittenberg, has become disengaged from the ghost's world of heroic virtue and the personal redress of injury. The difference here is between action mandated by a traditional regime of serial reciprocity and action that ensues from rational deliberation based on knowledge and reliable information.

The interpretation of Hamlet that I propose follows from Emerson's remarks about the way this character anticipates the 'speculative genius' of modernity and from Cornelius Castoriadis' discussion of the equivalency or equisignification between democracy and philosophy.

> Philosophy and democracy were born at the same time and in the same place. Their solidarity comes from the fact that both express the refusal of heteronomy – the rejection of the claims to validity and legitimacy of rules and representations just because they happen to be there, the refusal of any external authority (even, and especially, 'divine'), of any extrasocial source of truth and justice, in brief, the putting into question of existing institutions and the assertion of the capacity of the collectivity and of thought to institute themselves explicitly and reflectively.
>
> (Castoriadis 1991: 20)

When the figure of Hamlet steps forward to address the urban collectivity in early modern London with orations like 'what a piece of work is man' or 'to be or not to be', he enacts this fundamental and radical connection between critical speculative thought and the democratic impulse.

In order to see in what sense Shakespearean drama is 'democratic' it is necessary to have a clear idea of what we are talking about when we discuss democracy. Instead of debating Shakespeare's complicity with state power and the interests of imperial domination, instead of talking about whether Shakespeare loved the common people or hated them, we perhaps need to reflect first on what we think is the point of democracy, and on why anyone ever thought it could work. The first of these questions considers democracy as a moral idea. The second question is concerned with describing the attitudes, beliefs, practices, and institutions that would make democracy possible. It seems obvious that the second question depends crucially on what kind of answer we propose for the first.

The 'moral content' of democratic institutions is perhaps most conspicuous by its absence from contemporary political practice. It is also, of course, one of the principal unresolved issues in contemporary political theory. Leading neo-liberal theorists like Ronald Dworkin (1978) maintain that democracy has to provide procedural guarantees of fairness, but that democracy cannot privilege any substantive version of the good life. Richard Sennet has recently characterized as wrong-headed Sheldon Hackney's call for a national discussion on 'core values' and has suggested that what we need instead is a standard of civility that takes account of the irreconcilable differences within a culturally diverse population. Similar doctrines have been advanced by Barbara Herrnstein Smith (1988), and by Richard Rorty (1989), who apparently thinks that even a discussion of substantive conceptions of the good life would be misguided on both pragmatic and theoretical grounds. Communitarian critics of this view such as Hannah Arendt (1958), or more recently Albert Borgmann (1984), Alasdair MacIntyre (1984), Seyla Benhabib (1992), Charles Taylor (1989, 1992) and a number of others, maintain in various ways that a strictly procedural conception of democracy produces nothing more than a vacuous or negative freedom. Such freedom leaves people completely defenseless either to assimilation within the market economy or to exclusion and outright victimization. This fundamental disagreement over the moral content or the moral purpose of social life is already part of the prehistory of modern liberal democracy in the West.

I want to look briefly now at two possible sources for the idea of democracy in Shakespeare's England. First, there is a theological tradition that emerges in the context of Reformation Christianity and finds its fullest articulation in the ideas of Jean Calvin. Second, there is a vernacular and secular tradition that will eventually find its formal articulation in the social contract theories of Thomas Hobbes. Both of these traditions presuppose a type of subjectivity capable of acting on the basis of reflection, dialogue, and discussion rather than on habits of obedience to traditional authority. The point – or purpose – of collective action based on reflective deliberation, however, is quite different within these two traditions. I then hope to suggest that the pathos of a democratic and deliberative subjectivity is vividly represented *for us* in the figure of Hamlet.

To Calvin and his followers, stable social order could arise only from those who exercise disciplined rule over themselves and who remain faithful to their calling. But it's not at all obvious why the doctrines of Calvin should entail any particular interest in the political dimension of human life at all. Given the centrality of salvation by faith and predestination, fatalism or quietism seem to be the only logical attitude to adopt towards worldly politics. Nevertheless, Calvinism gave rise to an extraordinary movement of political activism all over Europe through the sixteenth and seventeenth centuries. According to Charles Taylor, it is perfectly true on Calvin's account that human beings cannot hope to bring about reconciliation between God and fallen humanity, but the reconciled person is nevertheless one who has a disposition to repair the disorder of things (C. Taylor 1989: 228). This is clearly related to the Calvinist sense of outrage and scandal over both personal and social disorder. The task of setting things right is the task of a community of well-ordered individuals, whose association will tend towards an approximation of democratic self-regulation.

Calvinist teachings on the civil order proper to a Christian commonwealth exhibit a somewhat equivocal view of political democracy. The existence of the franchise and the freedom of the estates to choose their own magistrates is a special gift or blessing from God. At the same time Calvin warned against innovation, disobedience, and sedition; the gifts of democracy could not be earned; still less could they be legitimately achieved through popular revolution. The most reliable way to acknowledge divine authority was through a qualified and thoughtful adherence to the *status quo*. In other words, history, rather than the notoriously wayward popular will, is the best guide to ascertaining what would constitute a legitimate form of political authority. Calvin's most favored model for such a well-ordered polity was not Athenian democracy, but rather ancient Israel. According to Calvin's interpretation of many *Old Testament* texts, the Jews enjoyed the blessings of a democratic franchise in the regulation of their community as the '"singular gift" of God to his people' (Höpfl 1982: 157). That gift was, however, also a special kind of historical and political vocation.

The regime of Calvinism fosters an impulse to democratic self-rule in the way the subject is constructed within a reshaping of Christian belief and practice. The discipline of continual self-examination is not limited to the continual audit of a person's inward spiritual condition. Introspection has a social and public dimension as well, and participation in the activities of the polity, as opposed to contemplative withdrawal, is the proper vocation for the disciplined and reflective subject of reformed Christianity. The Calvinist idea of self-fashioning through self-control extends to the practice of other-fashioning through mutual admonition and instruction. But although we are required to reflect upon and to regulate both private and public conduct, this does not necessarily mean easy conformity to local standards and contingent social imperatives. All things considered we ought to comply with customary practices, but with one important stipulation, namely that the customary practices and institutions are themselves subject to conscientious scrutiny and public deliberation. Subjects − or perhaps it would be better to refer to these entities as agents − are no longer tightly embedded in traditional social life. On the contrary, the traditional social world has itself become a proper topic for critical review with a view to repair and redress the scandal of disorder.

The theological tradition privileges democracy not in the sense of popular sovereignty, but rather in the more limited sense of a practice of open and public reflection about matters of collective social and moral interest. Democracy in this limited sense of deliberation among equals is also found in various forms of corporate life in the early modern period, where its purpose is the regulation of economic affairs. The political culture of guilds and municipal corporations constitutes a vernacular tradition of democratic thought. The key notion in the vernacular tradition is the proprietary interest citizens have, collectively and individually, in the direction of everyday practical activity. This proprietary interest leads to a strong, positive affirmation of the moral dignity of everyday life. At the same time it encourages the basic attitudes of strategic agency later to be codified by Hobbes in his articulation of the first two 'natural laws', namely 'To seek peace, and follow it' and 'By all means we can, to defend our selves.'

Despite his emphatic preference for monarchy, Hobbes believed that democracy actually could work, though he was not optimistic about its long-term prospects. For Hobbes the only proper standard for the assessment of any political regime was, as he put it, its aptitude for guaranteeing social peace both in the short term and over successive generations. If, for example, the citizens of ancient Athens thrived under a democracy, it was not because their govern-

ment was democratic, but rather because of their ongoing consent
and obedience to the undivided sovereignty of the popular assembly.
The crucial point for Hobbes is the unbreachable covenant between
sovereign authority and private individuals.

The theological tradition that I associate here with Calvin and
the vernacular tradition that I associate with Hobbes are alike in
the value they assign to heightened self-awareness and to a particular kind of discursive competence. They are also alike in affirming the dignity of everyday practical activity. Finally, the traditions
are similar in the sense they convey that ordinary citizens have a
political vocation, which implies something more than simply a
strategic interest in politics. The historical convergence of these two
traditions has, of course, been usefully articulated in Weber's *The
Protestant Ethic and the Spirit of Capitalism* and in many other historical
or sociological studies since the appearance of that work. What I
want to stress here, however, is the radical divergence of these two
traditions at the level of what I have been calling the moral content
of the democratic idea. Briefly stated, the point of democracy in the
theological tradition is in the repair or the restitution of a disordered
social world. The citizen's vocation in this sense is defined by an
active conscience that interacts with others to generate civic virtues.
In the vernacular tradition, by contrast, the point of democracy is
the efficient management of practical activity and the protection of
private liberty understood in terms of proprietary interests. In this
context the citizen's vocation can be understood simply as a form of
strategic agency.

Hamlet's radically philosophical orientation to questions of being
is, of course, quite ostentatiously manifested in many of the characters' speeches. The democratic impulse here is perhaps harder to
recognize unless we pay closer attention to comments about 'something rotten in the state of Denmark' and to Hamlet's conviction
that

> The time is out of joint, O cursed spite
> That ever I was born to set it right.

There is, of course, nothing in the injunctions of old Hamlet about
setting things right; the ghost just wants to get even. Hamlet's puri-
tanical revulsion over sexual disorder, dissimulation, and dishonesty
in the court, as well as his rather fitful concerns with the parlous
state of Danish society, express a somewhat wavering commitment
to the kind of political vocation required in the tradition of Calvin

and the reformers. The ghost interprets Hamlet's task within the regime of serial reciprocity, heroic virtue and honor. Hamlet struggles to assimilate this task to a more complex and exacting regime of social repair, self-institution, and individual conscience.

The pathos of this story, of course, is that Hamlet has no one to talk to except the audience who attend his performance in the theater. Setting things right would require rational public action on a grand scale. But in the fictional and archaic Denmark of the play there is no public sphere, no infrastructure of institutional practices that would empower the democratic subjectivity exhibited by Hamlet to take action for the restitution of a damaged social order. Nevertheless, the possibilities for rational public deliberation on the subject of political institutions and civil policy are dimly apprehended in the world of the play. Hamlet has several brief encounters with the vernacular tradition of practical democratic reflection in his scenes with the players, with Fortinbras' captain, and most vividly with the grave-diggers. What he is able to glimpse at these points in the story is a pattern of interminable social violence in the regime of heroic virtue and serial reciprocity. But as a singular individual, Hamlet's competence is limited to action precisely within the institutions of heroic virtue that his philosophy calls into question. The answer to the question of interminable social violence turns out to be not the regime of conscience and social redemption envisioned by Calvin but the regime of undivided sovereignty and state coercion forecast by Hobbes.

François Guizot recognized Hamlet as the archetypal representative of modernity, but he also realized that the complexity brought into being in the enlightened forms of social life could become a 'troublesome burden' (Guizot 1852: 178–179). Brecht takes the somewhat sterner view that Hamlet's failure is the result of an 'ineffective use of the new approach to reason which he has picked up at the University of Wittenberg' (Brecht 1964: 201). These judgments imply that the private and public calamities which ensue in this play are really the consequence of a faulty implementation of the possibilities of enlightened critical intelligence on the part of Hamlet. For Guizot, and even more certainly for Brecht, the possibility of a truly effective use of the 'new approach to reason' is their most fundamental intuition not only about *Hamlet*, but also about the broader movement of Western modernity. Stephen Dedalus offers a much more severe reading of the play as a diagnosis of modernity.

Nine lives are taken off for his father's one, Our Father who art in purgatory. Khaki Hamlets don't hesitate to shoot. The blood-boltered shambles in act five is a forecast of the concentration camp sung by Mr Swinburne.

(Joyce 1946: 185)

Stephen deliberately refuses admiration for Hamlet's 'speculative genius', insisting instead on the grotesque and indiscriminate violence of his revenge. What's distinctively modern about Hamlet is not confusion, indecisiveness, or an 'ineffective use of reason', – khaki Hamlets don't hesitate to shoot. What's appalling about this play for Stephen Dedalus, himself a latter-day Hamlet, is the exorbitance of the demand for the redress of historical grievances – nine lives taken off for one. Even the most brilliantly realized achievements of critical intelligence and imagination fail to withstand the force of archaic enmity.

The reception history of *Hamlet* instantiates and confirms the decrees of Lord Morpheus: the great stories always return to their original form. What remains unclear, however, is what role is left for these great stories after the supposedly definitive foreclosure of all 'master narratives' (Lyotard 1984: 31ff.). This question can be addressed by returning to Bill Watterson's *Calvin and Hobbes* (Figure 2) and to a deservedly famous strip in which Calvin, evidently impersonating Walter Benjamin, explains to Hobbes that he has discovered the meaning of all preceding history. The end of history, the grand purpose of all preceding human labor, strife, and creativity was to produce Calvin himself.

Thousands of generations lived and died to produce my exact, specific parents, whose reason for being, obviously, was to produce *me*. All history up to this point has been spent preparing the world for my presence. . . . Now I'm here, and history is vindicated.

I suggested earlier that Calvin is a kind of omega point in the history of modern Western liberal democracy. With the successful introjection of the cultural past performed by eating a grossly unappetizing plate of food, Calvin achieves the fully unencumbered, self-determining subjectivity for which Hamlet was only a kind of quaint experiment. Hobbes wants to know, however, what they should do now that the end of history has been achieved. The

answer is contained in the strip's final panel. Calvin and Hobbes sit together watching television and laughing. The on-screen voice of Elmer Fudd is heard: 'Ooh, you wascawwy wabbit!'

The end of history is a cartoon within a cartoon. More precisely it is the devolution of public cultural authority from print to animated film to television. The sovereign subject of late capitalism has no further need for master narratives and does not want the difficult pleasures of the great stories. Calvin, the angry white male of contemporary politics, no longer has anything to do except enjoy the ceaseless humiliation of another angry white male, the bumbling and infantile Elmer Fudd, by the irrepressible Bugs Bunny. Calvin's discovery of the end of history suggests an alternative to the 'bloodboltered shambles' as an ending for the story of big-time Shakespeare.

There's no doubt that Shakespeare has been essential for the successor cultures of Western modernity. The difficult pleasures of his work, however, are linked to the centrality and even the supremacy of print culture. While no one should take seriously the implication that the end of history has been achieved, there may be an important sense in which literature as a central institution for Western modernity has been suspended. The impoverishment of this institution coincides with opportunities for capital accumulation in larger but more fragmented cultural markets where hyperactivity and distraction are preferred to the more difficult pleasures of traditional literature. Shakespeare can compete and flourish as a commodity in the frenzied environment of commercial popular culture, but the Shakespeare of the culture industry is neither more nor less essential to consumers than Bugs Bunny.

The long-term authority of Shakespeare is an expression of communal solidarity with the past. But great stories are ominous as well as difficult, and they do not answer fully to every need for dialogue, no matter how urgently or how eloquently voiced.

HAMLET: What may this mean,
That thou, dead corse, again in complete steel
Revisits thus the glimpses of the moon,
Making the night hideous, and we fools of nature
So horridly to shake our disposition
With thoughts beyond the reaches of our souls?
Say why is this? wherefore? what should we do?

(1.4.51–56)

References

A Breefe Discourse, declaring and approuing the necessarie and involable maintenance of certain laudable custemes of London. London: 1584.

Adorno, Theodor (1978) 'Commitment', in Andrew Arato and Eike Gebhardt (eds) *The Essential Frankfurt School Reader*. New York: Urizen Books (originally published in *New Left Review*, 1962).

—— (1991) *The Culture Industry*, (ed.) J. M. Bernstein. London: Routledge.

—— (1984) *Aesthetic Theory*, trans. C. Lenhardt. London: Routledge & Kegan Paul.

Agnew, Jean Christophe (1986) *Worlds Apart: The Market and the Theater in Anglo-American Thought, 1550–1750*. Cambridge: Cambridge University Press.

Alford, Violet (1937) *Pyrennean Festivals*. London: Chatto & Windus.

—— (1959) 'Rough Music or Charivari'. *Folklore*, 70: 505–518.

Althusser, Louis (1984) 'Ideology and Ideological State Apparatuses', *Essays on Ideology*. London: Verso. First published 1970.

Archer, Ian (1991) *The Pursuit of Stability: Social Relations in Elizabethan London*. Cambridge: Cambridge University Press.

Arendt, Hannah (1958) *The Human Condition*. Chicago: Chicago University Press.

Artaud, Antonin (1958) *The Theater and its Double*, trans. Mary Caroline Richards. New York: Grove Press.

Avery, Emmett L. (1956) 'The Shakespeare Ladies Club'. *Shakespeare Quarterly*, 7: 153–158.

Babcock, Robert Witbeck (1931) *The Genesis of Shakespeare Idolatry, 1766–1799: A Study in English Criticism of the Late Eighteenth Century*. Chapel Hill: University of North Carolina Press.

Bachorik, Lawrence (1977) 'Davenant's Shakespeare: 1600–1668'. Diss: McGill University.

Backscheider, Paula (1993) *Spectacular Politics: Theatrical Power and Mass Culture in Early Modern England*. Baltimore: Johns Hopkins University Press.

Bagehot, Walter (1965) 'Shakespeare the Individual', in Norman St. John-Stevas (ed.) *The Literary Essays*, 2 vols, in *The Collected Works of Walter*

Bagehot. Cambridge, MA: Harvard University Press: I, 173–216 (originally published in *The Prospective Review*, July, 1853).

Bakhtin, Mikhail M (1981) *The Dialogic Imagination*, trans. Caryl Emerson and Michael Holquist. Austin: University of Texas Press.

—— (1983) *Rabelais and His World*, trans. Hélène Iswolsky. Cambridge, MA: MIT Press.

—— (1986) *Speech Genres and Other Late Essays*, Caryl Emerson and Michael Holquist (eds), trans. Vern McGee. Austin: University of Texas Press.

—— (1990) *Art and Answerability*, trans. Michael Holquist. Austin: University of Texas Press.

Bard on Trial Again, and Again He Wins (1988) *New York Times*, 28 November C-21.

Barish, Jonas (1981) *The Antitheatrical Prejudice*. Berkeley: University of California Press.

Bartholomeusz, Dennis (1982) The Winter's Tale *in Performance in England and America, 1611–1976*. Cambridge: Cambridge University Press.

Bate, Jonathan (1989) *Shakespearean Constitutions: Politics, Theatre, Criticism 1730–1830*. Oxford: Oxford University Press.

—— (ed.) (1992) *The Romantics on Shakespeare*. Harmondsworth: Penguin Books.

Batman uppon Bartholome, his Booke De Proprietatibus Rerum (1582). London: Thomas East.

Becker, Lawrence (1990) *Reciprocity*. Chicago: University of Chicago Press.

Bede (1943) *Opera Temporibus*. Cambridge, MA: Harvard University Press.

Belsey, Catherine (1985) *The Subject of Tragedy: Identity and Difference in Renaissance Drama*. London: Methven.

Benhabib, Seyla (1992) *Situating the Self: Gender, Community, and Postmodernism in Contemporary Ethics*. London: Routledge.

Benjamin, Walter (1969) *Illuminations*, trans. Hannah Arendt. New York: Schocken Books.

Bentley, Gerald Eades (1961) *Shakespeare: A Biographical Handbook*. New Haven, CT: Yale University Press.

Bernheimer, Richard (1952) *Wild Men in the Middle Ages: A Study in Art, Sentiment, and Demonology*. Cambridge, MA: Harvard University Press.

Bernstein, J. M. (1991) 'Introduction', in Theodor Adorno *The Culture Industry*. London: Routledge.

Berry, Herbert (1989) 'The First Public Playhouses, Especially the Red Lion'. *Shakespeare Quarterly*, 40: 133–148.

Bevington, David (1993) Review of Brian Vickers' *Appropriating Shakespeare: Contemporary Critical Quarrels*. *Shakespeare Quarterly*, 45 (1994): 354–359.

Biggins, Dennis (1962) '"Exit Pursued by a Bear": A Problem in *The Winter's Tale*'. *Shakespeare Quarterly*, 13: 3–13.

Billington, Michael (1989) 'A "New Olivier" Is Taking on Henry V on the Screen'. *New York Times*, Sunday, 8 January.

Billington, Sandra (1991) *Mock Kings in Medieval Society and Renaissance Drama*. Oxford: Clarendon Press.

Black, Antony (1984) *Guilds and Civil Society in European Political Thought From the Twelfth Century to the Present*. Ithaca, NY: Cornell University Press.

Blisset, William (1971) 'This Wide Gap of Time: *The Winter's Tale*'. *English Literary Renaissance*, 1: 52–70.

Bloom, Allan (1987) *The Closing of the American Mind*. New York: Simon & Schuster.

Bloom, Harold (1989) *Shylock. Major Literary Characters*. New York: Chelsea House Publishers.

—— (1990a) *Hamlet. Major Literary Characters*. New York: Chelsea House Publishers.

—— (1990b) 'Interview Conducted by Antonio Weiss'. *Writers at Work: The Paris Review Interviews*, 9th Series, George Plimpton (ed.). New York: Penguin Books.

—— (1994) *The Western Canon: The Books and Schools of the Ages*. New York: Harcourt Brace.

Bodley, Sir Thomas (1926) *Letters of Sir Thomas Bodley to Thomas James First Keeper of the Bodleian Library*, G. W. Wheeler (ed.). Oxford: Clarendon Press.

Boorstin, Daniel (1962) *The Image: A Guide to Pseudo-Events in America*. New York: Harper Colophon.

Booth, Stephen (1989) 'The Best *Othello* I Ever Saw'. *Shakespeare Quarterly*, 40: 332–336.

Borgmann, Albert (1984) *Technology and the Character of Contemporary Life: A Philosophical Inquiry*. Chicago: University of Chicago Press.

—— (1992) *Crossing the Postmodern Divide*. Chicago: University of Chicago Press.

Boulton, Jeremy (1987) *Neighborhood and Society: A London Suburb in the Seventeenth Century*. Cambridge: Cambridge University Press.

Bourdieu, Pierre (1977) *Reproduction: In Education, Society, and Culture*, trans. Richard Nice. London: Sage.

—— (1984) *Distinction: A Social Critique of the Judgment of Taste*, trans. Richard Nice. Cambridge, MA: Harvard University Press.

Bradbrook, Muriel (1932) *Elizabethan Stage Conditions*. Cambridge: Cambridge University Press.

Bradshaw, Graham (1994) *Misrepresentations: Shakespeare and the Materialists*. Ithaca, NY: Cornell University Press.

Braudy, Leo, (1986) *The Frenzy of Reknown: Fame and Its History*. Oxford: Oxford University Press.

Brecht, Bertolt (1964) *A Short Organon for Theatre*, in *Brecht on Theatre*, trans. John Willett. New York: Hill & Wang.

—— (1965) *The Messingkauf Dialogues*, trans. John Willett. London: Eyre Methuen.

Breight, Curtis (1991) 'Branagh and the Prince, or a Royal Fellowship of Death'. *Critical Quarterly*, 33: 4.

Bretnor, Thomas (n.d.) *A Newe Almanacke and Prognostication, for the Yeare of our Lord God, 1615*.

Bristol, Michael D. (1986) *Carnival and Theater: Plebeian Culture and the Structure of Authority in Renaissance England*. London: Methuen.

—— (1989) '*Two Noble Kinsmen*: Shakespeare and the Problem of Authority', in *Shakespeare, Fletcher, and The Two Noble Kinsmen*, Charles Frey (ed.). Columbia, Mo: University of Missouri Press.

——— (1990) *Shakespeare's America/America's Shakespeare*. London: Routledge.
——— (1994) '"Funeral Bak'd Meats": Carnival and the Carnivalesque in *Hamet*', in *Case Studies in Contemporary Criticism: William Shakespeare*, Hamlet, Susanne Wofford (ed.). Boston: Bedford Books, pp. 348–367.
Brooks, Van Wyck (1915) *America's Coming of Age*. New York: B. W. Huebsch.
Bruster, Douglas (1992) *Drama and the Market in the Age of Shakespeare*. Cambridge: Cambridge University Press.
Buckmaster, Thomas (1571) *A New Almanacke and Prognostication, for the yere of the Lord God MDLXXI*. London: Richard Watkins.
Buck-Morss, Susan (1977) *The Origins of Negative Dialectics: Theodor W. Adorno, Walter Benjamin, and the Frankfurt Institute*. New York: The Free Press.
Bulman, J. C. (1988) *Shakespeare on Television: An Anthology of Essays and Reviews*. Hanover, NH: University Press of New England.
Burke, Kenneth (1951) 'Othello: An Essay to Illustrate a Method'. *The Hudson Review*, 4: 165–203.
Burnim, Kalman A. (1961) *David Garrick, Director*. Pittsburgh: University of Pittsburgh Press.
Butler, Martin (1984) *Theatre and Crisis 1632–1642*. Cambridge: Cambridge University Press.
Canby, Vincent (1989) 'A Down-to-Earth "Henry V" Discards Spectacle and Pomp'. *New York Times*, 8 November.
Capp, Bernard (1979) *English Almanacs 1500–1800: Astrology and the Popular Press*. Ithaca, NY: Cornell University Press.
Castoriadis, Cornelius (1991) 'The "End of Philosophy"?', in *Philosophy, Politics, Autonomy*, David Ames Curtis (ed.). Oxford: Oxford University Press.
Cavell, Stanley (1987) *Disowning Knowledge in Six Plays of Shakespeare*. Cambridge, MA: Cambridge University Press.
Cerasano, Susan P. (1993) 'Phillip Henslowe, Simon Forman, and the Theatrical Community of the 1590s'. *Shakespeare Quarterly*, 44: 145–159.
Charnes, Linda (1993) *Notorious Identity: Materializing the Subject*. Cambridge: Harvard University Press.
Chartier, Roger (1987) *The Cultural Uses of Print in Early Modern France*, trans. Lydia G. Cochrane. Princeton: Princeton University Press.
——— (1988) *The Culture of Print*, trans. Lydia G. Cochrane. New York: Polity Press.
Cheal, David J. (1989) *The Gift Economy*. London: Routledge.
Clark, Katerina and Holquist, Michael (1984) *Mikhail Bakhtin*. Cambridge, MA: Harvard University Press.
Coleridge, Samuel Taylor (1849) *Notes and Lectures Upon Shakespeare and Some of the Old Poets and Dramatists With Other Literary Remains of S. T. Coleridge*, Mrs. H. N. Coleridge (ed.). London: William Pickering, 2 vols.
Colie, Rosalie (1974) *Shakespeare's Living Art*. Princeton: Princeton University Press.
Cook, Ann Jennalie (1981) *The Privileged Playgoers of Shakespeare's London*. Princeton: Princeton University Press.

Cox, Lee Sheridan (1969) 'The Role of Autolycus in *The Winter's Tale*'. *Studies in English Literature*, 9: 283–301.

Currie, Gregory (1989) *An Ontology of Art*. New York: St. Martin's Press.

Davis, Natalie Z. (1974) '"Women on Top": Symbolic Sexual Inversion and Political Disorder in Early Modern Europe', in *The Reversible World: Symbolic Inversion in Art and Society*, Barbara Babcock (ed.). Ithaca, NY: Cornell University Press, pp. 147–190.

—— (1975) 'Printing and the People'. *Society and Culture in Early Modern France*. Stanford: Stanford University Press.

—— (1981) 'The Reasons of Misrule: Youth Groups and Charivaris in Sixteenth Century France'. *Past and Present*, 50: 49–75.

De Grazia, Margreta (1988) 'The Essential Shakespeare and the Material Book'. *Textual Practice*, 2: 69–86.

—— (1991) *Shakespeare Verbatim: The Reproduction of Authenticity and the 1790 Apparatus*. Oxford: Clarendon Press.

Digges, Leonard (1605) *A Manual of Prognostication*. London.

Dircks, Phyllis T. (1985) *David Garrick*. Boston, MA: Twayne Publishers.

Dobson, Michael (1992) *The Making of the National Poet: Shakespeare, Adaptation, and Authorship, 1660–1769*. Oxford: Clarendon Press.

Dollimore, Jonathan (1984) *Radical Tragedy: Religion, Ideology and Power in the Drama of Shakespeare and his Contemporaries*. Chicago: University of Chicago Press.

Dollimore, Jonathan and Sinfield, Alan (eds) (1985) *Political Shakespeare: New Essays in Cultural Materialism*. Ithaca, NY: Cornell University Press.

Donaldson, Peter (1991) 'Taking on Shakespeare: Kenneth Branagh's *Henry V*'. *Shakespeare Quarterly*, 42, 1: 60–71.

Drainie, Bronwyn (1994) 'Stratford's Troubles Affect All of Us'. *Globe and Mail*, 22 September.

Drakakis, John (ed.) (1985) *Alternative Shakespeares*. London: Methuen.

Dreyfuss, Hubert (1991) *Being in the World: A Commentary on Heidegger's* Being and Time. Cambridge, MA: MIT Press.

Durkheim, Emile (1915) *The Elementary Forms of the Religious Life*. London: George Allen & Unwin.

Dutton, Richard (1991) *Mastering the Revels: The Regulation and Censorship of English Renaissance Drama*. Iowa City: University of Iowa Press.

Dworkin, Ronald M. (1978) *Taking Rights Seriously*. Cambridge, MA: Harvard University Press.

Edmond, Mary (1987) *Rare Sir William Davenant*. Manchester: Manchester University Press.

Eisenstein, Elizabeth (1983) *The Printing Revolution in Early Modern Europe*. Cambridge: Cambridge University Press.

Elster, Jon (1982) 'Belief, Bias, and Ideology', in *Rationality and Relativism*, Martin Hollis and Steve Lukes (eds). Cambridge, MA: MIT Press.

—— (1986) *An Introduction to Karl Marx*. Cambridge: Cambridge University Press.

Emerson, Ralph Waldo (1968) *Representative Men: Seven Lectures*, in *The Complete Works of Ralph Waldo Emerson: Centenary Edition*, 12 vols. New York: AMS Press.

—— (1987) 'Politics', in *The Essays of Ralph Waldo Emerson*, Alfred R. Ferguson and Jean Ferguson (eds). Cambridge: The Belknap Press.

Erickson, Peter (1982) 'Patriarchal Structures in *The Winter's Tale*'. *PMLA*, 97: 819–29.

—— (1991) *Rewriting Shakespeare, Rewriting Ourselves*. Berkeley: University of California Press.

Evans, Malcolm (1989) *Signifying Nothing: Truth's True Contents in Shakespeare's Text* (2nd edn., foreword by Terry Eagleton). Athens, Georgia: University of Georgia Press.

Ewbank, Inga-Stina (1964) 'The Triumph of Time in *The Winter's Tale*'. *Review of English Literature*, V, 2: 83–100.

Farmer, Richard (1821) *An Essay on the Learning of Shakspeare*, London: T. and H. Rodd (first published 1767).

Felperin, Howard (1972) *Shakespearian Romance*. Princeton: Princeton University Press.

—— (1985) '"Tongue-tied our Queen?" The Deconstruction of Presence in *The Winter's Tale*', in *Shakespeare and the Question of Theory*, Patricia Parker and Geoffrey Hartman (eds). London: Methuen.

Fiedler, Leslie (1966) 'Caliban or Hamlet: An American Paradox'. *Encounter*, 26: 23–27.

Fitter, Chris (1993) 'A Tale of Two Branagh's: *Henry V*, Ideology, and the Mekong Agincourt', *Shakespeare Left and Right*. London: Routledge.

Foucault, Michel (1972) *The Archaeology of Knowledge*, trans. A. M. Sheridan. New York: Pantheon.

Franklin, Colin (1991) *Shakespeare Domesticated: The Eighteenth Century Editions*. Aldershot: Scolar Press.

Freud, Sigmund (1959) *Beyond the Pleasure Principle*, trans. James Strachey. New York: Bantam Books.

Frey, Charles (1980) *Shakespeare's Vast Romance*. Columbia: University of Missouri Press.

Frye, Northrop (1957) *A Natural Perspective: The Development of Shakespearean Comedy and Romance*. New York: Harcourt, Brace & World.

Fuller, Graham (1989) 'Two Kings'. *Film Comment*, 25,6: 2–7.

Furness, Horace Howard (1922) *The Letters of Horace Howard Furness*. Boston: Houghton Mifflin (2 vols).

Gadamer, Hans-Georg (1975) *Truth and Method*. New York: Seabury.

Gaignebet, Claude and Florentin, Marie-Claude (1979) *Le Carnaval: essais de mythologie populaire*. Paris: Payot.

Gaiman, Neil *et al.* (1990) 'Men of Good Fortune'. *The Sandman*, 13. New York: D. C. Comics.

Gamson, Joshua (1994) *Claims to Fame: Celebrity in Contemporary America*. Berkeley: University of California Press.

Garber, Marjorie.(1974) *Dreams in Shakespeare: From Metaphor to Metamorphosis*. New Haven, CT: Yale University Press.

—— (1987) *Shakespeare's Ghost Writers: Literature as Uncanny Causality*. London: Methuen.

Gardner, Helen (1982) *In Defence of the Imagination*. Cambridge, MA: Harvard University Press.

Geduld, Harry M. (1969) *Prince of Publishers: A Study of the Work and Career of Jacob Tonson.* Bloomington: Indiana University Press.

Gentleman, Francis (1770) *The Dramatic Censor or Critical Companion* (2 vols). London: J. Bell.

Gesner, Carol (1970) *Shakespeare and the Greek Romance.* Lexington: University of Kentucky Press.

Giddens, Anthony (1984) *The Constitution of Society: Outline of a Theory of Structuration.* Cambridge: Polity Press.

Gimpel, Jean (1976) *The Medieval Machine.* Harmondsworth: Penguin.

Godfrey, Stephen (1992) 'Stratford Woos a Younger Crowd, but at What Cost?' *Globe and Mail*, 25 April.

Godfridus (1608) *The Knowledge of Thinges Unknowne. . . . Together with the Husband-man's Practise.* London: J. Baker.

Goffman, Erving (1974) *Frame Analysis: An Essay on the Organization of Experience.* Cambridge, MA: Harvard University Press.

Goodman, Walter (1989) 'The Shakespeare Mystery: Who Was He?' *New York Times*, 18 April, C–2.

Grady, Hugh (1991) *The Modernist Shakespeare: Critical Texts in a Material World.* Oxford: Clarendon Press.

Gray, Walter (1591) *An Almanack and Prognostication made for the Yeere of Our Lord God 1591.* London: Richard Watkins.

Greenblatt, Stephen (1980) *Renaissance Self-fashioning From More to Shakespeare.* Chicago: University of Chicago Press.

—— (1988) *Shakespearean Negotiations: The Circulation of Social Energy in Renaissance England.* Berkeley: University of California Press.

Gregory, C. A. (1982) *Gifts and Commodities.* New York: Academic Press.

Griffith, Elizabeth (1775) *The Morality of Shakespeare's Drama Illustrated.* London: printed for T. Cadell.

Guizot, François Pierre Guillaume (1852) *Shakespeare and His Times.* New York: Harper & Brothers. (Originally published in French as *Sur la vie et les oeuvres de Shakespeare*, Paris, 1821.)

Gurr, Andrew (1983) 'The Bear, the Statue, and Hysteria in *The Winter's Tale*'. *Shakespeare Quarterly*, 34: 420–425.

—— (1987) *Playgoing in Shakespeare's London.* Cambridge: Cambridge University Press.

—— (1990) *The Shakespearean Stage* (2nd edn). Cambridge: Cambridge University Press.

—— (1993) 'Three Reluctant Patrons and Early Shakespeare'. *Shakespeare Quarterly*, 44: 159–175.

Gurvitch, George (1964) *The Spectrum of Social Time*, trans. Myrtle Korenbaum. Dordrecht: D. Reidel.

Habermas, Jürgen (1992) *The Structural Transformation of the Public Sphere: An Inquiry into a Category of Bourgeois Society*, trans. Thomas Burger. Cambridge, MA: MIT Press (first published 1962 in German as *Strukturwandel der Öffentlicheit*).

Halperin, Richard (1991) *The Poetics of Primitive Accumulation: English Renaissance Culture and the Genealogy of Capital.* Ithaca, NY and London: Cornell University Press.

Harbage, Alfred (1935) *Sir William Davenant: Poet Venturer, 1606–1668*. Philadelphia: University of Pennsylvania Press.
—— (1941) *Shakespeare's Audience*. New York: Columbia University Press.
—— (1952) *Shakespeare and the Rival Traditions*. New York: Macmillan.
Hardison, O. B. (1965) *Christian Rite and Christian Drama in the Middle Ages: Essays in the Origin and Early History of Modern Drama*. Baltimore: Johns Hopkins University Press.
—— (1984) *Toward Freedom and Dignity: The Humanities and the Idea of Humanity*. Baltimore: Johns Hopkins University Press.
Hassel, R. Chris (1979) *Renaissance Drama and the English Church Year*. Lincoln: University of Nebraska Press.
Hawkes, Terence (1986) *That Shakespeherian Rag*. London: Methuen & Co.
—— (1992) *Meaning by Shakespeare*. London: Routledge.
Haywood, Eliza (1755) *The Female Spectator*. 4 vols. (fifth edn.). London.
Hazlitt, William (1817) *Characters of Shakspear's Plays*. London: R. Hunter.
Heilman, Robert (1956) *Magic in the Web*. Lexington: University of Kentucky Press.
Heinemann, Margot (1985) 'How Brecht Read Shakespeare', in *Political Shakespeare*, Jonathan Dollimore and Alan Sinfield (eds). Ithaca, NY: Cornell University Press.
Hexter, J. H. (1980) 'Property, Monopoly and Shakespeare's *Richard II*', in P. Zagorin (ed.) *Culture and Politics from Puritanism to the Enlightenment*. Berkeley: University of California Press, pp. 1–24.
Higgins, Anne (1989) 'Medieval Notions of the Structure of Time'. *Journal of Medieval and Renaissance Studies*, 19: 229–242.
Hjort, Mette (1993). *The Strategy of Letters*. Cambridge, MA: Harvard University Press.
Holderness, Graham, (ed.) (1988) *The Shakespeare Myth*. Manchester: Manchester University Press.
Holderness, Graham and Murphy, Andrew (1995) '"Shakespeare Country": The National Curriculum and Literary Heritage'. *Critical Survey*, 7: 110–115.
Holland, Norman (1964) *The Shakespearean Imagination: A Critical Introduction*. Bloomington: University of Indiana Press.
Holquist, Michael (1986) 'Introduction'. *Speech Genres and Other Late Essays*, trans. Vern McGee, Caryl Emerson and Michael Holquist (eds). Austin: University of Texas Press.
—— (1990) *Dialogism: Bakhtin and His Word*. London: Routledge.
Höpfl, Harro (1982) *The Christian Polity of John Calvin*. Cambridge: Cambridge University Press.
Horwitz, Tony (1993) 'Making Shakespeare Fun at 14: "Julius Caesar Killed in Bloodbath."' *The Wall Street Journal*, 5 February.
Howard, Jean (1994) *The Stage and Social Struggle in Early Modern England*. London: Routledge.
Howard, Jean and O'Connor, Marion (eds) (1988) *Shakespeare Reproduced: The Text in History and Ideology*. New York: Routledge.
Hughes, Merritt Y. (1940) 'A Classical Versus a Social Approach to Shakespeare's Autolycus'. *Shakespeare Association Bulletin*, 15: 219–226.

Hume, David (1757) 'Of the Standard of Taste', in *Four Dissertations*. London: A. Millar.

Hunt, Marvin (1988) 'Commotion in the Winds!' *Spectator*, 8 December: 8.

Hunter, G. K. (1964) 'Elizabethans and Foreigners'. *Shakespeare Survey*, 17: 37–52.

—— (1967) '*Othello* and Colour Prejudice'. *Proceedings of the British Academy*, 53: 139–163.

Hurd, Richard (1762) *Letters on Chivalry and Romance*. London: A. Millar.

Hutcheson, Francis (1973) *An Inquiry Concerning Beauty, Order, Harmony, Design*, Peter Kivy (ed.). The Hague: Martinus Nijhoff.

Hyde, Lewis (1983) *The Gift: Imagination and the Erotic Life of Property*. New York: Vintage Books.

I. F. (1598) *Perpetuall and Naturall Prognostications of the Change of Weather Gathered out of Divers Ancient and Late Writers, and Placed in Order for the Common Good of all Men*. London: Edward White.

Ingram, William (ed.) (1982) *Records of Early English Drama: Coventry*. Toronto: University of Toronto Press.

—— (1992) *The Business of Playing: The Beginnings of the Adult Professional Theater in Elizabethan London*. Ithaca, NY: Cornell University Press.

Innis, Harold (1951) *The Bias of Communication*. Toronto: University of Toronto Press.

Ioppolo, Grace (1991) *Revising Shakespeare*. Cambridge, MA: Harvard University Press.

Jameson, Frederic (1991) *Postmodernism: Or the Cultural Logic of Late Capitalism*. Durham, NC: Duke University Press.

Janton, Pierre (1988) 'Othello's Weak Function'. *Cahiers Elisabethains*, 34: 79–82.

Jay, Martin (1984) *Adorno*. Cambridge, MA: Harvard University Press.

Jones, Eldred (1965) *Othello's Countrymen: The African in English Renaissance Drama*. Oxford: Oxford University Press.

Jordan, Winthrop (1968) *White Over Black*. Chapel Hill: University of North Carolina Press.

Joyce, James (1946) *Ulysses*. New York: Random House.

Kastan, David S. (1982) *Shakespeare and the Shapes of Time*. Hanover: University Press of New England.

Kelly, Aileen (1992) 'Revealing Bakhtin'. *New York Review of Books*, 24 September.

Kermode, Frank (1982) 'On Being an Enemy of Humanity'. *Raritan Review*, 11: 87–102.

Kernan, Alvin (1987) *Printing Technology, Letters & Samuel Johnson*. Princeton: Princeton University Press.

—— (1990) *The Death of Literature*. New Haven, CT: Yale University Press.

Kirsch, Arthur (1981) *Shakespeare and the Experience of Love*. Cambridge: Cambridge University Press.

Krause, Sydney Joseph (1967) *Mark Twain as a Critic*. Baltimore: Johns Hopkins University Press.

Krier, Theresa M. (1982) 'The Triumph of Time: Paradox in *The Winter's Tale*'. *Centennial Review*, 26 (4): 341–353.

Kristeva, Julia (1982) 'Women's Time', in *Feminist Theory: A Critique of Ideology*, Nannerl O'Keohane, Michelle Z. Rosaldo and Barbara C. Gelpi (eds). Brighton: Harvester.

Lamb, Charles (1893) *Plays and Dramatic Essays*, R. Dircks (ed.). London.

Laroque, François (1982) 'Pagan Ritual, Christian Liturgy, and Folk Customs in *The Winter's Tale*'. *Cahiers Elisabethains*, 22: 25–33.

—— (1987) 'An Archaeology of the Dramatic Text: *Othello* and Popular Traditions', *Cahiers Elisabethains*, 32: 13–35.

—— (1991) *Shakespeare's Festive World: Elizabethan Seasonal Entertainments and the Professional Stage*, trans. Janet Lloyd. Cambridge: Cambridge University Press.

Le Roy Ladurie, Emmanuel (1979) *Carnival in Romans*, trans. Mary Feeney. New York: G. Braziller.

Leach, Edmund. (1961) *Rethinking Anthropology*. London: Athlone Press.

LeGoff, Jacques and Jean-Claude Schmitt (eds) (1977) *Le Charivari: Actes de la table ronde organisée a Paris (25–27 avril 1977) par l'Ecole des Hautes Etudes en Sciences Sociales et le Centre National de la Recherche Scientifique*, Paris: Mouton.

Levin, Richard (1979) *New Readings vs. Old Plays: Recent Trends in the Reinterpretation of English Renaissance Drama*. Chicago: University of Chicago Press.

Levinas, Emannuel (1987) 'Reality and its Shadow', in *Collected Philosophical Papers*, Alphonso Lingis (trans.). Dordrecht: Martinus Nijhoff.

Levine, Lawrence (1988) *Highbrow/Lowbrow: The Emergence of Cultural Hierarchy in America*. Cambridge, MA: Harvard University Press.

Liberace, Lee (1973) *Autobiography*. New York: Putnam.

Limon, Jerzy (1986) *Dangerous Matter: English Drama and Politics in 1623/24*. New York: Cambridge University Press.

Livingston, Paisley (1991) *Literature and Rationality: Ideas of Agency in Theory and Fiction*. Cambridge: Cambridge University Press.

Loewenstein, Joseph (1988) 'The Script in the Marketplace', in *Representing the Renaissance*, Stephen Greenblatt (ed.). Berkeley: University of California Press.

Loomba, Ania (1989) *Gender, Race, Renaissance Drama*. Manchester: Manchester University Press.

Lounsbury, Thomas R. (1902a) *Shakespeare and Voltaire*, New York: Charles Scribner's Sons.

—— (1902b) *Shakespeare as a Dramatic Artist: With an Account of His Reputation At Various Periods*. New York: Charles Scribner's Sons.

—— (1906) *The Text of Shakespeare: Its History from the Publication of the Quartos and Folios Down To and Including the Publication of the Editions of Pope and Theobald*. New York: Charles Scribner's Sons.

Lowenthal, Leo (1961) *Literature, Popular Culture and Society*. Palo Alto: Stanford University Press.

Lynch, Kathleen M. (1961) *Jacob Tonson: Kit-Cat Publisher*. Knoxville: University of Tennessee Press.

Lyotard, Jean-Françoise (1977) 'Jewish Oedipus'. *Genre*, 10.

—— (1984) *The Postmodern Condition: A Report on Knowledge*, trans. Geoff Bennington and Brian Massumi. Minneapolis: University of Minnesota Press.

MacCary, Thomas W. (1985) *Friends and Lovers: The Phenomenology of Desire in Shakespeare Comedy*. New York: Columbia University Press.

MacFarlane, Alan (1978) *The Origins of English Individualism: The Family, Property, and Social Transition*. Cambridge: Cambridge University Press.

MacIntyre, Alasdair (1984) *After Virtue: A Study in Moral Theory* (2nd edn). Notre Dame: University of Notre Dame Press.

—— (1990) *Three Rival Versions of Moral Inquiry: Encyclopedia, Genealogy, and Tradition*. Notre Dame: Notre Dame University Press.

McLuhan, Marshall (1962) *The Gutenberg Galaxy: The Making of Typographical Man*. Toronto: University of Toronto Press.

Mack, Maynard (1950) 'The World of *Hamlet*'. *Yale Review*, 41.

Maguire, Nancy Klein (1987) *Renaissance Tragicomedy: Explorations in Genre and Politics*. New York: AMS Press.

Malone, Edmond (1790) *The Plays and Poems of William Shakespear, in Ten Volumes*. London: H. Baldwin.

Mann, Thomas (1937) 'Freud and the Future', in *Essays of Three Decades*, trans. Helen T. Lowe-Porter. London: Secker & Warburg. First published in English translation in *Freud, Goethe, Wagner*. New York: Alfred Knopf, 1937. Lecture originally given in German in Vienna, 1936.

Marcus, Leah (1986) *The Politics of Mirth: Jonson, Herrick, Milton, Marvell, and the Defense of Old Holiday Pastimes*. Chicago: Chicago University Press.

—— (1988) *Puzzling Shakespeare: Local Reading and its Discontents*. Berkeley: University of California Press.

Markham, Gervase (1986) *The English Housewife: Containing the Inward and Outward Virtues Which Ought to be in a Complete Woman . . .* , Michael R. Best (ed.). Montreal: McGill-Queens University Press.

Marsden, Jean, (ed.) (1991) *The Appropriation of Shakespeare: Post-Renaissance Reconstructions of the Works and the Myth*. Hemel Hempstead: Harvester Wheatsheaf.

Mauss, Marcel (1967) *The Gift*, trans. Ian Cunnison, with an Introduction by E. E. Evans-Pritchard. New York: W. W. Norton & Co.

May, Lee (1993) 'Who Was the "Real" Shakespeare? It's Oxford vs. Stratford in Battle of the Bard'. *Atlanta Constitution*, 1 April: E-1.

Montagu, Elizabeth (1769) *An Essay on the Writings and Genius of Shakespeare, Compared with the Greek and French Dramatic Poets with some Remarks upon the Misrepresentations of Mons. de Voltaire*. London: First edition published anonymously.

Montrose, Louis Adrian (1980) 'The Purpose of Playing: Reflections on a Shakespearean Anthropology'. *Helios*, NS 8: 51–74.

Moodie, Susanna (1989) *Roughing It in the Bush*. Toronto: McClelland and Stewart Inc.

Morson, Gary Saul and Emerson, Caryl (1990) *Mikhail Bakhtin: Creation of a Prosaics*. Palo Alto: Stanford University Press, pp. 287–288.

Mowat, Barbara (1976) *The Dramaturgy of Shakespeare's Romances*. Athens, Georgia: University of Georgia Press.

Muchembled, Robert (1985) *Popular Culture and Elite Culture in France: 1400–1750*, trans. Lydia Cochrane. Baton Rouge: LSU Press.

Mullaney, Stephen (1988) *The Place of the Stage: License, Play, and Power in Renaissance England*. Chicago: University of Chicago Press.

Neavoll, George (1993) 'Celebrating Shakespeare's Birthday'. *Portland Press Herald*, 23 April.

Neely, Carol Thomas (1980) 'Women and Men in *Othello*: "What Should such a Fool/Do with so Good a Woman?"', in *The Woman's Part: Feminist Criticism of Shakespeare*, Carolyn S. Lenz, Gayle Greene and Carol Thomas Neely (eds). Urbana: University of Illinois Press, pp. 211–239.

—— (1985) *Broken Nuptials in Shakespeare's Plays*. New Haven, CT: Yale University Press.

Neill, Michael (1989) 'Unproper Beds: Race, Adultery and the Hideous in *Othello*'. *Shakespeare Quarterly*, 40: 383–413.

Nelson, T. G. A. and Haines, Charles (1981) 'Othello's Unconsummated Marriage'. *Essays in Criticism*, 33: 5–7.

Newman, Karen (1987) ' "And Wash the Ethiop White": Femininity and the Monstrous in *Othello*', in *Shakespeare Reproduced: The Text in History and Ideology*, Jean Howard and Marion O'Connor (eds). London: Methuen & Co.

Nicoll, Allardyce (1980) *The Garrick Stage: Theatres and Audience in the Eighteenth Century*, Sybil Rosenfeld (ed.). Manchester: Manchester University Press.

Nightingale, Benedict (1989) 'Henry V Returns As a Monarch For This Era'. *New York Times*, 5 November.

Nussbuam, Martha (1993) 'Non-relative Virtues: An Aristotelean Approach', in *The Quality of Life*, Martha C. Nussbaum and Amartya Sen (eds). Oxford: Clarendon Press.

Orkin, Martin (1987) '*Othello* and the Plain Face of Racism'. *Shakespeare Quarterly*, 38: 166–188.

Ornstein, Robert (1986) *Shakespeare's Comedies: From Roman Farce to Romantic Mystery*. Newark: University of Delaware Press.

Parker, Patricia (1985) 'Shakespeare and Rhetoric: "Dilation" and "Delation" in *Othello*', in *Shakespeare and the Question of Theory*, Patricia Parker and Geoffrey Hartman (eds). London: Methuen & Co.

Parkes, Don and Thrift, Nigel (1980) *Times, Spaces and Places*. Chichester: Wiley.

Patterson, Annabel (1984) *Censorship and Interpretation: The Conditions of Writing and Reading in Early Modern England*. Madison: University of Wisconsin Press.

Pavel, Thomas (1986) *Fictional Worlds*. Cambridge, MA: Harvard University Press.

Percy, Thomas (1765) *Reliques of Ancient English Poetry*. London: J. Dodsley.

Quinones, Ricardo (1972) *The Renaissance Discovery of Time*. Cambridge, MA: Harvard University Press.

Rabkin, Norman (1967) *Shakespeare and the Common Understanding*. New York: The Free Press.

Rackin, Phyllis (1987) 'Androgyny, Mimesis, and the Marriage of the Boy Heroine on the English Renaissance Stage'. *PMLA*, 102: 29–42.

Ragland, Fanny E. (1884) 'Prize Examination on the Play of *Othello*'. *Shakespeariana*, I, 251–254.

Randall, Dale B. J. (1985) ' "This is the Chase": Or, The Further Pursuit of Shakespeare's Bear'. *Shakespeare-Jahrbuch*, 121: 89–95.

Rappaport, Steve (1989) *Worlds within Worlds: Structures of Life in Sixteenth Century London*. Cambridge: Cambridge University Press.

Rey-Flaud, Henri (1985) *Le Charivari: Les rituels fondamentaux de la sexualité*. Paris: Payot.

Robertson, J. M. (1931) *The State of Shakespeare Study: A Critical Conspectus*. London: George Routledge & Sons.

Robinson, Herbert Spencer (1932) *English Shakespearian Criticism in the Eighteenth Century*. New York: H. W. Wilson Company.

Rogin, Michael (1985) 'The Sword became a Flashing Vision'. *Representations*, 9: 150–195.

Rorty, Richard (1989) *Contingency, Irony, Solidarity*. Cambridge: Cambridge University Press.

Rose, Gillian (1978) *The Melancholy Science: An Introduction to the Thought of Theodor W. Adorno*. New York: Columbia University Press.

Rowe, Nicholas (1948) *Some Account of the Life of Mr William Shakspear (1709)*, The Augustan Reprints, Extra Series, no. 1. Los Angeles: William Andrews Clark Memorial Library.

Rymer, Thomas (1957) *The Critical Works of Thomas Rymer*, Curt A. Zimansky (ed.). New Haven: Yale University Press.

—— (1974) *A Short View of Tragedy*, in *Shakespeare: The Critical Heritage*, 6 vols., Brian Vickers (ed.). London: Routledge & Kegan Paul, pp. 2, 27.

Salingar, Leo (1966) 'Time and Art in Shakespeare's Romances'. *Renaissance Drama*, 9: 3–35.

Sauer, Thomas G. (1981) *A. W. Schlegel's Shakespearean Criticism in England, 1811–1846*. Bonn: Bouvier Verlag Herbert Grundmann.

Schechner, Richard (1988) *Performance Theory* (revised and expanded edn). New York: Routledge.

Schlegel, Augustus William (1846) *A Course of Lectures on Dramatic Art and Literature*, trans. John Black. London: Henry G. Bohn.

Schoenbaum, Samuel (1975) *Shakespeare: A Documentary Life*. New York: Oxford University Press.

Schwartz, Beth C. (1991) 'Thinking Back Through Our Mothers: Virginia Woolf Reads Shakespeare'. *ELH*, 58.

Seary, Peter (1990) *Lewis Theobald and the Editing of Shakespeare*. Oxford: Clarendon Press.

Sedgewick, Eve Kosofsky (1985) *Between Men: English Literature and Homosocial Desire*. New York: Columbia University Press.

Sennett, Richard (1992) *The Fall of Public Man*. New York: W. W. Norton (first published 1972).

'Shakespeare for Mere Mortals' (1993) *The New York Times*, 3 September: A–8.

Sharpe, Buchanan (1980) *In Contempt of All Authority: Rural Artisans in the West of England, 1586–1660*. Berkeley: University of California Press.

Sherbo, Arthur (1986) *The Birth of Shakespeare Studies: Commentators from Rowe (1709) to Boswell-Malone (1821)*. East Lansing, MI: Colleagues Press.

—— (1992) *Shakespeare's Midwives: Some Neglected Shakespeareans*. Newark: University of Delaware Press.

Sinfield, Alan (1985) 'Royal Shakespeare: Theatre and the Making of Ideology', in *Political Shakespeare: New Essays in Cultural Materialism*, Jonathan Dollimore and Alan Sinfield (eds). Ithaca, NY: Cornell University Press.

—— (1991) *Faultlines: The Politics of Dissident Reading*. Berkeley: University of California Press.

—— (1994) 'Untune that String: Shakespeare and the Scope for Dissidence'. Review of Graham Bradshaw, *Misrepresentations: Shakespeare and the Materialists. Times Literary Supplement*, 22 April: 4–5.

Smith, Barbara Herrnstein (1988) *Contingencies of Value: Alternative Perspectives for Critical Theory*, Cambridge, MA: Harvard University Press.

Smith, D. Nichol (ed.) (1963) *Eighteenth Century Essays on Shakespeare* (2nd edn). Oxford: Clarendon Press.

Snow, Edward.(1980) 'Sexual Anxiety and the Male Order of Things in *Othello'. English Literary Renaissance*, 10: 384–412.

Snyder, Susan (1979) *The Comic Matrix of Shakespeare's Tragedies*. Princeton: Princeton University Press.

Sobran, Joseph (1989) 'Orthodox Shakespeare Fan Mad Without Seeming So'. *Daily Oklahoman*, 18 April.

—— (1991) 'There's More Than One Variety of Intolerance'. *Daily Oklahoman*, 11 June.

Stallybrass, Peter (1986) 'Patriarchal Territories: The Body Enclosed', in *Rewriting the Renaissance: The Discourses of Sexual Difference in Early Modern Europe*, Margaret W. Ferguson, Maureen Quilligan and Nancy Vickers (eds). Chicago: University of Chicago Press.

Stavropoulos, Janet (1987) 'Love and Age in *Othello'. Shakespeare Studies*, 19: 125–141.

Stendhal (1925) *Racine et Shakespeare*, Pierre Martino (ed.), Vol. 18 in *Oeuvres Complètes* (37 vols.). Paris: Edouard Champion.

Stockholder, Kay (1987) *Dream Works: Lovers and Families in Shakespeare's Plays*. Toronto: University of Toronto Press.

Sturges, Hale (1936) *The Publishing Career of Jacob Tonson, the Elder, 1678–1720*. Ann Arbor: University Microfilms.

Summers, Joseph H. (1984) *Dreams of Love: On Shakespeare's Plays*. Oxford: Clarendon Press.

Taylor, Charles (1989) *Sources of the Self*. Cambridge, MA.: Harvard University Press.

—— (1992) 'The Politics of Recognition,' in *Multiculturalism and the Politics of Recognition*, Amy Guttman (ed.). Princeton: Princeton University Press.

Taylor, Gary (1989) *Reinventing Shakespeare: A Cultural History from the Restoration to the Present*. New York: Weidenfeld & Nicolson.

Tennenhouse, Leonard (1986) *Power on Display: The Politics of Shakespeare's Genres*. London: Methuen.

Theobald, Lewis (1949) *Preface to the Works of Shakespeare (1734)*, The Augustan Reprints, Extra Series, no. 2. Los Angeles: William Andrews Clark Memorial Library.

Thirsk, Joan (1978) *Economic Policy and Projects: The Development of a Consumer Society in Early Modern England*. Oxford: Clarendon Press.

Thompson, E. P. (1972) 'Rough Music: Le Charivari Anglais'. *Annales: Economies, Sociétés, Civilisations*, 27: 285–312.

Thomson, Peter (1992) *Shakespeare's Professional Career*. Cambridge: Cambridge University Press.

Thorsell, William (1994) 'From Remarks at the Woodrow Wilson School of Public and International Affairs, Princeton University on 4 October'. Reprinted as 'A little less Adam Smith, a lot more William Shakespeare', *Globe and Mail*, 19 October.

Tierney, John (1991) 'Era Ends as Times Square Drops Slashers for Shakespeare', *The New York Times*, 14 January.

Todorov, Tzvetan (1984) *Mikhail Bakhtin: The Dialogical Principle*, Trans. Wlad Godzich. Minneapolis: University of Minnesota Press.

Tokson, Elliot (1982) *The Popular Image of the Black Man in English Drama 1550–1688*. Boston: G. K. Hall.

Topsell, Edward (1607) *The Historie of Foure-Footed Beastes*. London: William Iaggard.

Trousdale, Marion (1976) 'Style in *The Winter's Tale*', *Critical Quarterly*, 18: 30–42.

Turner, Victor (1982) *From Ritual to Theatre: The Human Seriousness of Play*. New York: Performing Arts Journal Publications.

Tusser, Thomas (1573) *Five Hundreth Points of Good Husbandrie*. London: Rychard Tottel, p. 54.

Twain, Mark (1909) *Is Shakespeare Dead?* New York: Harper & Brothers.

—— (1986) *Huckleberry Finn*, John Seelye (ed.). Harmondsworth: Penguin.

Underdowne, David (1985) *Revel, Riot, and Rebellion: Popular Politics and Culture in England 1603–1660*. Oxford: Clarendon Press.

Uphaus, Robert W. (1981) *Beyond Tragedy: Structure and Experience in Shakespeare's Romances*. Lexington: University Press of Kentucky.

Vickers, Brian (1993) *Appropriating Shakespeare: Contemporary Critical Quarrels*. New Haven, CT: Yale University Press.

Von Martin, Alfred (1944) *Sociology of the Renaissance*, trans. W. L. Luetkens. London: Kegan Paul, Trench, Trubner & Co.

Wade, Nicholas (1990) 'Henry V v. Henry V: Branagh's Victory at Agincourt', *New York Times*, 6 February.

Wall, Wendy (1993) *The Imprint of Gender: Authorship and Publication in the English Renaissance*. Ithaca, NY: Cornell University Press.

Warton, Thomas (1754) *Observations on* The Faerie Queen *of Spenser*. London: R. and J. Dodsley.

Weimann, Robert (1978) *Shakespeare and the Popular Tradition in the Theater*, Robert Schwartz (ed.). Baltimore: Johns Hopkins University Press.

—— (1988) 'Bifold Authority in Shakespeare's Theater'. *Shakespeare Quarterly*, 39: 401–418.

Werstine, Paul (1990) 'Narratives About Printed Shakespeare Texts: "Foul Papers" and "Bad" Quartos'. *Shakespeare Quarterly*, 41.

Wiles, David (1987) *Shakespeare's Clown: Actor and Text in the Elizabethan Playhouse*. Cambridge: Cambridge University Press.

Williams, George Walton (1985) *The Craft of Printing and the Publication of Shakespeare's Works*. Washington: Folger Books.

Williams, Raymond (1982) *The Sociology of Culture*. New York: Schocken.

Williamson, Marilyn (1986) 'The Romances: Patriarchy, Pure and Simple', in *The Patriarchy of Shakespeare's Comedies*. Detroit: Wayne State Press.

Wilson, F. P. (1970) *Shakespeare and the New Bibliography*. Revised by Helen Gardner (ed.). Oxford: Clarendon Press.

Wolff, Janet (1981) *The Social Production of Art*. London: Macmillan.

—— (1983) *Aesthetics and the Sociology of Art*. London: George Allen & Unwin.

Woodbridge, Linda (1984) *Women and the English Renaissance: Literature and the Nature of Womankind, 1540–1620*. Urbana: University of Illinois Press.

Woods, Leigh (1987) *Garrick Claims the Stage: Acting as Social Emblem in Eighteenth-Century England*. Westport, CT: Greenwood Press.

Woolf, Virginia (1929) *A Room of One's Own*. London: Hogarth Press.

—— (1932) *To the Lighthouse*. London: Hogarth Press.

Würzbach, Natascha (1990) *The Rise of the English Street Ballad, 1550–1650*, trans. from the German by Gayna Walls. Cambridge: Cambridge University Press.

Zuidervaart, Lambert (1991) *Adorno's Aesthetic Theory: The Redemption of Illusion*. Cambridge, MA: MIT Press.

Index